D0149230

The Fixer

The Fixer

Secrets for saving your reputation in the age of viral media

Michael Sitrick

With Dennis Kneale

REGNERY PUBLISHING
A Division of Salem Media Group

Regnery® is a registered trademark of Salem Communications Holding Corporation

Cataloging-in-Publication data on file with the Library of Congress

Originally published in hardcover 2018, ISBN 978-1-62157-286-2
ebook ISBN 978-1-62157-435-4

Published in the United States by
Regnery Publishing
A Division of Salem Media Group
300 New Jersey Ave NW
Washington, DC 20001
www.Regnery.com

Manufactured in the United States of America

10 9 8 7 6 5 4 3 2 1

Books are available in quantity for promotional or premium use. For information on discounts and terms, please visit our website: www.Regnery.com.

This book, like the last, is dedicated to my best friend,
life partner, and wife, Nancy, whose love, sacrifices,
and support over all these years made it possible for me
to accomplish what I have.

Contents

A Note to the Reader

It's not unusual, when a client calls, for him or her to ask whether the conversation will be confidential. My response is always the same: "Of course, confidentiality is critical in the business we're in. You couldn't kiss and tell and stay in this business."

How then, one might ask, can I maintain confidentiality and write a book about the cases with which we have been involved? This is the same question I addressed in my first book, *Spin*. Much of what we do is public. In those instances where we discuss things that are not, we have masked the identity of the clients or had them review and approve what we have written.

Michael S. Sitrick

Meeting Mike

Dennis Kneale

February 2016

On a startlingly bright Saturday morning, after a lovely, sunlit drive north out of Los Angeles and into the Pacific Palisades of southern California, past a guarded gate and a carefully plotted patchwork of large homes nestled among the craggy cliffs and canyons of the Santa Monica Mountains, I arrive at the House that Mike Built.

Out front, a large glass sculpture obscures the view of the front door, almost as if guarding it. Inside, the place overflows with paintings and sculptures: originals by Peter Max, LeRoy Neiman, and Mark Kostabi and limited-edition prints by Picasso, Warhol, Chagall, Miró, and Norman Rockwell. Out back a dark infinity pool seems to spill endlessly past a serene pond, which gives way to a stunning vista of lush mountainside plunging down to the Pacific Ocean.

This is the home of Michael S. Sitrick of Sitrick And Company, which does a thriving business in the art of strategic communications, practicing PR as persuasion. He is the "Ninja Master of the Dark Art of Spin" (*Gawker*), "The Flack for When You're Under Attack" (*Forbes*), and the "prince of PR" and the "Wizard of Spin" (fifteen years apart, in the *Los Angeles Times*). Most fitting of all, perhaps, he has been called the "Winston Wolfe of Public Relations" (*Fortune*), referring to the "fixer" played by Harvey Keitel in *Pulp Fiction*. Though his firm provides communications services in a wide range of cases—launching companies, bankruptcy reorganizations, corporate governance, hostile takeovers, regulatory fights, government investigations, reputation management, lawsuits, and high-profile divorces—Mike Sitrick is known best for crisis advice, and he is legendary as the best in the business.

He has spent nearly three decades building Sitrick And Company (spelled with that upper-case A), which has evolved and thrived with the explosion of the Internet, *TMZ*, 24/7 celebrity journalism, and the rise of social media. In Mike Sitrick's view, most companies in crisis deserve a fair trial in the court of public opinion, a shot at redemption, and a chance to make things right, though he has turned some clients down. He has been a spectral presence in some of the highest-profile stories and hottest controversies to ignite the media:

- The scandal at Hewlett-Packard after its chairman was accused of spying on board members and reporters
- The feud between Disney's then-CEO, Michael Eisner, and Roy Disney, board member and nephew of Walt Disney himself, culminating in Eisner's stepping down as chairman and the early retirement of one of the most powerful CEOs in Hollywood a year later

- The tumult at BlackBerry
- Scandal in the Catholic Church
- The mosque at Ground Zero
- The restoration of the estate of Michael Jackson after his drug-overdose death
- The exposure of the doping of Olympic athletes by the Russian government

The clients involved in these stories have authorized Mike Sitrick to talk about their cases or the facts have previously been made public. He can't—and *won't*—discuss cases that are pending or in which the details or his involvement have not become public.

The tougher the case, the more impossible the situation, the more likely Mike Sitrick is to take it on and try to pull off a miracle. Some people who know him attribute this to an urge to stick up for people who get picked on—a soft spot he developed as a Jewish kid protecting his younger brother on the multiethnic streets of the South Side of Chicago in the 1950s and '60s.

I'm honored to help Sitrick share the secrets of his craft in a book that is equal parts how-to and tell-all—or tell-*almost*-all; this guy knows secrets he never will tell. We have known each other for more than fifteen years, having met when I was the managing editor of *Forbes* in New York and he visited me with a client's story to sell.

Sitrick published an earlier book on his approach in 1998— eons ago in Internet time. He signed the copy he sent to me after we first met, way back then. I still have it and brought it with me on this visit to his home. On the first page, he wrote: "Dennis, enjoyed our lunch. Hopefully, a couple of cases we work on together will be in my next book. Mike, 5/17/99." Which was kind of prophetic, it turns out.

Sitrick's new effort is all the more important in this age of the Net and social media, when any misstep can blow up into a world-wide embarrassment on Facebook, when the Outrage Brigade on Twitter, armed with virtual torches and pitchforks, can destroy the career of any CEO, company, or celebrity.

I show up at Sitrick's home at 9:30 a.m. expecting four hours of first-round interviewing. He ushers me in the front door, mutes the smartphone that is grafted to his ear, and says he has an emergency conference call coming up. He is almost six feet tall and trim, his lack of a potbelly impressive given my struggle with my own. His face bears stubble from a working vacation at his house in Hawaii, and the new goatee gives him a devilish glint.

I follow him into his home office, where paintings waiting to be hung rest on the floor and a cup of coffee waits, getting cold. Sitrick turns away from me and sits down to hover over a screen and keyboard, editing a statement drafted by the emergency client's general counsel and waiting for the call to commence.

Sitrick had agreed to set aside this time for me to help him map out some Big Thoughts for the book, but he is preparing to brief a star *New York Times* reporter and has no time to talk. An entertainment executive has launched a holy war on Sitrick's wealthy client, resorting to dirty tricks that could get that executive fired. Sitrick also has a second situation, another feud between rich guys, which he is about to offer to a *Wall Street Journal* reporter. A Sitrick client hopes to damage his foe by linking him to misdeeds alleged by a third guy.

Oh, and there's this delicate matter: a bitter divorce case in which the angry ex-wife has just filed an eighty-six-page motion that, among other incendiary items, accuses her ex-husband, Sitrick's client, of child abuse. The attorneys assure Sitrick it is a trumped-up charge she filed only after losing badly in court; she is just trying to punish him. He asks them to provide more details and evidence, and they do.

None of which bears on the emergency conference call that is about to begin. His phone rings and Sitrick, now wearing a headset, answers it. The call goes on for almost an hour, and I eavesdrop shamelessly, though only on Sitrick's side of the interchange. This is a privilege I am afforded only because I have signed a non-disclosure agreement to work for Mike on this book. Mike, who from the onset said we would have to mask the identity of the company and its executives, briefed me later on the parts of the conversation to which I wasn't privy.

The young CEO of a hotshot financial firm, a unicorn worth a few billion dollars, is being ousted, a step that's necessary to insulate his company from fallout over what he says were well-intentioned misdeeds in trying to accommodate torrid growth. As half a dozen people listen in, including Sitrick and his colleague Sallie Hofmeister (formerly a reporter and editor at both the *New York Times* and *Los Angeles Times*), a company lawyer explains the predicament and says the SEC might yet get involved. I've got butterflies in my stomach; no reporter ever would get to hear a frank exchange like this. We lust to get on the inside, to know the "real" story, but we rarely do, if ever.

All hell is about to break loose. The company is getting hammered in the media, which will interpret the founder's abrupt departure as a calamity both for him and for the company. Everything seems to ride on getting one thing right—the press release.

For the ousted CEO, his reputation is at stake. He doesn't want potential compliance problems mentioned at all, and he wants the release to emphasize his continuing, integral role at the company he created. The company, though, can't ignore the material issues, some of which have already been reported in the media. Some on the call argue for the company to make a *mea culpa*, but that might set off the founder and blow up the entire deal, to say nothing of the fact that it would create problems for the company with regulators and others.

Sitrick is just an advisor on the sidelines, but he soon takes over as quarterback. You can't announce that the founder will stick around as a "close advisor," he says. What if he gets in trouble with regulators? And what good will a *mea culpa* do, especially if it sets off the founder? Instead, he tells them, the company should say it is taking a series of steps to strengthen its internal policies, procedures, and controls. This, it turns out, is one of Sitrick's rules: focus on the fix.

Sitrick taps at the keyboard and waters down the phrase to say the CEO will be available to ensure "a smooth transition." He starts to put it in the lead paragraph of the release (the "lede," as journalists call it) as a sweetener to get the buy-in of the departing chief, but after some deliberation, he buries it further down in the announcement. He adds the line about taking steps to strengthen internal controls.

Then someone suggests Sitrick tighten up the details of the release, show it to the exiting CEO, and tell him this is as favorable as it will get. "We get these guys on the phone and we say we can live with this, but we can't go further than this, then have Mike weigh in on why, from a PR standpoint, this is the best thing, not just for the company but for [the CEO] himself." The exec on the call makes a direct appeal to Sitrick: "Mike, he has tremendous respect for you, tremendous respect. If he hears you...it could make the difference."

"I have no problem with that," Sitrick responds, "because I believe this is in his best interest as well as the company's. If I were advising him, I'd tell him the same thing."

This was, in Sitrick's view, critical. His one absolute in business is never to lie, not even a little. They agree to reconvene for another call in an hour, after some further consultations. It blows through his entire Saturday, and some of Sunday, but that happens a lot.

All of this agonizing over a seemingly simple press release, over minutiae that the uninformed might dismiss as...who cares? But to Sitrick the details are paramount. In today's business world, the "story"—the public account of an event or a company or a senior executive—is as important as the reality. One of Sitrick's favorite sayings is that perception *is* reality.

Online, as Sitrick has seen, a misimpression can be repeated a million times, and a lie left uncorrected becomes the truth, festering forever on Google. Decades of brand-building and corporate "good will" can be wiped out if an online beating goes undefended. A harsh truth, if not softened by nuance and perspective and the rest of the story, becomes the only truth, a truncated version of what happened. It can damage your reputation. Permanently.

Even the best-run, biggest companies have been known to blow it in their response to a crisis. They start out in denial, shut down, and raise the shields just when they should open up and at the least find out what reporters want to know. As Sitrick tells it, the easy thing to do is to advise a client to refuse to comment, stay silent, don't talk to the press—because this shields the advisor, who would get the blame if the client talks to reporters and gets skewered. Sure, there are cases where "no comment" is the right option, when you don't know the facts or the facts don't clearly support an acceptable statement, when your client is in a particularly sensitive legal situation, or you are negotiating a settlement with the government. Most times, however, Sitrick says, the better instinct is to find out what the reporter wants, get the facts, and then, if the facts support you, speak up.

But while the need has never been greater for image protection and rapid response, Sitrick believes the business world suffers from a scarcity of smart advice in crisis communications. His take: this isn't a game for amateurs, but an awful lot of amateurs play this game. This has been his view throughout his entire PR career, and he has held it more firmly as his experience has increased.

Through more than a thousand cases (he has lost count), Sitrick has developed a battle-tested regimen for crisis response. He understands the power of storytelling and harnesses it for the purposes of persuasion. The media, both old and new, want to tell a story, and he sees his job as helping them get a better one for their audience (and for his client). I have seen from the other side of the desk that he knows how to undercut and counterpunch his clients' adversaries, how to turn the media to his clients' favor, and how to preempt or mitigate a bad story. He gets the importance of responding instantly and repeatedly, and he uses accurate, fact-sourced details to establish his version's credibility.

Rather than telling his clients to duck and cover, Mike Sitrick tells them that if they don't tell their story, someone else will tell it for them. Failing to respond early and strategically leaves empty space and airtime to be filled by someone else: your adversaries, short-sellers, media grandstanders, Wall Street shills.

That points up a key difference between Sitrick and most other people in the crisis business, a difference that I have observed as a reporter, editor, and television news anchor. Many companies and PR people regard the media as their enemy and reporters as arrogant and evil. Many reporters, in turn, view companies and PR people warily, suspicious they are out to block a good story.

Sitrick, on the other hand, has a clear affection for journalists. He even started out as one, albeit briefly. I have dealt with hundreds of journalists, and Mike Sitrick is, hands down, a better storyteller than most of them, at all times staying within the four corners of the truth. *And reporters need good stories.* He respects them and refuses to trash them. (Although, when they get it wrong, he tells them so, demanding a correction when warranted, even if he has to go over their heads.) Sitrick figures most of them work hard, they try to get it right, and often they believe they are fighting for the underdog, a trait with which Sitrick can identify.

Sitrick sees reporters as essential to getting out his clients' version of the truth, and he stresses the value of understanding their deadline pressures, their competitive zeal, and their fear of getting beaten on a story. Stories are the currency he carries—exclusives, interviews, counterpunch tips, profiles—when he meets with members of his vast network of reporters and editors. This guy delivers the goods, acting as gatekeeper to some of the biggest stories and scandals of the past decade and beyond.

On occasion, Sitrick and his partners on a case will fight an ongoing story by developing and placing a different one, a counternarrative offering compelling new details. His firm's ex-journalists, lawyers, and executives are particularly adept at this technique. They also have been known to divert negative news by creating a bona fide news event. Mike Sitrick trains his people to approach their practice as a litigator approaches a trial, gathering the evidence, presenting the facts, preparing for cross-examination, and crafting a compelling closing argument—which is, in essence, a story that sees things his client's way.

From day one, in fact, Sitrick staffed his firm largely with exjournalists because, as he likes to say, it is easier to teach PR to a journalist than to teach news judgment to a PR person. His partners include former reporters and editors from the *Wall Street Journal, Bloomberg, Forbes, Barron's,* the *New York Times,* the *Los Angeles Times,* the *San Francisco Chronicle,* and the *Houston*

Chronicle as well as on-air talent from CNBC, Fox Business Network, NBC, and CBS. Of eighteen partners profiled on the Sitrick website recently, more than a dozen are veteran journalists.

Sitrick gets a callback from that *New York Times* star reporter, greeting him as if they were about to catch up on the latest gossip, and tells a story that would arouse any reporter's interest in the rich-guy feud: details of "character assassination," "harassment," "anonymous attacks." The reporter is loving it.

Meanwhile, I pad over to the kitchen, where his wife, Nancy, is pouring me a cup of coffee. She is even trimmer than Mike is and looks much younger, and the first thing you notice is the great haircut—an attractive bob, one side longer than the other and curving under toward her jawline. She has had it for ten years, and every time she thinks of trying a new style, someone compliments her on it (as her visitor had just done), and she stays put.

They met in college when she was just eighteen and he was nineteen. They have been together ever since, marrying a month after Mike graduated with a B.S. in business and journalism from the University of Maryland and six months before Nancy graduated. They have raised three daughters, who now have seven offspring of their own. "You're my play date today," Nancy tells me. My arrival means her husband has something else to do while she goes out to meet friends for the day.

At the end of a hallway leading to the family room are framed photos of grown kids and sons-in-law and grandkids—two sets of twin girls in two separate families, plus a boy for each set of twins and their newest addition, a baby girl from their daughter in Hawaii—smiling at the beach and posing for groupies rather than selfies. These are some of the only photos in which you'll see Mike smiling. In almost every shot in the many profiles published about him, he stares into the camera like some badass.

I mention to Nancy that, despite my having known Mike for fifteen years, he has never said much about his family. That's his way, she explains. He internalizes, masking his emotions and restraining any burst of anger, a persona he learned from his father, a longtime Chicago radio executive and adman. Sitrick has never been known to lose his temper, even when dealing with the most ferocious investigative reporters. Few people really know her husband, Nancy believes. And then she seems to issue me a challenge: "I always tell people, 'You'll never know Mike.'"

From what I have been able to piece together before today's visit, I know this much:

He is the oldest of three sons, and even today he consults on business matters now and then with his brothers, David and Ronald, both of them successful lawyers. And although Mike Sitrick has known some of the most renowned business leaders in the world, he credits his own father as his most important mentor. Now in his nineties, Herman Sitrick taught Mike the ethics of hard work, accountability, and responsibility. When Mike, early in his career, told his father about a problem he was going to bring to his boss, his father replied, "Your job is not to bring problems to your boss. It's to bring solutions." It is an adage he has lived by ever since. Herman still has his own ad business in Chicago, and he still goes in to the office every day. Like his oldest son, Herman Sitrick married young, and seventy-one years later, he and Marcia were still married, until she passed just prior to the publication of this book.

Mike endured the culture shock of a move from the South Side of Chicago to Birmingham, Alabama, in his senior year of high school, when his dad got a top job running a group of radio stations. After a freshman year at the University of Alabama, he transferred to the University of Maryland at College Park, a fateful decision: that's where he met Nancy.

He figures marrying Nancy was the smartest decision of his entire life, one that set him up for everything else that came his way. "My wife, my best friend, and my soul mate," he calls her in the dedication to her in his first book, "without whose love and support during all these years, none of what I have accomplished would have been possible."

Sitrick wrote for his college paper, local radio and TV, and then free-lanced for the *Baltimore News American*, and the *Washington Star*, passing up a full-time job at the *Chicago Tribune* to take a PR job in the University of Maryland agriculture division. (It paid $160 a week; the *Tribune* offered $125 a week. Mike told me he loved journalism, but preferred being able to eat.) He jumped quickly to Western Electric in Chicago and then, still in his early twenties, went to work in the administration of Chicago's legendary Mayor Richard J. Daley, where he rose to deputy director of public information for one of the city's largest agencies. Mike later joined a local PR firm and then, at the age of twenty-seven, became the head of PR at National Can Corporation, then a Fortune 500 company. In 1981 he took the job that largely determined the rest of his career: vice president, and then senior vice president, of communications at Wickes Cos.

Nine months later, after the brilliant turnaround artist Sanford Sigoloff swooped in to take over the firm and guide it back to health, Wickes filed for Chapter 11 reorganization. Mike Sitrick handled communications strategy, which included putting Sigoloff at center stage and focusing the story on what he was doing to save Wickes. The fine points Sitrick learned about the U.S. Bankruptcy

Code and the insights he gained into the emotional and psychological effects of a turn in Chapter 11 helped him start his own firm. He got one of his first cases before he even had incorporated—Roy Disney's Shamrock Holdings, which was making a run at Polaroid in 1989—and he went on to build one of the largest and most successful practices in restructuring and strategic communications.

I met him a decade later, when I was a top editor at *Forbes* magazine. I had reluctantly agreed to meet with Mike Sitrick at the request of someone I knew well, a crush from my college newspaper days, expecting yet another PR guy with an axe to grind and a client to bill. I was thinking, "So he comes to you through someone you trust, just like the mob does in *Goodfellas*."

I was braced to resist his overtures. Something inside a journalist makes him want to resist when a PR spinner comes calling. Resistance isn't futile, it's a virtue. And something about Mike Sitrick himself made me even more resistant, as we met at a bar near the *Forbes* offices and he settled into a chair, shrouded in shadows and the purple-blue tinge of neon lights. Maybe it was his three-thousand-dollar tailored suit and the fancy, perfectly knotted necktie.

He had an unreadable poker face, with a fingerprint-sized birthmark on his left cheekbone that made it look as if he recently had been in a fight, and you should see the other guy. Rather than unspooling enthusiastic flights of fancy, he uttered plain, unadorned sentences in a low and gravelly voice. He could have been a great stand-in for Al Pacino in *The Devil's Advocate*, which had come out two years earlier.

Which is all to say that Sitrick wasn't your typical PR guy at all. He wasn't a glad-handing, backslapping, hale fellow well met. He didn't dabble in small talk; he was too focused to bother with it. He didn't ask questions about me personally or talk about the Yankees. He even hates golf—four hours knocking a tiny ball around strikes him as a waste of time.

This guy had no time for any of that. Friends say his only real interests are his firm and his family, notwithstanding his impressive art collection and the vintage guitar in an old, scarred case in his office. It is one of nine he owns. (When he was nineteen, he was offered a recording contract in Nashville, but was told he'd have to drop out of college and go on tour. His mother vetoed the idea, telling him, "You'll go on tour, okay, but it will be Vietnam.")

Sitrick sat there with a story to sell, and he laid it out as if he were spinning a yarn. I was working on a vodka martini with olives, he was drinking seltzer, and now my resistance was subsiding because I kind of liked the tale he was telling. Today neither one of us can remember it, but I am sure it had all the requisite Sitrickian elements: a central hero getting beaten up in the ring, a point of conflict with larger things at stake, a foe that was being unfair or unethical or misleading, detailed evidence that the other side was wrong, and, whenever possible, a man-bites-dog twist.

Over the years, when I was at *Forbes* or in my later anchor stints at CNBC and Fox Business, I worked with Mike Sitrick on a dozen or more stories. Sometimes his solutions don't involve public relations at all but leaps of strategy—one reason Sitrick calls his style of PR "strategic communications," a term a lot of people throw around, though it is practiced by very few. These strategic directives come out of nowhere, his partners say, and go beyond just managing the story itself to solving the larger problem that triggered the story to begin with.

Too often, in Sitrick's view, PR people focus only on the task at hand, doing the chores they were asked to do instead of looking at an issue strategically. To him the real point is the problem the client is trying to solve. What is the client's ultimate goal and how can we use our skills and our contacts to help achieve that? It's the strategy that's important. Communications is just the means to an end.

Classic case: the rescue of Twinkies. On Christmas Eve 2008, Sitrick got a call while on vacation with his family in Mexico. A lawyer for a Sitrick client, Twinkies maker International Bakeries Corporation, told him that GE Capital had just reneged on providing $125 million in credit. This could derail the entire six-hundred-million-dollar refinancing package that IBC had spent a year assembling to be able to get out of Chapter 11. Without the GE credit, the company could go belly-up. The lawyer wanted Sitrick's advice on how to handle media for the lender-liability lawsuit his client was about to file.

Sitrick responded with a question: hadn't GE recently received bailout money from the Troubled Asset Relief Program after the global financial meltdown? A quick Google search showed the company had received two kinds of federal infusions, with the implicit promise of recirculating that money in the form of loans to help rebuild the U.S. economy. How could GE now justify withholding this help from IBC, a company that employed almost thirty thousand workers? "What do you think GE will say, when asked by the *Wall Street Journal*, 'Didn't you get $800 million in federal assistance to enable you to lend money to save jobs?' We need to get the unions involved, contact local congressmen and senators, Chuck Schumer and Hillary Clinton."

So they scrapped the lawsuit idea, and Mike instantly mapped out a plan to make this a jobs issue. Playing up the thousands of jobs at risk at IBC, he and the team with whom he was working put pressure on GE Capital by bringing this matter to the attention of U.S. Senators Hillary Clinton and Chuck Schumer of New York and Edward Kennedy of Massachusetts, who in turn wrote strong letters to GE's management. They also got the company's union leaders and the Twinkies-packing rank and file involved, who contacted local state and federal representatives. Within weeks, IBC won the GE backing and completed its Chapter 11 reorganization to emerge as a renewed company, able to fight another day.

Sitrick's colleagues say it's a "Mike thing." In a meeting with a client, Mike suddenly will say, "I know what we could do," and then sets out an audacious plan. The first response is incredulity—we can't do that! But it soon becomes clear that, by golly, *it will work*. Their ringleader has been "thinking outside the box" since long before it became a business cliché.

Even Mike Sitrick himself says he doesn't quite know how he comes up with these catapulting ideas. His neural network is running scenarios and simulations based on thousands of past moves in the crisis chess game, figuring out a pathway and pursuing it until a new adaptation becomes necessary. He is his own machine-learning algorithm.

Much of what Sitrick does, therefore, may not be teachable. He is guided by gut and a tingly Spidey-sense, an intuitive knack for divining, in each confrontation, which methods to deploy at which junctures, when to counterattack and when to let the frenzy run itself out. His cases don't all conform to the same template. Each one is different, every person under fire has unique needs and assets, and the particular facts dictate what follows.

Yet *some* things can be put down on paper, surely, or displayed on a Kindle or iPad screen. Knowingly or not, Sitrick has developed the process for managing a crisis and shaping the story, forming his team with his well-honed approach. And now we endeavor to put his ethos and methods into a book for anyone else to learn. The way Sitrick sees it, this book isn't just for PR people, it is for CEOs, senior executives, celebrities, entrepreneurs and business owners, and anyone else who must deal with the media—or who would want to do so by choice.

In the months after that first attempted interview at his home in Pacific Palisades, Mike Sitrick explained for me the art and science of his strategic communications and crisis-quelling techniques, stealing time for interviews from his constant emailing and conference calls. His aim was to boil down a lot of what he knows and teach it to others by offering a glimpse of what he does, guided by some central tenets, incisive points, adaptable guidelines, and tested techniques.

He starts with a fast overview of his regimen for response. It will be the guidepost for this entire book, showing up in the various case studies we will assemble, analyze, and explain. Now, Sitrick could just sprinkle these gems out over the course of the next two hundred or so pages and force you to search for them, but who has the time? And so he serves it up right here at the beginning. If you don't read to the last page of this book, you are dead to us, but at least you have the gist, right here, and you can fake the rest. Here they are, Sitrick's Ten Rules for Engagement:

Rule 1: First, get the facts.

Rule 2: Identify your objective.

Rule 3: Act preemptively.

Rule 4: Use a Lead Steer.

Rule 5: Focus on the fix.

Rule 6: Social media often are a means to an end.

Rule 7: If you don't tell your story, someone else will tell it for you.

Rule 8: Put your opponent on the Wheel of Pain.

Rule 9: "No comment" can be PR malpractice.

Rule 10: Never lie.

Not all of these rules apply to every situation, and each case requires a different assortment of these guidelines, plus extra considerations particular to the case. Nor are all of these rules absolute. Mike Sitrick also emphasizes three corollaries:

First, don't wait until a reporter's deadline to respond. The longer you wait, the less influence you will have on the story.

Second, understand the rules of "background," "not for attribution," and "off the record" and the differences between them.

Third, in rare instances you can kill a story, but only by harnessing pertinent and incontrovertible facts that demonstrate the reporter has it wrong.

Social media exercise significant influence, but Mike believes that to bring about major change—such as legislation, indictment or criminal charges, congressional hearings, or even the firing or exoneration of a top executive—in most instances a story that began on social media needs to be picked up or re-reported in "old" (traditional) media. He offers three examples:

- There is no question that Donald Trump's use of social media contributed to his election as president, but even with his twenty-two million or so Twitter followers (who put him in the top fifty tweeters), it was the mainstream media's reporting of Mr. Trump's tweets that made them so effective. Twitter limits messages to 140 characters, but the stories resulting from these tweets were almost always considerably longer and often on the front page or leading the evening news. The mainstream media coverage of these messages either brought them to people's attention for the first time or reinforced them while giving them the credibility of being in the *New York Times*, *Los Angeles Times*, *Washington Post*, or CBS Evening News. Then there is the fact that according to various reports, many if not all, Twitter accounts include bots and inactive accounts, which reduces the number of real, active followers.

- One client of Sitrick And Company dismissed the criticism heaped on him by two Hollywood blogs as meaningless gossip, only to discover that *Vanity Fair*, which, of course, had a much wider audience, used these blogs as a basis for its story, citing them at the beginning of the article. This took the story from a limited audience in Hollywood, to a national story, which was then picked up by other media throughout the U.S.

- When a television news program was criticized in various social media outlets for a story of national interest, nothing much happened until the criticism was repeated and expanded in the traditional media. The news organization questioned the veracity of the criticism, but in the end the scandal resulted in widespread firings of the program's staff and ultimately helped push the program off the air.

In handling more than a thousand cases, Sitrick has devised an approach that is as focused and high-precision as a police procedural—*Dragnet* meets *CSI*—and he has been able to lay it down through examples and case histories, which you will read here. Along the way, you also will hear about his Five Stages of Crisis and Three First Steps when confronted by the media.

The question isn't whether you'll face a crisis one day, especially if you are at the top of your game. The question is what will you do when crisis comes? Crisis arrives unexpectedly, swelling and subsiding in an almost mathematical, recurring pattern. A crisis can be quelled and refocused with a common set of responses if you know the right fixes and when to deploy them.

That is Sitrick's forte, the thing he was born to do, although crisis-management is only one part of his portfolio of strategic communications services. In the chapters that follow, we will try to *show* you how he does it, not just *tell* you how he does it. So suit up and strap in. This guy moves fast.

Chapter 1

Dolby v. BlackBerry

In my long career in strategic communications—especially that aspect involving crisis communications—my accessibility to clients has never been more important or more instantaneous than it is today, and it all began with the first wireless wonder, the BlackBerry. Remember when it ruled the wireless world? Corporate IT chiefs prized its proprietary network, bulletproof security, and cumbersome link to the Internet. Devotees called it the "Crack-berry," so addicted were they (I among them) to the feel of the gadget's pebbly keyboard and navigational thumbwheel.

The BlackBerry was conceived by a company formed in 1984 by Mike Lazaridis—a man former GE CEO Jack Welch called a genius—and his childhood friend Douglas Fregin. Research in Motion, or RIM, was based not in the innovative hills of Silicon Valley but in the polite, cold climes of Waterloo in Ontario, Canada.

When RIM introduced the first BlackBerry in 1999, pagers still clung to businessmen's belts and typing on your cell phone required tapping the "2" key three times just to form the letter "c." The BlackBerry was downright magical, winning fans and investors. The company's stock started trading on the Nasdaq the same year, with a total market value of a quarter-billion dollars. Ten years later RIM had more than twenty-five million customers and a seemingly unbreakable hold on the wireless-gadget market. Its market value had soared to $55 billion. Annual earnings would peak at over $3 billion.

RIM, however, had a patent problem. For five years starting in 2006, while selling millions of BlackBerrys, the company neglected to pay licensing fees for the portfolio of patents behind the microchip that produced the devices' digitally-compressed high-fidelity sound. These patents belonged to one of the premier sound engineering companies in the world, Dolby Labs. In 2011, after years of unsuccessful efforts to get RIM to pay patent fees, Dolby decided it had to take action. Never in its forty-five-year history had the company brought a patent infringement suit, but RIM's resistance was setting a bad precedent.

Dolby Labs was run for more than thirty years by a financial executive who worked for the founder, Ray Dolby. He kept its focus on the lab, eschewing the production of consumer electronics powered by its sound technology. Its noise-reduction technology provided crystal-clear sound to the music and movie industries.

Dolby had adapted to the digital wave, continuing to innovate as Moore's Law took us into the handheld age. Its digital-compression techniques used only half the storage or bandwidth of previous technologies, and sometimes only one-tenth as much, with no loss of sound quality.

The company's income came largely from licensing its proprietary technology to dozens of electronics makers, the music industry, movie theaters, and more, receiving a small cut of a product's revenue as a fee. By 2011 the annual patent-fee revenue coming into Dolby Labs approached $800 million a year and accounted for more than 80 percent of its total business. Virtually every major electronics maker—from Apple and Android to Nokia, Microsoft, and Motorola—was a Dolby licensee.

Every major electronics maker, that is, but one—RIM, one of the biggest. From 2006 through 2010, RIM sold almost *ninety million* BlackBerrys (four million in 2006, more than six million in 2007, almost fourteen million in 2008, twenty-six million in 2009, and thirty-six million by 2010). Dolby's licensing subsidiary, named Via, had been negotiating with RIM's patent department since 2006 but with no progress.

Prizing its peaceful relations with its licensees, Dolby had always been reluctant to sue, but in 2009 its chief financial officer, Kevin Yeaman, rose to CEO. Two years later he brought in a new general counsel, Andy Sherman from CBS Interactive. That's when Dolby began to take a harder look at its patent portfolio practices.

The overseas market was booming, a new wave of Asian brands was on the rise, led by HTC of Taiwan, and Dolby felt it had to put the rest of the world on notice that it would be a vigilant protector of its intellectual property. It needed a way to make RIM pay up without hurting Dolby's image as a nice-guy partner.

Andy Sherman took the matter to the board, which reluctantly agreed they had to sue. They fretted over how the combative move might be viewed by other licensees, how the trade press would cover it, and whether mainstream media would notice at all. They needed to know more than just how to manage the message; they needed to determine what the message should be.

That is when a board member, Sandy Robertson, proposed hiring me. My partner Lew Phelps, who would work with me on the case, viewed it as a natural for me. It had a dramatic backdrop: the booming smartphone market defined by wireless wars among Apple, Samsung, Android devices, and the rest, not to mention BlackBerry. And BlackBerry had been very much in the news over its loss of market share. The last thing it could afford was a further loss of consumer confidence. The case of *Dolby International v. Research in Motion*, in fact, perfectly illustrates Rule Eight of my Ten Rules for Engagement: put your opponent on the Wheel of Pain. We were able to assess the situation, spot RIM's pressure point, and achieve the result our client wanted faster than any of us ever expected.

Sandy Robertson remains a living legend: the eminence grise of Silicon Valley investment banking, who has used my services a dozen times or more in the previous twenty years. In *A History of Silicon Valley*, Arun Rao writes that the tech industry "was historically served by four independent, San Francisco–based boutique investment banks from the 1960s to the late 1990s…Hambrecht & Quist, Alex Brown & Sons, Robertson Stephens, and Montgomery Securities. These four firms became known as the Four Horsemen."

Imagine being the guy who introduced Eugene Kleiner to Tom Perkins and helped them raise their first fund of a mere $8.4 million for what became the fabled Kleiner Perkins Caufield & Byers. Sandy's firm, Robertson Stephens, helped bankroll the Internet boom, underwriting seventy-four firms and raising $5.5 billion in 1999–2000 alone.

Sandy told the Dolby board he had every confidence that I would know the right knobs to twist and levers to pull in the case of *Dolby v. RIM* and that I would look at not just how to get out the right story but also, perhaps, how to get what Dolby wanted most of all: for RIM to settle, paying Dolby what it owed.

Sandy Robertson and I had first met more than twenty years earlier in a touchy case. He was advising a U.S. chipmaker that was about to sell itself to a Japanese company, even though the CEO himself sat on an industry committee created to keep the U.S. semiconductor industry out of the hands of Japanese rivals. This was back in 1989 or so, when America's getting bested by the Japanese, first in cars and now in memory chips, was a blow to national pride. If the story of this sale caught fire in the media, it could endanger the deal, so the legal counsel to the CEO had brought in my firm to manage public perception.

A Pre-Emptive Move

As soon as Sandy Robertson heard of my background, he later told me, he had heard enough. After graduating college and doing a little reporting for the old *Washington Star, Baltimore News American*, and a Baltimore radio station, I spent a year in two PR jobs and then, at age twenty-two, started working in the administration of the famed Chicago Mayor Richard J. Daley. Robertson, a Chicagoan himself, assumed that here was a PR man who knew how to knock heads and break a few kneecaps when necessary. In this case, however, all that was needed was preemptive action and a nifty bit of jujitsu.

I told my new clients that, to avoid a story pointing out the irony of this company selling out to the Japanese, we needed to preempt it by giving an exclusive to a mergers and acquisitions reporter rather than announcing it broadly via a press release that might alert, say, a Washington-based reporter who was more attuned to the political implications. I figured if we could break the story in the *Wall Street Journal*, other media would follow that lead and report what the *Journal* had written, overlooking the controversy.

Though I hadn't named this type of maneuver at the time, it was based on two of Sitrick's Ten Rules for Engagement—Rule Three, act preemptively, and Rule Four, use a Lead Steer. So I called a *Wall Street Journal* editor over the weekend to offer an embargoed exclusive for Monday. The *Journal* broke the news the next morning, focusing on the transaction and what it meant for the company and the industry. Nothing was said about a Japanese company's buying a U.S. chipmaker whose CEO was chairman of a committee created to prevent that very type of transaction. The political issue was raised only in passing by one of the scores of media outlets covering the story, and even then, it was dismissed by the CEO. No other media raised the issue, controversy was averted, and the merger sailed through.

In the years since that deal, Robertson had matched me up with a series of investment banking clients, letting us go off into the sunset together, as he would put it. His A-list of clients never ceased to impress me, and his eye for creative solutions was an asset. I've always believed that no matter how good you think you are at giving advice, you must listen closely to your clients, because the insights coming back in your direction can be even more valuable than your own. In Sandy Robertson's case, this offered a particularly bountiful bonus to me by letting me become his close friend and expand my base of knowledge.

Robertson's high demands and lofty expectations made me and my team better. He wanted more than a PR spinner—he demanded inventive, strategic thinking and an ability to pitch solutions and ideas that had eluded other PR or legal experts. Robertson liked to say that while other PR firms promoted your positives on a day-to-day basis and we of course did that too, where we really shined was when things were really tough. Our good work paid dividends in numerous ways. First and foremost, it benefited our clients. It also resulted in referrals. Sandy would generously tell people in recommending my firm, "There is nobody better"—yet another benefit of doing good work and achieving results for one's clients.

Robertson put me on a conference call with Dolby's Andy Sherman, who told me the company was preparing to file a patent-infringement lawsuit against RIM. When he told me the amount of damages they were seeking—and, quite frankly, I determined there was no other news that would enable major media coverage— I saw that they needed to rethink their strategy. I told Andy that, with all due respect, the amount he was seeking, at least from a news standpoint, reminded me of the scene in *Austin Powers, International Man of Mystery* when Dr. Evil, awakened after thirty years in suspended animation and still thinking in terms of 1960s prices, announces a plan to steal a nuclear warhead and "hold the world ransom for ONE MILLION DOLLARS!" Snickers all around. I suggested that the damages sought weren't large enough to garner much media coverage, certainly not in the major media. Dolby needed to get the attention of the C-suite—and make the CEO want to make this suit go away.

Then it struck me: what if Dolby were to bring a suit before the International Trade Commission or in federal court, seeking an injunction to ban shipments of BlackBerrys into the United States and Germany, where the suit was to be filed? "That would get their attention. They could never withstand the market uncertainty," I told Sherman and his lawyers on the call. "You probably won't even have to argue for it in court—because I seriously question whether RIM can withstand the pressure." Then I recommended that we not specify the amount we were seeking in damages. We'd just say, "damages to be determined at trial."

This is where we pulled out Rule Eight: put your opponent on the Wheel of Pain. We knew that RIM couldn't afford bad publicity just now. The last thing it needed was a threat that its products might not be allowed to enter the United States and Germany.

Think about it, I told my new clients: threatening a ban on U.S. imports of BlackBerrys would prompt a flood of reporters' calls to the company asking whether its business might come to a halt. Investors would fret that RIM's revenue and cash flow could suffer. Suddenly RIM's CEO would become aware of an existential threat, all because of a patent licensing dispute.

The jujitsu part of the plan was using BlackBerry's hefty size and fame against it. The gadget still had millions of diehard fans, "Crackberry" addicts who might worry that their supply would be cut off if U.S. and German imports were halted. And the news would come at a clutch moment for RIM, just as it was about to report earnings.

The strategy came together quickly after my suggestion. Dolby's law firm drafted the complaint against RIM and prepared to file it in two courts simultaneously. The first, in the federal district court in San Francisco, near Silicon Valley, would spark nationwide major media and tech coverage. The second, in Mannheim, Germany, would unleash wider coverage overseas, letting Dolby send a tough-guy message to manufacturers in the rest of the world.

Meanwhile, I had Lew Phelps prepare to brief members of the media after the initial two stories were posted to get maximum follow-up coverage. Lew had waged PR patent battles with me before. Today he is white-haired and raspy-voiced, an actor you might cast in a remake of Hemingway's *Old Man and the Sea*. After a decade as a reporter for the *Wall Street Journal* in the 1970s, he had served as a public relations head at three Fortune 500 companies in energy and railroads and of his own firm before joining Sitrick And Company in 1997.

In training my people to think strategically about a case and look beyond a media pitch to figure out the real problem they are trying to solve, I have them ask four key questions:

- What is the client's objective?
- How can we use our skills to contribute to achieving that objective?
- What is the best strategy to bring to this situation?
- So what? Why should anyone care?

In Dolby's case, the objective wasn't to get media coverage of its patent fight with RIM, it was to get RIM to pay Dolby its licensing fee. I thought the threat of a ban on BlackBerry imports stood a good chance of achieving that objective. We had elevated a request for an injunction into high drama. Sure, we would put out the *de rigueur* press release on the wires—after the initial stories broke—and it needed to deliver the right message. New lawsuit, injunction to block BlackBerry imports, RIM avoiding the patent payments, tough yet conciliatory tone, and a quotation from a reluctant yet resolute Andy Sherman as Dolby's top lawyer: "Litigation was regrettably our last resort after RIM declined to pay for the use of Dolby's technology. We have a duty to protect our intellectual property."

Mass Press Release or Exclusive?

In this case, however, I thought that sending that press release out on PR Newswire or Business Wire to hundreds of media outlets as a means of announcing the lawsuit would be a waste of a precious resource: a bona fide exclusive. Taking that approach, I told our client, would get us a lot of small news items, none of them telling the whole story. But if we placed the right story—a powerful story with great, exclusive details—we could get one or two good, long stories setting up the factual template for hundreds of followers. If you first put out a press release, nobody gets the exclusive. In this case and others like them: opportunity squandered.

This is a mistake many PR firms make. They fear angering, say, the *New York Times* by handing an exclusive to the *Wall Street Journal* or vice versa; why risk the ire of other reporters by favoring one of their rivals with a scoop? This reluctance, in my view, is the result of giving higher priority to your relationships with reporters than to serving your clients. While we "spread the love," so to speak—giving an exclusive to the *New York Times* one day, to the *Wall Street Journal* the next, then to *Bloomberg Businessweek*, *Fortune*, *Forbes*, or the *Financial Times*—what dictates the choice is whatever is best for our clients. I tell everyone who comes to work here, if you can't put our client's interests ahead of your own, you are in the wrong firm.

My firm hands out scoops boldly and with lethal efficiency. We know that if we pick an outlet with enough clout—a "Lead Steer," as I like to call it—the story will get even more coverage after the exclusive break, because the herd of reporters will follow in those first tracks. I talked about Lead Steers in my first book. Quite simply, I believe the media have a herd mentality. And like any herd, they follow a lead steer. A lead steer can be a respected reporter or a media outlet. More on that later.

I personally arranged for the Dolby scoop to go exclusively to two of the premier media platforms in the business world—the *Wall Street Journal* and CNBC. Just after 9:00 a.m. Eastern Time, the *Journal* would post the story online, and at exactly the same time, Jon Fortt, then the tech correspondent for CNBC out in Silicon Valley, would break the story on the air. Lew Phelps arranged for a reporter at *Bloomberg News* to post a story minutes later. After that story broke, he would follow up with a few key media outlets around the world, starting with other top U.S. media, moving to English-language editions in China and Asia, and then to Europe. Finally, we would issue the press release worldwide.

One complication: most media outlets won't report on a new lawsuit unless they have proof that it has been filed. So a few moments after Dolby's lawyers simultaneously filed the lawsuit against RIM in San Francisco and in Germany on the morning of June 15, 2011, a Dolby lawyer called me (reaching me on my Black-Berry, of course). Within a few minutes, I had a PDF of the cover page of the lawsuit, time-stamped and with a case number. I emailed the PDF to my contacts at the *Journal* and CNBC and called Lew Phelps to unleash him on his reporters minutes after the *Journal* and CNBC stories appeared. Then we waited.

The coverage went off exactly as we had planned. Shortly after 9:00 a.m. in New York, the *Wall Street Journal*'s website ran a byline scoop: "Dolby Sues Rim over Patents," by Chip Cummins. At about the same time on CNBC, an urgent, red, full-screen alert emblazoned with the headline "Breaking News" took over the picture, and anchor Melissa Lee tossed to San Francisco, telling viewers, "All right, we have some breaking news here. We want to go to Jon Fortt with the latest. Jon, what's the latest here?"

"All right," Fortt responded, taking the handoff, "the news *here*, Dolby Laboratories is suing Research in Motion, claiming patent infringement on its audio compression technology. Now, Dolby is saying they want the courts to halt sales of RIM devices, including most of their phones and the BlackBerry Playbook, say-ing they're infringing" on Dolby patents.

Fortt had led with the lawsuit *and* the import ban. Then he hit a second critical point—the isolation of RIM as the sole company not signing a license agreement. A "*Who's Who* of the phone industry" had licensed the patents, said Fortt, including Apple, Nokia, and Samsung. He also said Dolby had been trying to get RIM to sign for years to no avail, adding, "This is a big suit. It comes at a big time, just a day before RIM is scheduled to report earnings. They've already lowered guidance."

As Fortt tossed the story back to New York after a flawless, unscripted, eighty-nine-second hit, Lew Phelps and I looked at the real-time stock chart at the bottom of the screen, which showed RIM's pre-market stock price now in the red and falling on the news. A CNBC anchor then picked up the story from Fortt and turned to her co-anchor for an ad-lib: "Interesting to see the choppy pre-market action in RIM. Oftentimes these patent litigations last for years." Her co-anchor returned serve, alluding to a Nokia patent flap that Apple had settled the day before, agreeing to pay one billion dollars by some estimates.

The real money at stake in *Dolby v. RIM* wasn't anywhere near that sum, nor did the CNBC anchor say it was, but suddenly the Dolby assault on the BlackBerry maker looked like a billion-dollar story.

Lew Phelps had been working his contacts in the United States and overseas while on vacation at a cabin on Squam Lake in northern New Hampshire, putting in forty-two hours in a week that was supposed to be idle. This is what our clients expect of us, and it is what I expect of my people: we do whatever it takes, however many hours and nights and weekends it takes, to deliver for the client. There will be time to rest and sleep later.

Phelps had set up a Washington-based reporter for *Bloomberg* beforehand with an embargoed interview with the Dolby general counsel, with the understanding it would run after the *Journal* and CNBC ran their stories. As they communicated, at one point the *Bloomberg* writer asked Phelps where he was, and Phelps sent her a quick cell phone photo of the dock out back and the lake, which had served as the idyllic setting for the film *On Golden Pond.* "This is where I am," he texted. The reporter responded with a photo of her cluttered desk in the Bloomberg Washington bureau, her brownbag lunch in the frame.

In the first twenty-four hours, the Dolby-sues-BlackBerry story was published by more than five hundred publications and websites around the world, from Reuters, *Bloomberg,* Forbes.com and the *Washington Post* in the United States to Agence France-Presse in Paris to the *Financial Post* in Canada (RIM's home turf) to techie outlets *TechCrunch* and *ZDNet* and local papers (the *San Jose Business Journal* and the *San Francisco Business Times*).

Most of the stories carried the key points set out in the news release, and they often used Andy Sherman's restrained sound bite, with its parental tone. In every story, moreover, RIM's response was the same—no response at all: "RIM declined comment on the suit."

RIM had begun the week on Monday with its stock price at $36.56 a share. The stock price fell almost 3 percent in two days after the lawsuit news broke, while the broader market fell only 1 percent in the same stretch. The stock ended the week down 25 percent after RIM reported bad earnings and reduced its profit outlook for the second time in two months.

RIM's defiance ended quickly and with a whimper. Two days after Dolby filed the lawsuit and sparked hundreds of stories worldwide, the BlackBerry maker's general counsel called Andy Sherman and told him, "We will settle if you call off the media blitz. We'll even pay our back licensing fees." The Wheel of Pain had done its job. Dolby also had a new Exhibit A to put on the bargaining table when it negotiated patent fees with other makers. On September 12, 2011, Dolby dropped the lawsuit against Research in Motion with the statement, "We are pleased to welcome RIM into Dolby's family of mobile technology licensees," warning, "We believe in and will continue to protect the value of our intellectual property."

At Andy Sherman's request, my staff printed the more than five hundred stories sparked by the RIM lawsuit and our strategy—a stack of papers two inches thick. Months later, Sherman told Lew Phelps with a smile that when other patent licensees balk at Dolby's fees, he places the stack of stories in front of them, pats it, and says, "Don't make me turn Sitrick loose on you." I'm not sure he actually does this, but it was a nice thing to say, regardless.

It was a surprising victory for a firm taking on a titan fifteen times its size, and it led to a second surprise. A couple of years later, RIM's co-founder and co-CEO Mike Lazaridis and co-CEO Jim Balsille hired Sitrick And Company to handle the transition from their roles as co-CEOs to directors of the company.

When I mentioned to them that I had advised Dolby in its patent fight with RIM, Lazaridis responded he was well aware of that fact, adding that he had been unaware of the patent dispute until the media reported it. "We fired the lawyer who was responsible for this," he told me. I continued to work for Mike after the transition and through his attempted purchase of BlackBerry and the launching of his new Quantum fund. We still represent him today.

Chapter 2

Exonerating Pattie

Part One

In the annals of boardroom dramas, the case of Hewlett-Packard Co. and how it allegedly spied on journalists and its own board of directors stands out as a tale of mistrust and manipulation, of deception and misdirection. Beneath the headlines, it also was a melodrama of personal feuds and tricks.

I was spending a sunny Sunday afternoon in September 2006 with my extended family at our beach house in Malibu when my phone rang. Answering, I heard a soft, tentative voice: "May I speak with Michael Sitrick, please?"

"This is he."

"This is Patricia Dunn, I don't know if you know who I am."

"I'd have to live on Mars not to know who you are, Pattie. Nice to meet you. How can I help you?"

Patricia Dunn was the nonexecutive chairman of the board of directors of Hewlett-Packard Co., the largest computer maker in the world, which was, at the moment, caught in a horrendous media hailstorm. She told me she had some concerns about how well H-P's PR people were handling the crisis and was contacting me at the suggestion of three different people, wondering whether my firm and I might be available to help H-P.

H-P had a disturbing problem with leaks emanating directly from the board of directors, which had understandably upset Mark Hurd, then the CEO, and the board. Hurd had asked every board member if he or she had been leaking information, and each had denied doing so. Thus, everyone knew someone among them was lying. These leaks spawned mistrust, unnerved management, and, some have said, may even have violated federal securities regulations. An investigation of the leaks had gone wildly awry, and those missteps had now become the big story.

Here's the short version of what happened. Hurd's predecessor, Carly Fiorina, had asked for an internal investigation of who was leaking confidential information, but it went nowhere. After Fiorina's firing and the elevation of Pattie Dunn to nonexecutive chairman, board members asked Dunn to oversee a new investigation into the leaks. She was directed to work through the company's internal security department, and she did. The head of internal security retained an outside investigator to undertake the operation. Unbeknownst to Dunn, this outside firm used questionable methods to review directors' phone records and conduct surveillance of a reporter and a board member. Agents engaged in "pretexting"— impersonating some of their targets to trick the phone company into providing records they had no legal right to inspect. Worse from a media standpoint, they also cracked into the cell phone records of nine journalists.

Some of these acts may have violated California law, despite assurances from legal advisors to Pattie Dunn, the board, and brass that everything the investigators were doing was kosher. (To our knowledge, the legal advisors were not aware of the pretexting or any of the other acts that may have violated the law.) At this moment it appeared that criminal indictments were looming.

The H-P scandal was one of the biggest business stories in years, and it was unfolding with blinding speed, already sparking a board resignation, a congressional inquiry, multiple criminal investigations, and hundreds of stories. No matter how anyone tried to spin this one, it was a huge, unmitigated screw-up. Clearly, we were getting to this crisis late.

As my partner Terry Fahn and I prepared to take on the Pattie Dunn case, we could see that three of Sitrick's Ten Rules for Engagement would be particularly important—Rule 1: First, get the facts; Rule 4: Use a Lead Steer; and Rule 7: If you don't tell your story, someone else will tell it for you.

First, I had to find out whether what was being said about my new client was true. If not, then what were the facts? How do we go about correcting the record so the wrong story doesn't keep getting repeated, and then how do we get a compelling, fact-based counter-narrative that tells the correct facts? And where do we place that story? In trying to exonerate Pattie Dunn, we would do long, detailed interviews with respected writers for the *Wall Street Journal* and the *New Yorker*, premier platforms in journalism, and then we would put Pattie face to face with Lesley Stahl in an exclusive interview on CBS's *60 Minutes*.

I have seen the cycle of crisis and response speed up and shorten significantly in recent years, especially since the rise of the web and social media. The damage done by delaying your response is now far worse and happens far more quickly than before, yet the time required for recovery hasn't gotten any shorter. Our strategy for Pattie Dunn corrected the record and changed the narrative and, more importantly, public perception. In one of the most satisfying campaigns of my career, we helped a wronged client clear herself of the charges against her, even as she battled a terminal case of ovarian cancer.

That Sunday, as Pattie began filling me in, I saw that she was in much more danger than she realized. It seemed entirely possible that she could be blamed, and the more she told me, the greater my concern grew.

She had endured a rough week. H-P had disclosed the leak investigation in a filing with the Securities and Exchange Commission on Wednesday, September 6, triggering a wave of hysterical and "shocked" media coverage. On Friday, the eighth, two days before Pattie's first call to me, H-P had confirmed targeting the phone records of nine journalists. Cue hordes of outraged reporters.

The company's solution was to put Pattie Dunn out in front of this, intentionally or unintentionally adding to the impression this was Pattie's show. On the Friday before she called me, H-P's PR people had told her over the telephone that the company needed to talk to the press and that she would be the spokesman. "When?" she asked. "Now," the PR person responded. The next thing she heard was, "Pattie, say hello to Damon Darlin of the *New York Times*."

This struck me as particularly odd. If my partners and I had been on the scene, we would have prepared her for the interviews the way a lawyer would prepare his client for testimony: we would have presented questions she likely would be asked and would have worked with her to make sure her answers were clear, concise, and accurate. If a question was legally sensitive, we would have advised her to tell the reporter she couldn't comment for just that reason, and if she didn't know the answer to tell the reporter that and not speculate. We would have also been on the phone during the call with her so we could follow up. Pattie told me the H-P crew didn't do any of that. They just let her wing it.

"Mike, That Won't Ever Happen"

Twenty minutes into our first phone call, I realized that the interests of Dunn and H-P could be divergent and that she very well might need her own advisors, both for legal counsel and for PR strategy. I warned her that she should brace for this possibility. Pattie responded in her ever-optimistic way: "Mike, that won't ever happen."

"Then if it doesn't, it won't matter," I said. "Humor me." She agreed, in an abundance of caution, to retain her own lawyer. "But I want someone based in San Francisco," she said. I recommended James Brosnahan of Morrison Foerster. Jim's awards over his distinguished career—too numerous to mention here—include being named one of the top thirty trial lawyers in the United States by *Legal 500 US* and induction into the California Trial Lawyers Hall of Fame. Having worked with him on numerous criminal and civil cases, I admired his savvy not only in a court of law but also in the court of public opinion. I told Pattie about a high-profile case the two of us had worked on, and how, during depositions, every time he walked behind this difficult and obnoxious witness, he would "accidentally" kick the back of the guy's chair, unsettling him. I got Jim and Pattie on the phone together that afternoon, and she retained him.

Sitrick And Company started out representing Hewlett-Packard, but we insisted on a "carve-out" clause that would allow us to represent Dunn should her interests conflict with the company's. Immediately upon hanging up from the call with Pattie Dunn, I had a partner at my firm, Terry Fahn, begin the fact-finding deep dive with which we begin every case. Fahn happened to be visiting the Malibu beach house that Sunday with his family. Clad in swim trunks and flip-flops, he grabbed his laptop and began searching hundreds of sources online for all that had been reported and repeated in the media about the H-P scandal.

We had to have as many facts as possible, gathered from media coverage and by interviewing the client and her team, to know which inaccurate impressions we needed to correct and how we might use the facts to correct the story. Rule 1: First, get the facts.

It was all too clear that this story had already spun out of control. When that happens, wrong "facts" and impressions are repeated over and over, and it can be impossible to correct each individual misstatement. We needed to educate the reporters who already had written stories about what they got wrong and correct the story—"redirect the narrative," if you want it in fancy PR terms—but doing so would be especially tricky. The facts of this case were damaging, and reporters have an especially intense interest in a story about a company spying on...*reporters.*

Fahn, a firm veteran who had interned under me when he was only nineteen during the Orange County bankruptcy, was well equipped for the research, having done a lot of it in his years as a litigator at a respected Los Angeles–based law firm before joining me. The more he turned up, the more we both believed that Pattie was getting railroaded. The leak-plugging probe had been undertaken at the urging of the board, with its full approval and knowledge. It had been overseen by H-P security executives and monitored by H-P's general counsel, and it had been conducted by outside contractors H-P's internal security had used for years. Pattie, the board, and the brass had been assured that everything the investigators were doing was both legal and proper. She had a full-time job at the top of Barclay's wealth management, and as an outside director and the *nonexecutive* chairman of H-P, she had no operating authority, no one reporting to her, no assistant, and no office at the company.

So how had Pattie Dunn become the scapegoat?

There it was at the top of a September 6 column in the *Wall Street Journal*: "an extensive investigation into press leaks that was undertaken by new board Chairman Patricia Dunn." The sole H-P executive quoted, she had told the reporter: "The situation is regrettable. But the bottom line is that the board has asserted its commitment to upholding the standards of confidentiality that are critical to its functioning. A board can't serve effectively if there isn't complete trust that what gets discussed stays in the room."

It's not uncommon after a scandal of this scale for the company to feel it has to find a scapegoat. I had no evidence that this was the case here, but still I worried that Pattie might become H-P's target for blame, whether intended or unintended. She told me she trusted H-P's Mark Hurd implicitly. She had helped put him in the job, she respected him greatly, and he was her good friend. Later the same day, I had a call with Hurd and listened as the CEO said all the right things about Pattie. Yet my instincts told me I needed to protect Pattie.

Rather abruptly I realized that this well-meaning, earnest woman was just doing what the company's CEO and her dysfunctional board had asked her to do: plug the leaks. She used H-P's internal security group, which reported to the company's general counsel. The internal security group hired the investigators. The general counsel and the CEO were copied on all reports. But now

Pattie was being depicted as power-mad and out of control. To me, it just didn't seem right.

This almost instant, empathic reaction came to me naturally. At my firm, we often adopt a protective and reassuring approach if we feel clients have been wronged. From the moment I began examining the spying scandal and searching for ways to respond, I felt intuitively that the media had it backwards, that there must be another villain at work.

————

The seeds of this scandal had been planted more than a year earlier, five years into the tumultuous reign of superstar CEO Carly Fiorina.

H-P had been founded in the proverbial Silicon Valley garage on January 1, 1939, by two engineers, William Hewlett and David Packard, and Fiorina was the first outsider to run the company. As she once told *Forbes* magazine in a cover profile, "Leadership is a performance." Words to live by when she ran for the Republican nomination for president in 2016.

On January 24, 2005, a page-one story by Pui-Wing Tam in the *Wall Street Journal* revealed intimate details of a strategic retreat for H-P directors and senior management. It told of directors' qualms with Fiorina, who had been resisting their push for her to delegate more and let retired director Tom Perkins rejoin the board.

Furious about the leak, Fiorina had an outside lawyer look into the breach. He questioned directors, but everyone professed innocence, including, obviously, the leaker. When Fiorina was fired in early February (in a parting insult, private details about her sudden, unceremonious exit were leaked to the press), the board elevated Pattie Dunn to the new position of nonexecutive chairman and set up a search for a new CEO. They also reappointed Tom Perkins to the board.

The seventy-four-year-old Perkins, a co-founder of Silicon Valley's Kleiner Perkins Caufield Byers, was the fifth (ex-)husband of the romance novelist Danielle Steele and himself the author of *Sex and the Single Zillionaire*, a "supremely trashy novel," as the *New York Times* called it. The billionaire venture capitalist was "a wild, old cowboy," in Pattie's view, flouting the rules and flaunting the inappropriate, while she was earnest and strait-laced. Perkins, she told me, had complained that she was too much "by-the-book."

Code Name: "Kona"

A month later, at the urging of seven of her nine fellow directors, Pattie Dunn asked H-P security officials to look further into the boardroom leaks. She suggested bringing in the renowned Kroll & Associates, but H-P security recommended a small firm that had worked with them before. The board gave the project the code name "Kona" because it got underway as Pattie was on vacation in Hawaii.

On March 30, H-P tapped former NCR Corp. executive Mark Hurd as its new CEO. Hurd was told about the investigation and voiced his support. By September, Kona had faltered, and in November, Hurd was told the results were inconclusive.

Then came another big leak. On January 23, 2006, one day shy of the anniversary of the leak in the *Journal* that had so infuriated Fiorina, CNET.com reported secret details of a board retreat held a few days earlier. Hurd and the H-P directors were outraged. To them it felt like a betrayal. The chairman, Patricia Dunn, with everyone's support, asked H-P security to start a new investigation, code-named "Kona II."

By May, the results of Kona II were in. The leaker, according to the report, was George A. "Jay" Keyworth II, the longest-serving H-P board member (since 1986) and reportedly a close friend of Tom Perkins. H-P's own PR people had introduced Keyworth to Kawamoto (obviously not for that purpose), and the two had kept in touch.

Tom Perkins had asked Pattie Dunn to withhold the leaker's identity and give Keyworth a wrist-slap in private. Pattie sought the advice of the board's outside counsel and the company's general counsel, as well as Mark Hurd. All of them recommended that she take the matter to the board, which she did. On the day the board met, Hurd huddled with Keyworth beforehand, telling him the investigation had found the culprit and hoping the director would step up, take the hit, confess, and apologize.

Keyworth didn't say a word.

In the board meeting a few hours later, Pattie Dunn revealed that the investigators had identified Jay Keyworth as the leaker. Tom Perkins jumped up from the table, resigned, and stormed out. If he thought his fellow directors would ask him not to quit, he was disappointed. They took a hard line, voting immediately to accept Perkins's resignation. The board then asked Jay Keyworth to resign. Unfazed, he refused, saying that the shareholders should decide.

Pattie believed that this turn of events outraged Tom Perkins, who was accustomed to getting his way, and set him on a path of revenge—not because of the leak probe, but because she had not bowed to his request to keep the outcome of the investigation under wraps.

Hewlett-Packard had to disclose Perkins's resignation in a filing with the SEC, and it could have revealed the findings of the leak investigation then. In my opinion, it should have done so. Instead, H-P issued a terse statement in which Hurd praised the man who just had quit:

H-P (NYSE:H-PQ) (Nasdaq:H-PQ) announced today that Thomas J. Perkins resigned from its board of directors on May 18, 2006, with immediate effect.

The board has 10 members following his resignation.

Mark Hurd, H-P chief executive officer and president, said, "On behalf of H-P, I wish to thank Tom for his service and dedication to our company. Since he first joined the company nearly 50 years ago, going on to serve as leader of H-P's early computer operations, an executive at H-P Labs and ultimately as a director, we have benefited from Tom's business insights and understanding of technology. He has been instrumental in championing improvements that are leading to a stronger H-P. I am particularly grateful for the support he has provided to me over the past year."

Pattie, Jim Brosnahan, and I were perplexed by this announcement. It was so incomplete that the SEC eventually censured H-P for violating disclosure requirements. Worse, though, the company's reticence left it vulnerable by creating an asset—the secret of its investigation—that now was in the possession of a person—Tom Perkins—who was upset with the company, its board, and management and could give it to the media. We believed that Perkins was stoking this controversy with manufactured outrage merely as a tactic for getting back at Pattie and forcing her off the board. We felt this was an important element in the story.

Turning this story around would have been easier if we had been hired before the crisis exploded. Am I suggesting that H-P should have hired us before there was a crisis to manage? Yes, actually, I am. While not specifically talking about H-P, here, in my experience, companies often know that a crisis is coming, but fear and denial are powerful components of human nature. They immobilize senior executives, encouraging them to hunker down in the foolish hope that the crisis will go away. Which it rarely ever does, unless you can pull off a miracle. Or, they use the same PR firm they have been using to promote their products to handle the crisis, which in nine times out of ten it is ill-equipped to do. By the time Pattie brought us in, this genie had escaped the bottle. There was no stopping this story now, but we felt we could turn it.

In tending to hundreds of clients in crisis, I have developed a sense of the underlying cycle that drives most crisis cases, a cascading series of reactions and actions that play out with an almost mathematical order. You no doubt have heard of the five stages of grief. I have identified five stages of crisis:

Stage One: Denial. Companies often don't realize a crisis is about to descend; executives don't feel it is that bad, or they think if they ignore it, it will just go away. Maybe it will be just a one-day story.

Stage Two: Shock and silence. Stunned that controversy has jolted their company, executives go silent. They may feel that they don't know enough to comment. Their media advisors may tell them that reporters are out to get them. They may believe that nothing they can say will make it any better (which may be true); they might even make it worse. Or the lawyers will tell a company's leadership to forgo saying anything publicly. Sometimes going silent is required, but more often, "no comment" is bad advice (see Rule 9).

Stage Three: Turning inward. The company decides it will ignore the media and communicate only to its customers and employees. This can be problematic for two reasons: (1) There is a high probability that those communications will be "leaked to the media," in which case someone else will be framing and explaining your message. (2) Even if the internal communication is not leaked, if the situation attracts media attention, someone else will be framing your message. The *Wall Street Journal* is saying things are terrible, while your internal message says things are just fine. Whom are your employees likely to believe?

Stage Four: Help! Belatedly, the brass turns to its lawyers or board to recommend a crisis communications consultant to deal with the situation, which has deteriorated into a full-blown emergency. This is when Sitrick's Rule 1 for Engagement kicks in. Get the facts. This should have been the first thing management did when the crisis hit.

Stage Five: Healing and fixing. With outside help, the company focuses on getting the "facts" communicated to its various constituents, including the fact that it has corrected what went wrong.

By the time Pattie Dunn made her opening call to me, the H-P scandal had tumbled into Stage Four. I knew then that getting a grip on this story and redirecting it was going to take some drastic moves that usually were unheard of in these cases.

Events were outpacing us, though. That day, *Newsweek* issued a press release announcing a devastating cover story that would appear on newsstands September 11, excoriating Pattie Dunn with the headline "The Boss Who Spied on Her Board." It played up "Pattie Dunn's obsession" with plugging leaks and said, "Lying, spying, name-calling, finger-pointing—all of it is a tragicomedy that Shakespeare might've penned had he gotten an M.B.A."

A real hatchet job, in our view, and wrong on so many counts. Pattie wasn't the boss, and she didn't oversee the spying. The story had Dunn jousting with an ex-board member, the billionaire venture capitalist Tom Perkins, heroically resigning to protest the spying and turning into a whistleblower.

On that same Monday, September 11, as outrage spread in the media, the U.S. House Committee on Energy and Commerce sent a letter to Patricia Dunn demanding thousands of documents within a week and seeking "an interview related to these matters." Reading the letter, I couldn't help but notice that the four congressmen's signatures were large enough to rival John Hancock's on the Declaration of Independence. Everybody was jumping on her case.

Positioning and Wording Are Paramount

At 1:46 p.m. that same day, Terry Fahn sent me an email with the subject line "URGENT call." H-P's internal PR head, he told me, had set a call for 3:30 p.m. with Mark Hurd, Pattie Dunn, and others. "They want us to look over and comment on a press release, script, and media plan. Let's talk when you get back." The sad but not surprising announcement would be that Pattie Dunn, ever the good soldier, was going to hand over her prized title of chairman to Mark Hurd in a few months and stay on the board.

Positioning and wording are paramount in a press release, and no detail is too picayune to question and agonize over. Terry Fahn has kept draft documents from this time, and they show the painstaking approach that we took, easing the harshness of the event, and changing and adding responses to their proposed questions and answers.

In the avalanche of media coverage the next day, Tuesday, the twelfth, Fahn and I handled calls and emails from roughly seventy reporters and producers, including five at CNBC, three at *Bloomberg*, two apiece at Reuters, the *New York Times*, and the *Washington Post*, and one at the *Wall Street Journal*. It was crucial to avoid anyone's reporting "no comment" or "couldn't be reached for comment." Fahn and I both knew it was *our job* to respond as early, as often, and in as much detail as possible, especially to the biggest players. After filling a spreadsheet with every reporter's name, affiliation, email address, and phone number, Fahn made sure to return every single call and every email that I couldn't. He has told me he learned this from me. It's a matter of going the extra mile to represent and protect the client, to say nothing of showing respect for the reporter. He spent an entire hour on the phone with one NPR host, and heard a softer tone from him soon after.

One noteworthy name on Fahn's call list: Rich Bonin, senior producer for *60 Minutes*, who worked with Lesley Stahl. I had known Bonin for years and had worked on *60 Minutes* stories with him. He had been working on a story about Carly Fiorina, whose new memoir offered her side of the story of her ouster from H-P in February 2005. Now Pattie Dunn was in trouble at the same company, and, according to Bonin, both women were saying that Tom Perkins had played a role in the turmoil. By coincidence, Bonin also was working at that moment on a story about the largest private yacht in the world. Its owner: the very same Tom Perkins.

Interestingly, I had already been talking with Dunn and Brosnahan about the high-risk, unheard-of move of putting Pattie on *60 Minutes* in the middle of the scandal. It was the ultimate Lead Steer—on the air for four decades, still ranked as one of the most-watched programs in America, airing every Sunday night to eleven million viewers, and celebrated for taking on CEOs and rapacious businesses with an investigative vengeance. And, if Pattie appeared, it would be watched by most, if not every journalist covering the story. After talking to Jim and Pattie, I approached another *60 Minutes* veteran, Vicki Gordon, executive story editor, about the possibility of Pattie appearing on the program if Jim and Pattie approved. Needless to say, it wasn't a hard sell.

As I explain to my clients, choosing a Lead Steer is not just about audience size, it is about the respect the journalist and the media outlet command among other journalists. Getting a favorable story from someone who is known for "softball" interviews won't influence other journalists to write about your client in a favorable way, as a Lead Steer media outlet or journalist would. Tell your story through the *New York Times*, *Wall Street Journal*, *Financial Times*, *Washington Post*, *Los Angeles Times*, or *60 Minutes*, and it could change the direction of the herd and ultimately change public perception.

That was our thinking in putting Pattie on *60 Minutes*. I approached Vicki Gordon because I knew her well, having worked with her on numerous stories. I trusted her and she trusted me, and I trusted Bonin and *60 Minutes* to be fair. Bonin was aware that Vicki Gordon and I were communicating. Though he worked in Washington and Gordon worked in New York, they were good friends.

When I called Gordon, I told her I was representing Pattie Dunn (she laughed and said, "What a surprise") and wanted to explore putting her on *60 Minutes*. Because our client faced possible criminal charges, I explained that we would have to have an off-the-record meeting first to ensure that we all felt comfortable with one another. I told her I wanted to make sure Brosnahan in particular didn't feel this could undercut his legal strategy.

Serving our clients often depends on maintaining this close network of trusted journalists at the most important media platforms. If we trust the reporters, we're more confident that even the toughest stories will be fair, that the client's version of the story will get told, that there won't be any surprises, ambush interviews, or cheap shots.

In Pattie's case, I had to think bigger. It was risky, but we had no choice. Sitrick And Company was getting to this party late.

When Pattie had first called Jim Brosnahan, he was in a trial in San Jose, working sixteen-hour days. "Who's Pattie Dunn?" he asked the assistant who informed him of her call. The assistant responded, "She's on the cover of *Newsweek* magazine."

Brosnahan had worked with me on half a dozen or more cases by now. He was a courtroom killer-with-kindness, able to lacerate his adversary but without overdoing it. Moreover, he was a strategist with a view beyond just the legal issues. Jim Brosnahan was willing to go further than most lawyers in devising a media strategy. I readily yielded to him on legal matters, because the bigger goal is to win the case in court, even as we support the client in the court of public opinion. He in turn yielded to me on media matters, as long as it didn't jeopardize the legal outcome. The two of us worked together like a precision instrument.

Telling Pattie's Story

On Friday, September 22, ten days after Dunn had agreed to give up her chairman's title by the following January, her situation got even worse. The H-P board decided it was necessary for her to hand the chairmanship over to Hurd immediately and to resign from the board. H-P's conflict with Dunn now was clear. Also resigning from the board was the chief leaker, Jay Keyworth, but the media made less of that development, focusing instead on Pattie Dunn. In fact, it was beginning to look like California Attorney General William Lockyer might pursue criminal indictments, perhaps targeting Pattie Dunn at the top. We needed to take more drastic measures to draw attention to Pattie's story and the injustices she faced.

Now, more than ever, the idea of putting Pattie Dunn under the hot lights of *60 Minutes* appealed to me. It offered us the chance fundamentally to alter the main story line across the entire mediascape with a single stroke.

Now that H-P had forced Pattie Dunn off the board, Jim Brosnahan and I both emphasized to her that she just had been wronged. Even at this point, however, she refused to blame the H-P board. She simply did not want to believe that her fellow directors would turn on her. Brosnahan saw this as touching resilience, thinking she had one of the most affirmative life attitudes of anyone he had ever met. Pattie would need to draw on it, big-time, to have any chance of getting through what was coming her way.

Chapter 3

Exonerating Pattie

Part Two

To hear many journalists tell it, most PR people are lacking in a skill that is central to dealing with the media: the art of storytelling.

This basic but critical talent shapes much of what I do and defines my firm's approach to strategic communications: getting the facts out, ensuring our client's story is understood and told properly, and sometimes combatting or averting a negative story by telling a better one. To be clear: this doesn't mean making things up, veering from the facts, or even shading the truth. It means being able to put together a series of facts in an interesting, cohesive, understandable, and compelling way. This also involves acting preemptively to answer the question "So what?"

As a journalist, you are taught the "the five W's and how"—to answer the questions *who, what, when, where*, and *why*, and sometimes *how*. In my firm, you are also taught to answer the question

"So what?" Why should anyone care—the reporter, his or her readers, viewers, listeners, or anyone else?

This is one of the reasons that so many of the professionals at Sitrick are former journalists with twenty years' experience or more. We also have a senior member of the firm who is a former litigator. Same skills. They all know how to put together a good story and tell it. Some clients think the former journalists have some invisible pull with their former colleagues, an ability to reach out to some editor by a back channel. Many do, and if they can, so much the better, but my main interest in hiring them is their knowledge of what makes news and how to tell a good tale. Teaching them what PR is turns out to be the easy part. As I've already said, it is easier to teach a journalist PR than teach a PR person what news is.

Every big story is a battle among conflicting versions of events. Our job is to ensure our client's version gets seen and heard. Shaping the story and redirecting it to ensure that our client's message is told and received requires us to come up with a *better* story through better facts, a more thorough explanation, and a more plausible alternative.

In the case of Pattie Dunn, that is what we did. We needed to find a new narrative. We needed to demonstrate that what had been reported was wrong, to get the real facts in the public square, and to show what Pattie *did* and, more importantly, what she *didn't* do. That process starts with the same rule most of my cases start with: first, get the facts. Once you know the facts, you can ascertain what is true and what is not, and if the facts support it, you can use that information to counter a negative story and generate a positive one.

For the first few days after we were retained, my team and I intensified our fact-finding mission in extensive briefings with Pattie Dunn and her attorney, Jim Brosnahan. After sifting through the coverage to identify what was right and what was wrong, I reached out to the network of reporters who had written about the case to arrange individual off-the-record briefings. Our goal was twofold: to educate them on the facts of the case and, in the process, to tell them what they had gotten wrong, in the hope that they wouldn't repeat it. Yet we didn't ask the reporters for corrections. Ordinarily, if a reporter gets something wrong we ask for a correction or clarification. Here, however, everyone was basically writing the same thing. It would be a daunting and likely losing battle to convince a reporter that not only did he get it wrong, but everyone else had gotten the facts wrong too, and now he alone should publish a correction when maybe nobody else would. Plus, I didn't want to do this piecemeal. Instead, we chose to concentrate on establishing a relationship. The plan from the start was to use a Lead Steer so we could try to change the direction of the herd.

So during a weekend break in Brosnahan's trial in San Jose, I flew up from Los Angeles and snagged a conference room in his hotel, using it as a "war room" where Jim and I could meet one at a time with a few select reporters we had lined up for backgrounders. We let them ask almost anything they wanted and gave them direct access to Pattie Dunn's attorney, only days after the scandal had been splashed all over the front pages of newspapers throughout the country.

I made sure the briefings were entirely off-the-record, meaning that the reporters agreed not to use the information in any way in print or on the air and not to share it with anyone outside their news organization. Any sharing of the information within their news organization likewise had to be treated as off the record. They accepted these conditions so they could learn more about the case from the people who had the inside track. And, of course, if they refused, they wouldn't get the interview, and the journalists who accepted the conditions would have a leg up on them.

If the information were handed to the reporters on a "not-for-attribution" basis, it could be used in print or on the air; they just couldn't say who had told them. "Off-the-record" was much stricter and, quite frankly, safer at this point, since we were still in the fact-gathering process. It is mission-critical that anyone dealing with the media understands these arcane and little-discussed ground rules, one of which is you must have agreement before the interview begins.

A lot of people in the PR field would have done these briefings en masse to save time, but as any young associate in my firm could tell you, you can't really do effective briefings of this type in a crowd; you must do it one-on-one. This more intensive and more personal approach is a staple of my firm. Even when we deal with reporters on the record, we avoid press conferences. As I will tell clients, if they ask, first of all, what happens if you hold a press conference and no one bothers to show up? (Not a risk in the Pattie Dunn case, to be sure.) Second, if you have one obnoxious question and one bad answer, everyone in the room has it, and once it is posted, all of their readers have it—including journalists and bloggers who didn't bother to show up.

But the most important reason I avoid press conferences is that they are impersonal. I believe it is critical to establish a personal relationship with reporters. I prefer one-on-ones. I like the intimacy and the ability to let a reporter get a feel for my client and understand that my client is giving this journalist his or her full attention, that this interview is special. And the reporters who do their homework, who ask the really good questions, don't like to share the results of their work with competitors. You can't serve everyone, of course, but you can pick out the most important ones.

From the pinnacle of business coverage at the *Wall Street Journal*, the *New York Times*, *Financial Times*, and *Bloomberg* to the pulse of the markets at CNBC and Fox Business News to the business magazines (*Forbes, Fortune, BusinessWeek*), as well as the newer online outlets like *CNET* and *TechCrunch*, we kept our network of contacts informed. We weren't offering them fluff—that's not what we do. We were offering them substance, the real stuff.

More Than Just Getting Ink

The goal, however, wasn't just to get some ink. We did everything with an eye on strategy, focusing on what information mattered and which publications would be most effective in communicating which story. Part of this process is figuring out which target audience you need to influence. Jim Brosnahan and I focused on what would benefit the client and, yes, the media. After all, you need to make it worthwhile for them.

Brosnahan also has told people that we study cases like lawyers, trying to achieve total command of the facts, and he praises my knowledge of the law, which I have gathered by working with him and other accomplished attorneys over the years. Jim and I both feel that we make an effective team: I recognize that it doesn't do any good to win the PR war and have our client go to jail or lose a case and pay a substantial judgment. Thus, while I am not shy about providing my views, in the end, of course, I yield to him on legal strategy and work within his needs. In turn, he has told me he holds unstinting faith in my advice on media strategy.

In the off-the-record meetings that Brosnahan did with reporters, we emphasized how an awful lot of the reporting on the H-P story was entirely wrong. The more we learned, the more we felt the story as reported wasn't the real story at all.

The real story, I now believed, was that Pattie had been blamed wrongly for actions taken by others. *She* hadn't launched the leak-plugging mission, she had acted at the behest of the *board*, with the full knowledge of the company's CEO. Pattie had gotten it started as she was asked to do, after consulting with H-P's security officials, who ran the investigation and oversaw a contractor they had recommended and hired. In fact, Pattie wasn't an employee of the company and didn't have anyone who reported to her. She didn't even have an office at H-P.

My partner Terry Fahn and I also recognized that Pattie Dunn's personal story, though moving and impressive, couldn't be used to counter the mounting allegations against her. We would have to be able to demonstrate that she was innocent of that of which she had been accused.

The daughter of a onetime Las Vegas showgirl, Pattie was only eleven years old when her dad, an entertainment booker for casinos, died in 1964. Afterward, she and her mom lived in their car for a while. Pattie put herself through college on scholarship and started as a temp at Wells Fargo's wealth-management business.

After Barclays Bank bought it, she worked her way up from secretary to global CEO of the unit, a by-the-book fiduciary overseeing a trillion dollars in assets. Pattie also was a three-time cancer survivor, having been diagnosed with breast cancer in 2000, melanoma in 2002, and stage IV ovarian cancer in 2004.

An impressive and touching personal backstory, surely, but as I said earlier it wouldn't help our situation if Pattie Dunn were guilty of all the misdeeds of which anonymous sources in the media were accusing her. This too is something many people both on the client side and on my side of the business don't understand. An advisor will try to play up how their client went from rages to riches or how much money their controversial client gives to charity, but her rags to riches story or his charitable giving doesn't matter if she is guilty of what she has been accused of or say, he embezzled ten million dollars as charged. Fortunately for us, Pattie Dunn wasn't guilty.

So we set out to change the narrative by getting out the real facts of the case, refuting the notion that Pattie personally had caused this mess by emphasizing that she had been directed to use H-P's internal investigation unit, which hired the outside contractor, and that she was acting at the urging of the board and the company's CEO, Mark Hurd. The internal investigative unit didn't report to Pattie. No one did. She was nonexecutive chairman. The investigative unit reported to the company's general counsel, who in turn reported to Hurd, the CEO. Pattie didn't even know what pretexting was, let alone order it.

We also let it be known that Tom Perkins had not quit the board in protest over the investigation, as had been reported in the media. He had quit because Pattie refused to do as he had asked—withhold the leaker's identity and give Keyworth a wrist-slap in private. Instead, at the advice of counsel, she brought it before the board.

This was the new story we would bring to our Lead Steer, the producers at *60 Minutes*, if Pattie and Jim Brosnahan would go along with my plan. I also had Jim and Pattie give interviews to two other Lead Steers in their respective realms, the *Wall Street Journal* in business news and Jim Stewart for the *New Yorker* in general-interest magazines.

We had learned that in the months since Perkins had resigned from the H-P board he had hired a PR advisor and a former Justice Department lawyer. Terry Fahn had spotted a gossipy item in the *New York Times* on September 12 that looked like a smoking gun. Perkins's lawyer was reported to have sent Perkins an email gloating about the bad press Pattie Dunn was getting, celebrating the

Newsweek cover and a *Houston Chronicle* column mocking her. The email's other recipient was George Keyworth, a close friend of Perkins and the H-P director who had been identified as the leaker. The *Times* reported that Perkins had forwarded his lawyer's note to two dozen people, including an H-P board member, H-P's chief strategy officer, and even the reporter who had written the searing *Newsweek* cover story. The same *Newsweek* writer was also at work on a book about the largest private yacht in the world— owned by none other than Tom Perkins.

To some observers this might have seemed a little too cozy. The *Newsweek* writer, covering a major story in which Pattie Dunn's reputation was at stake, used as a central source the person who was attacking her, Tom Perkins, whose cooperation he needed for his book on Perkins's yacht—all 289 feet of it. Some PR people might have seized on this and publicly attacked the *Newsweek* writer for a conflict of interest. But we didn't. *Newsweek* had disclosed the writer's book project at the top of its cover story. The conflict was there for all to see. It would just look like whining, and it didn't address the most important question: whether the story was true. While I almost never criticize a reporter publicly (though I will make an issue of his getting the facts wrong) and never make it personal, I would have made his conflict an issue had we discovered it and had *Newsweek* not disclosed it. Attacking reporters on a personal level may make you or your client feel good, but there is no other upside—and there is enormous downside. Reporters are human; they have feelings. And they wield the power of the pen. Though they would never admit it, they can make it personal too— and the client will be the loser.

Although we could have disputed several passages in the *Newsweek* story, that was not the right forum. We didn't want our side consigned to the obscurity of an insert or a correction, preventing us from "breaking" the story in a way that would have the impact we wanted. So we let it go and decided to pursue the Lead Steers we had picked for making our case.

On the day that Pattie Dunn was forced to quit the board, September 22, 2006, Perkins's lawyer went on CNBC with Maria Bartiromo in the 4:00 p.m. hour, backhandedly praising Pattie Dunn's "courageous and graceful" act in "taking full responsibility for the investigation that she initiated, conducted, and supervised." He also gave Mark Hurd "the benefit of the doubt." On September 26, in an op-ed in the *Journal*, Perkins's lawyer claimed that Perkins had resigned in protest, saying it was "unconscionable for a chairman to spy on her own directors."

Despite Perkins's lawyer's comments, Pattie never took "full" responsibility for the investigation. She had not "initiated" it—the entire board and the CEO *asked her* to start it—and she hadn't "conducted" it—H-P's contractors had, at the direction of the company's internal investigation unit. Pattie Dunn didn't "spy on her own directors." In fact, she herself had been a victim of the same pretexting.

Lodging a Multi-Prong Campaign

I wanted to be sure that we could make these counterpoints on critical platforms: in Pattie's congressional testimony, in interviews with key reporters, in an op-ed under her byline for the *Journal*, and in briefing producers who were now setting up their shoot for *60 Minutes*. In quelling a crisis in the age of the Internet and omnimedia, you have to fight a multi-front war.

On September 28, just six days after H-P bounced her off the board, Pattie Dunn was set to testify in a congressional hearing on the "spy scandal." Nine other figures had invoked their Fifth Amendment right against self-incrimination, but Pattie refused to take that stance. She felt she had a good counter-story and wanted to tell it. Jim Brosnahan and I agreed and thought she would make a credible, articulate, clear-spoken witness. We began prepping her immediately.

Brosnahan and I worked with Pattie on the written statement for the hearing, an opening salvo of eight thousand words that hit many of the central themes that we had identified. Sample: "I was a director of the company, not an officer or employee, and had no authority to enter into contracts.... I did not at any point consider myself [the probe's] 'supervisor.'"

Meanwhile, people on the team briefed congressional staff and a few congressmen in the days leading up to the hearing. I believe in the power of repetition: first, you tell them what you will be telling them, then you tell them, then you tell them what you just told them. We also ran Dunn through practice sessions, reviewing answers and arguments and troubleshooting questions. The last session was held in the Washington office of Brosnahan's firm right before her appearance.

In that hearing, testifying live and under oath, Pattie Dunn simply soared. Poised and calm before a phalanx of congressmen, she more than lived up to the faith that Jim Brosnahan and I had placed in her, coming off as cool, unflappable, authoritative, and at times funny. Here is one of my favorite exchanges:

> *Dunn*:...And I would add that I had no reason to think that anything illegal was going on. There were batteries of experts telling me that that was not the case.
> *Oregon Representative Greg Walden*: And I understand that you were advised that way and some of those batteries of experts are now looking for work. And I understand that. (LAUGHTER)
> *Dunn*: I'm one of them. (LAUGHTER)

Moreover, she performed a slam-dunk when Congressman Walden asked why her version of events differed from that of the outside investigator of the leak, Ron DeLia, who had taken the Fifth and refused to testify before the committee:

> *Dunn*: Sir, I am here testifying under oath. Mr. DeLia is not. I think I will leave it at that.
> *Walden*: Well, I'm not sure we can leave it at that. Answer my question about Mark [Hurd's] role in this.... You've indicated you kind of deferred to him.... What was your understanding of his role in this approval process?
> *Dunn*: This particular element of the investigation could not go forward without his approval.

Pattie's performance through seven hours of questioning was by most accounts triumphant, and in a news photo of her snapped as she left the hearing room, with Brosnahan and me just behind her, she is beaming in a satisfied, gleaming way. Afterward, I kept her away from the hordes of reporters at the hearing but made Brosnahan available for a fast press conference. Our star client had just nailed it in her congressional testimony, and Jim did equally well with the media afterwards.

The congressional hearing only bolstered the case, I felt, for putting Pattie on *60 Minutes*, and after the press conference, Jim Brosnahan and I went to a private, off-the-record meeting with the show's producer, Rich Bonin, and the venerable on-air star Lesley Stahl, who had flown in from New York to discuss the interview.

Brosnahan knew that putting Pattie on *60 Minutes* would be controversial. "This isn't exactly in the criminal defense playbook," he said to me. Shortly after I had broached the idea of putting Pattie on the famously aggressive program, he had told her straight out, "Pattie, if we do this, every lawyer that you meet at every cocktail party, no matter where it is, will come up to you and tell you two things: This is a total mistake, and Brosnahan must be out of his mind."

Then again, Pattie was the perfect witness—articulate, smart, with an honest story to tell. Plus, by going on *60 Minutes*, she would show America she had nothing to hide. This was another upside of taking the risk for Dunn. So at the meeting with the producer and Stahl, Jim Brosnahan agreed to let his client be interviewed the following week, on Wednesday, October 4, barely in time to air it on Sunday, the eighth.

That evening at 6:09 p.m. Eastern Time, in the aftermath of Pattie Dunn's congressional testimony, we put something on the PR Newswire that underscored the differences building between H-P and its now-former chairman. It was a copy of a letter Jim Brosnahan had just sent to H-P lawyers citing "a number of inaccuracies" in the company's recent Form 8-K disclosure statement (which the SEC requires a public company to file when there are "major events that shareholders should know about") regarding the leak investigation and demanding that H-P revise it. He wanted a clarification that the probe had begun *before* Pattie became chairman and an acknowledgment that H-P Security had gotten involved earlier than H-P had previously indicated. He also wanted H-P to delete the false statement that Dunn had heard the term "pretext" at a briefing the previous June. We took this step because we felt H-P needed to correct the record. It had the added benefit of making news: the correction request itself, or any changes that H-P made in response we knew would spark a news story, correcting the record in the court of public opinion.

As everyone prepared for the next big hurdle, the *60 Minutes* interview, the *Journal*'s Alan Murray called me to tell me he was going to do a story on H-P and Pattie Dunn. Though I had promised her exclusively to *60 Minutes*, I knew that the *Journal* was going to write something with or without Pattie, and we couldn't afford to have her side of the story left out yet again. My approach is always to be honest and up-front with reporters and editors. Dishonesty by omission is not only wrong, it can have severe consequences. So I let Bonin, the senior producer at *60 Minutes*, know that Dunn would be talking to the *Journal* and I let Murray know about *60 Minutes*.

Many years earlier, in another case, the CEO of one of the world's largest companies, embroiled at the time in one of the biggest crises in the world, secretly retained Sitrick And Company to provide advice to him and his chief operating officer, on the condition that no one else in the company could know. One day he called to tell me that *Newsweek* and *Business Week* were both working on company profiles and that his outside PR firm and internal people said they shouldn't tell either magazine that the other was doing a story. Each should think it had an exclusive. "What do you think?" he said. "Well," I told him, "besides being wrong on about five other levels, one of the magazines is going to publish first—and then the other one will kill you." The CEO took my advice and ordered his senior PR executive to tell them both.

Rich Bonin was unhappy to hear of the *Journal* story, but he understood. He wanted his show to be the first outlet anywhere to interview Pattie Dunn since her resignation from the H-P board, but he appreciated the heads-up. As it turned out, Bonin and I got lucky; the *Journal* wouldn't publish until the morning after the *60 Minutes* interview aired.

Then on October 4, just hours before the interview with Lesley Stahl was to be videotaped in a hotel suite in San Francisco, Pattie Dunn and four others were charged by the attorney general of California with four felony counts. Now the stakes suddenly were higher—anything she said in the interview could be used against her in court.

Nobody Gets Indicted and Goes on *60 Minutes*, or Do They?

Richard Bonin feared he might lose the Dunn interview altogether. Nobody gets indicted and goes on *60 Minutes* hours later. Yet I now felt we had even more compelling reasons to proceed with the Lesley Stahl interview. It was a chance to preempt the inevitable follow-up stories on her indictment. We just would have to be extremely careful about not giving any answers that could pose problems for Pattie's defense.

Before I line up any exclusive, especially if it's on a sensitive issue, I ask myself a battery of questions: *Can you trust the journalists? Are they honest, with high integrity? Do they have any hidden agendas? Would they try to make a name for themselves by pulling some cheap stunt?* I knew from years of working with the people on *60 Minutes* that the answers to those questions were the right ones.

After some discussion, Jim Brosnahan let the interview go forward. This surprised Bonin, and later he would say that decision showed him just how much faith Jim and I had in Pattie Dunn. We knew she could carry the ball. Pattie, for her part, still wanted to do the interview, despite the fresh indictment. She told me she didn't want her grandchildren to think she had done something wrong, because she hadn't. She needed to clear her name, and she may not have much time.

Few people knew it, but the indictment wasn't the worst news of the week for Pattie Dunn. The worst news had come a day earlier, when her doctors notified her that her stage IV ovarian cancer had returned.

On Wednesday, October 4, a *60 Minutes* crew set up in a suite at the Four Seasons in San Francisco. I was huddled in an adjacent bedroom with Jim Brosnahan, his partner Raj Chatterjee, and Terry Fahn, transfixed before a monitor and waiting to watch the interview unfold. Rich Bonin stationed himself in the hallway between the living room and the bedroom.

During breaks in the interview, I chatted with Rich Bonin as Terry Fahn showed another producer a copy of his smoking gun, the *Times* story on how Tom Perkins had sent out the mean email gloating about all the bad media coverage Pattie Dunn was getting. This was a hit job, he reminded her. The interview resumed.

Bonin wrote the script on his flight back East later that day so he could have the Pattie Dunn interview in the can in time for airing that Sunday, October 8, 2006. Most *60 Minutes* stories take six to eight weeks to put together; this one took four days.

The night the interview aired, I watched it at home in Los Angeles with my wife, Nancy. The interview opened with Stahl asking why Pattie was willing to be interviewed despite her indictment just hours before. Dunn answered, "I have a story to tell. I'm innocent. I need people to understand what happened, and I'm glad to have the chance to do it." When Stahl said that Mark Hurd "pointed the finger at you," Dunn calmly answered, "Well, it's a mischaracterization of my role."

Pattie also got in this really good lick: "The idea that I supervised, orchestrated, approved, all of the ways in which this investigation occurred, is just a complete myth. It's a falsehood. It's a damaging lie." The story took up the angle of the personal feud waged by Tom Perkins and his friend George Keyworth against Pattie, with Stahl describing how Perkins had stalked out of the board meeting "in a huff."

Then came the clincher, the dismount, the ending of the entire piece, when Lesley Stahl, in voiceover, played the cancer card: "Pattie Dunn appeared in a San Jose courtroom on Thursday. She's not just fighting for her reputation, she's also fighting for her life. This has all happened as she battles stage IV ovarian cancer." Then Stahl, on camera, said to Dunn, "And you're charged with all this. It's just all piling on you at once. And you're so strong."

> *Dunn*: What's the alternative?
> *Stahl*: Well, breaking down, getting in the back of a closet and sitting there. I can think of lots of things that other people might do.
> *Dunn*: Oh, the Golden Gate Bridge is always out there. It's not going away. I mean, you just have to fight back.

Pattie's parting shot may have been her best moment: "Having a criminal indictment is the last thing I ever expected in my entire life. But if I hadn't had four diagnoses of cancer, I would probably think it was the worst thing that could ever happen to anyone, and I know it's not." Cut to commercial. Turning to Nancy, I was surprised to see tears streaming down her cheeks. I told her, "We won." "What does that mean?" she asked. "It means, we won," I said. "This interview will turn the tide." And turn the tide it did.

You could feel it from that moment, in fact. The next morning, Monday, October 9, the *Wall Street Journal* ran the page-one story by George Anders and Alan Murray that we also had been working on, and it marked another turn in Pattie's favor. Then two days later came an op-ed in the *Journal* bylined by Patricia Dunn herself, laying out her story and calling out Tom Perkins directly:

> Some have said they feel I have been made a scapegoat. That is not for me to say. What I will say is that throughout the process I asked the right questions of the right people at the right times.... One more thing: Tom Perkins did not resign from the H-P board because of concern over the leak investigation—he resigned because he was upset that the full board had been given the chance to decide his friend's fate.

In the weeks that followed, others came to Pattie's defense. In mid-November, the veteran columnist Nicholas von Hoffman, in the *New York Observer*, surfed the shifting tide, writing a column headlined "Try a Little Sympathy for H.P.'s Patricia Dunn."

On December 8, the *Washington Post* reported that H-P had settled its case with the California attorney general, agreeing to pay a $14.5 million fine. That is about as much money as H-P takes in every hour, twenty-four hours a day, seven days a week, fifty-two weeks a year. The story quoted Attorney General William Lockyer making sounds of settlement for Pattie, saying he was "sympathetic to her health problems."

A few weeks later, in January 2007, I set up an off-the-record dinner between Pattie Dunn and one of the most respected financial journalists of his generation, the Pulitzer Prize winner James B. Stewart. He was pursuing a "reconstruction," a long, thoughtful "it all began when..." piece that would run in the *New Yorker*, one of the most prestigious magazines in the world. A Lead Steer can be a media outlet or a reporter, a columnist or a correspondent. Jim Stewart—a reporter, columnist, and author—is the model of a Lead Steer, respected by his peers and by his readers. People would ask me, why the *New Yorker*? My answer: because Jim Stewart was writing the piece.

My long-term professional relationship with Stewart aside, Brosnahan and I stayed by Pattie's side for the entire interview. She was still under indictment, after all. This was something that Jim Stewart, a former lawyer, understood.

Stewart published his twelve-thousand-word epic, "The Kona Files," in the February 19, 2007, issue of the *New Yorker*, which hit the stands on February 12. It presented the story fairly and in great detail, giving Pattie Dunn plenty of room to make the case that Sitrick And Company had been building the past five months. Jim Brosnahan, Terry Fahn, and I had spent days going back and forth with the magazine's famously meticulous fact-checking department. We grappled with 161 questions, prodding and poking at assertions and technicalities and nuances in every single one.

Then on February 27, Tom Perkins put his spin on the scandal in a jocular luncheon speech at a tech conference in San Francisco. "In spite of being indicted on four counts by the California attorney general, it is clear that former Chairman Patti Dunn won the battle," Perkins is reported to have said. The comment enraged Jim Brosnahan, and me as well, as we both still were in Pattie-protection mode. The next day we issued a scorching response on PR Newswire, noting that Dunn was undergoing chemotherapy and fighting for her life, even as she had to fight criminal charges that were largely the result of Tom Perkins's smear campaign. Brosnahan declared war:

> Yesterday, a man named Tom Perkins attacked my client. He did so unfairly. He did so falsely when he knows she cannot answer him. I am sorry that Patricia Dunn must

endure Mr. Perkins' cowardly attacks, but he has made the biggest mistake of his career. He is a bully, and he is bullying the wrong people.

In Brosnahan's eyes, Perkins had misrepresented his reasons for quitting, he had hurt Pattie Dunn unfairly, and he deserved to be called out and confronted for it.

A Distaste for Bullies

My own distaste for bullies traces back to my boyhood days on the South Side of Chicago. When I was maybe thirteen, my younger brother, David, nine-and-a-half years old at the time, was beaten up by five boys on the way home from school. David, sobbing, called our father at work. Dad said, "Put Mike on the phone," and he told me, the oldest of his three sons, "You do what it takes to make sure this never happens again." "Dad," I responded, "there were *five* of them." My father said, "I don't care. He's your brother. Fix it."

So I took my brother back to the house of the kid who was the leader of the group that beat him up and told him to go up to that kid and punch him in the nose. If those other kids tried to help, I'd take care of them. When three of the other kids ran up to help their leader, I stepped in and said, "You'll have to come through me," and they backed off. I was two years older than they were, and that was a big difference at the time.

Even today, I know that sometimes you have to punch someone in the nose, figuratively, to get his attention, and when it is necessary in my work, that's what we do.

Jim Brosnahan, in branding Tom Perkins a bully, vowed to get him on the stand at trial and cross-examine him, but he never got that chance. Just two weeks later, in mid-March, the newly elected California attorney general, Jerry Brown, dropped all charges against Pattie Dunn. Never mind her battle with cancer—this was a flimsy case. The AP headline read, "California Criminal Case against Former H-P Chairwoman Fizzles."

A month after the charges were dropped against Dunn, she made a speech at a financial conference in San Francisco. She wouldn't discuss the case except to say that prosecutors underestimated her: "Little did they know who they were dealing with."

More than a year later, on May 23, 2008, the SEC found that H-P had violated federal disclosure laws when it had withheld the reasons that Tom Perkins had resigned from the board. The company signed a cease-and-desist order, while neither admitting nor denying guilt. The SEC didn't impose any fine.

Pattie Dunn lived quietly after the crisis, enjoying her last five years free of scandal and scrutiny. She died of ovarian cancer at age fifty-eight. It was a sad coda to an especially triumphant exoneration. And even as I write this, a wave of sadness washes over me. She was truly a wonderful and special person who is missed by all who knew her.

Chapter 4

Inside "Disneywar"

The Walt Disney Company knows a lot about castles and kings, princesses and evil queens, having produced a matchless collection of live-action movies, children's TV series, and, most distinctively, animated films, which we used to call "cartoons." Maybe Disney should have considered this story-line:

> Once upon a time, in a magical kingdom, a powerful king reigned over the land. All was well for more than a decade: his people prospered, his shareholders prospered, and everyone was happy. But then things started to get worse, and he banished those who questioned his rule. And then, the king made the mistake of messing with the wrong guy.

Michael Eisner became Disney's CEO in 1984, transforming the company over the next decade from a dormant, inconsistent also-ran into a Hollywood juggernaut. But in later years Disney stagnated, and Eisner became renowned for his feuds.

His clashes included the fracturing of his relationship with a talented protégé, Jeff Katzenberg, the animation chief who quit in 1996 to form DreamWorks with Steven Spielberg and David Geffen. Though Katzenberg reportedly would have settled for $90 million, Eisner vowed he wouldn't get a dime, and Katzenberg later sued and settled out of court for $280 million. There was Eisner's relationship with super-agent Michael Ovitz, whom he brought in as his number two. Their prompt falling out sparked an embarrassing lawsuit and a $140 million payout. Not to mention strained relations with Harvey Weinstein of Miramax and Steve Jobs of Apple and Pixar.

Katzenberg, Ovitz, Weinstein, Jobs—Eisner had survived his scrapes with all those stars of Hollywood and the business world. He didn't fare nearly as well, however, against an unassuming heir whose surname was known the world over but who himself was barely known at all: Roy E. Disney, the septuagenarian son of Roy O. Disney, who had co-founded the company with his younger brother, Walt. Roy E. Disney and his longtime partner and financial advisor, Stanley P. Gold, mounted an unrelenting three-year campaign against Eisner, advised by my firm from the start.

At first, their modest goal was to force the Disney CEO to listen up and share a little power with the board. But in late 2003, Eisner tried to maneuver Roy E. Disney off the board. Rather than waiting to be forced off, he abruptly resigned and took his campaign public.

Roy Disney's crusade would result in Eisner's surrendering the chairman's title to an outside director after amassing the highest shareholder no-confidence vote ever lodged against a CEO. The following year, Eisner would retire as CEO and quit the board a full year before his contract was set to end. Robert Iger then took the Disney helm, healing the divisions that Eisner had inflicted and driving the company to renewed record growth. This would pay off fabulously for Disney investors.

With Michael Eisner's departure, Roy Disney got what he really wanted all along, and the dispute was dropped so quickly, quietly, and completely that it seemed like just a dream—Dorothy waking up at the end of *The Wizard of Oz*. (I know *The Wizard of Oz* is an MGM film, but the analogy still works.)

Of all the campaigns I have waged in the past three decades or so, the Eisner fight was among the most satisfying. It was a stunning win for a small SWAT team that took on one of the biggest media and entertainment companies in the world and one of the most powerful CEOs in all of Hollywood.

Let me admit up front that by most measures, Roy Disney had no rightful claim to stewardship of the company. Nor did he claim or desire to. He also didn't have much clout—on paper, at least—given his family's stake of less than 1 percent in the company. In board meetings, he rarely spoke up, and although he was chairman of Disney's animation division, he didn't run the day-to-day business.

And he was starting this fight late, with the annual shareholder meeting just a few months away. Yet Roy Disney prevailed because of the genius of Stanley Gold, the longtime chief of Shamrock Holdings (the financial holding company for Roy Disney's assets) and one of the most brilliant strategists I have ever worked with, aided by his chief outside legal counsel, David K. Robbins, and the small team of Shamrock executives he put together. Stanley also generously credits, in no small measure, the strategy we put in place to generate waves of favorable media coverage of our campaign, which built enormous support among Disney fans, institutional investors, Wall Street firms, and even Disney's own employees—or "cast members," as it calls them.

The "DisneyWar," as James B. Stewart titled his book about the saga, is a textbook case of effective shareholder activism. In particular, the story of how Roy Disney got his groove back shows the power of public perception, which we leveraged in three ways:

1. *Following my Rules of Engagement, three of which were especially important.* Rule 3: Act preemptively to get your story out there first. Rather than wait for the Disney Company to throw Roy Disney off the board, we preempted it, having Roy quit and state his reason for doing so. Rule 6: Social media often are a means to an end. We fought much of this battle on the Internet, providing one of the first case studies of how to use this new platform in corporate governance contests and incorporate it into one's efforts to tell the story to traditional media as well. A custom-made website let us trot out dozens of statistics and metrics underscoring Disney's lagging performance. Rule 8: Put your opponent on the Wheel of Pain.

2. *Dealing with the media.* Using off-the-record backgrounders to educate reporters about our side of the story, identifying major news hooks both for daily stories and long-form feature stories, giving exclusives, spacing out announcements over a few days to generate new rounds of coverage, hosting a rally, reporting on a meeting with someone important, and issuing a response to breaking news.

3. *Using multiple vehicles to reach our audience.* We used digital and social media, direct mail, email, traditional media (including gossip columns), face-to-face meetings, and even the hosting of our own annual meeting the day before the Disney annual meeting to get our message across.

Telling Roy's Story

The campaign we waged with Disney and Gold created a whole story, in a way, out of Roy's opinion, and that opinion was that the Walt Disney Company had lost its way. The beloved company no longer was a trustworthy maker of uplifting, fun family fare. Instead, it was adrift, a bureaucratic, soulless business machine. The argument was old-fashioned, but this was Roy Disney. His family name was on the door. Stanley Gold, recognizing that we were talking to investors as well as Disney loyalists, tied Roy's lamentation to Disney's lackluster financial performance and lagging stock price in the years since the stock market crash in 2000. Disney had underperformed.

This was the storyline that Sitrick And Company wanted to get out preemptively before the Mouse House could ease Roy off the board. The story's strength was that it was what Roy Disney truly felt.

For me the storyline is paramount. Too much of the PR profession focuses on process and PowerPoint presentations. We don't do PowerPoints, except under duress. Too few people dealing with the media understand what makes a good story, much less how to tell it compellingly. Storytelling is the currency I trade in—offering up exclusives, countering a bad story with a better one demonstrating that the first story was wrong. In essence, pulling a Rule 3, preempting one story with my own.

Knowing the best story to sell requires knowing *all* the facts and knowing what reporters are looking for. Once I have the best storyline in hand, I ask the following questions: *Who is our audience? What are we trying to accomplish by reaching it? Why should anyone care?*

Getting ink isn't enough, though many PR firms measure their performance by how many stories they can place in how many outlets. That isn't a strategy, it's a food fight. Throw everything against the wall to see what sticks. Those people who say any publicity is good publicity are, in my view, just making excuses for the bad press they have generated or received.

Most battles like Roy Disney's focus on Wall Street, institutional investors such as mutual fund companies and pension funds that own a given stock, and analysts who recommend stocks and the financial press. But everyone under Roy Disney's flag knew from the start that this campaign also needed to target legions of passionate Disney fans, calling them to arms to help Roy Disney rescue his family's legacy.

To rally them, we deployed a relatively new weapon in corporate governance battles at the time: the Internet. We created a new website, SaveDisney.com, as a gathering place and megaphone for the entire campaign, providing daily announcements, exhortations to join the fight, instructions on how to vote against Eisner, and one-stop shopping for the media ("click here for copies of shareholder letters, press releases and links to recent news clips").

Remember, this was in 2003, before the web had come into its own as a business platform, before Mark Zuckerberg "friended" his first pal on Facebook, which didn't launch until early 2004, before Jack Dorsey sent the first tweet flitting across Twitter in early 2006.

This was a time to fight. Roy Disney had a story to tell, and we were committed to telling it to the fullest degree. In the contest of Roy the Royal Nephew against Eisner, SaveDisney.com allowed my team to create headlines and coverage multiple times a week as the story grew. The website itself prompted stories heralding a new advocacy role for the web and became a template for many activist campaigns to follow.

The climax of the campaign, though, was still to come: a shareholder protest, a pro-Roy Disney and anti-Eisner pep rally that would be staged the day before Disney's annual shareholder meeting in Philadelphia. The SaveDisney confab has been called a brilliant stroke, a real event close enough to the actual shareholder meeting—across the street, actually—to ride on its coattails. Brilliant or not, it worked, and it was indicative of the kind of "fun" you can have working with a genius like Stanley Gold.

I have worked alongside Stan in many cases in the years since our first one in 1989, when he and Roy Disney were bidding unsuccessfully for Polaroid, but still made millions on their stock. We have cooperated on so many cases and our strategies meld so well that I lose sight of which parts were his and which were mine; the safe bet is the smarter ideas were his.

Stanley Gold, Roy Disney's close friend and advisor, is a shrewd financier and a great field marshal. Some clients don't know what they want, and I have to step up and create it, but Stan Gold always knew exactly what he wanted. I could add to it, build on it, and execute from there.

Disney and Gold were, in fact, among the first clients to sign on with Sitrick And Company after I went out on my own. I had handled all aspects of communications at Wickes Companies as one of a handful of senior vice presidents in a company of sixty thousand employees, as Wickes in the mid-1980s undertook a bankruptcy reorganization, acquisitions, divestitures, litigation support, and crises—all of which would become core segments of my business.

Gold, for his part, relied on Sitrick And Company for media strategy and communications with key constituents. He had known me well for twenty-five years by this time and had kindly recommended me to other clients. He would tell other CEOs that my firm will be 100 percent on your side, and that I will be available twenty-four hours a day, which is pretty much true. When you call me in the middle of the night, I have been known to wake up three staffers, put them to work, and show up on your doorstep at eight o'clock the next morning with a draft of a new press release.

Clients prize this doting devotion. For all the sophisticated technique and black arts involved in the type of strategic communications we practice, the single most important element is service: *serve the client, do whatever it takes—as long as it is legal and ethical.* I probably shouldn't have to add that last qualifier, but these days you dare not fail to do so.

As we circled our target at Walt Disney Company, my collaboration with Stan Gold must have irked Michael Eisner, for at one point in late 2002, as I later was told, at a board meeting as directors discussed a new *Los Angeles Times* story critical of Eisner's tenure, the Disney chief executive and chairman fixed his gaze on Gold and announced that he knew where the story had come from: "I know this is *Sitrick*, Stanley." I admit that I loved hearing that story from Stanley Gold, who chuckled as he told it. Yet in this instance, I had not planted any story, truth be told. There would be plenty of time for that.

The initial audience in the Roy Disney fight was select: Disney directors. Roy had been on the board since 1967, holding the title of vice chairman, and was also chairman of the Disney animation unit. Gold had been on the board since 1987. They had been in business with Eisner since 1984, when Roy Disney, under freakishly similar circumstances, resigned from the Disney board to push for the ouster of the CEO (Walt's son-in-law, Ronald Miller). This was five years before I began working with them.

Disney and Stanley Gold had helped recruit Michael Eisner, a hotshot executive at Paramount, who brought along his protégé Jeff Katzenberg. The first decade was great, but the bursting of the

Internet bubble in 2000 and the 9/11 terror attacks a year later had delivered a one-two punch to the company's theme park business. The film studio was struggling, and the ABC network, acquired in 1995, was floundering. Disney stock, at forty dollars per share as the year 2000 began, had fallen 60 percent, to fifteen dollars, by mid-2002.

Stan Gold and Roy Disney began making noises about Disney's lagging performance. Roy disclosed plans to sell 43 percent of the family stake over a five-year period. You don't sell off 43 percent of your stake if you believe in the company's future, do you?

Who's Who

As part of my preparation for storytelling, I look at the characters involved, and in the Disney feud we had two vivid ones in Roy and Stan. Roy Disney played the good cop, Stanley Gold the bad cop. Roy was avuncular, folksy, and beloved among the Disney animators in the days before Pixar (and by everyone I ever met who knew him). He also was the spitting image of Walt Disney (without the mustache).

Stanley Gold, as the bad cop, was financially shrewd and fearless, with an ever-present cigar clenched between his teeth, although it was never lit. (Though he will hate reading this, Stan is likewise beloved by everyone close to him, as well.) While other Disney directors were reluctant to criticize Eisner, Gold wrote several letters to board members starting in August 2002, unapologetically expressing his concerns. He made sure to send a copy of each letter to Michael Eisner personally, a classic Stanley Gold touch.

Eisner at first tolerated Disney and Gold, but gradually he moved to consolidate power and rid the board of obstinate characters—this was our view, at least, of what he was doing. Disney had reduced its board to twelve members from seventeen, in the process offloading Andrea Van de Kamp, a Sotheby's executive and chairman of the Performing Arts Center of Los Angeles, who had been a vocal critic. According to an article in the *L.A. Times,* Van de Kamp, in an email to Eisner and some board members, said she was being singled out by Eisner for having sided against him—and with directors Stanley P. Gold and Roy Disney—on various issues. A new rule banned directors from talking to the media. Eisner also had the board reclassify Stanley Gold as no longer an outside director, removing him from a powerful board committee.

Then, again in our view, Michael Eisner blew it, to put it rather bluntly. He pushed for a new corporate bylaw that imposed a retirement age of seventy-two for board members, then brought up the issue with the board's nominating committee. Roy Disney already was seventy-three years old at the time, though the new retirement age rule didn't apply to board members who also were part of management, as Roy was. Worse, rather than delivering the news personally, Eisner sent another director, John Bryson, whom Roy knew only casually, to deliver the news. Meeting Roy for lunch on a Friday in November 2003 at a nondescript wine bar in a mall in Pasadena, Bryson told him the slate of directors up for election at the next shareholder meeting would not include Roy's name.

In all my years of counseling companies and CEOs, I have come to realize how important hurt feelings can be. Always keep in mind: *business is a relationship, and how you make other people feel often is as important as the facts of any case.* Disney was so offended that something inside the usually docile man snapped. His wife, Patty, later told the *New York Times* Sunday magazine (in a sympathetic profile) that Roy "was gray when he walked in.... He looked like he had been kicked in the gut." After his lunch with Bryson, Disney told Stanley Gold that one of the first thoughts he had was "I'm not the one who should be leaving. Eisner is the one who should be leaving."

Stanley Gold understood immediately that Roy Disney was going to make Eisner regret insulting him. He summoned me for a meeting the next morning, a Saturday, at the Shamrock offices in Burbank with Roy and Patty Disney, their son, Roy Patrick, Stanley Gold, longtime Shamrock lawyer David Robbins, and a few other Shamrock executives.

Roy Disney was direct, telling everyone, "I want him out." To me, Roy seemed not so much angry as he was hurt, injured by Michael Eisner's disregard. The question, though, was how could we push Michael Eisner out of his job? He controlled the board, and no one investor had a large enough stake to oust him.

And as Robbins pointed out, with Disney's annual meeting set for March, it was too late to stage a proxy battle and offer a rival slate of directors to be voted on by Disney shareholders. Stanley Gold then suggested an effort to organize a no-confidence vote, a campaign to persuade shareholders to vote their shares so as to withhold approval of Michael Eisner's reappointment to the board.

It would be purely a symbolic protest, with no binding effect on Disney directors, and given that the company had *two billion shares* outstanding, and some 2.8 million individual shareholder accounts, it would be extremely difficult to make much of a statement at all. Robbins, the lawyer, and I knew the challenge was especially daunting, given that the largest no-confidence vote in corporate history was 20 percent, and Robbins pointed this out. Stan Gold pulled the cigar out of his mouth, fixed his gaze on the both of us and said, "That's why I have you two." "Great," I whispered to David, "guess that's that," both of us chuckling, but we knew Stan was not kidding. Roy Disney told his new team to get ready for a fight.

I have known David Robbins since the late 1980s and have always viewed him as one of the savviest corporate lawyers I've met. He has a deep knowledge of corporate law and raider tactics, yet Robbins can also go beyond the fine print and improvise. He in turn likes my creative approach to strategic communications. Roy and Stanley felt we made a good team. We agreed.

David and I also agreed that we should *keep it focused on business, not personal, issues.* Shareholders care about stock price, not personal antagonisms. This is almost always my approach, the exception being "personal" issues like embezzlement or the like. There was nothing remotely like that here. Let the other side go *ad hominem* and whisper that Roy Disney was "Walt's idiot nephew," a cheap shot that someone had made many years before, though it was entirely unwarranted and completely inaccurate. We would make sure it blew up in their faces, striking back with the contrary evidence and pointing out to reporters that the other side's personal attacks reveal the lack of facts behind their case.

Disney and Gold wanted to strike back forcefully, and we knew our first blows would have to fall with military precision and balletic grace. The plotting started at a meeting of thirty people, including myself, my partner Terry Fahn, David Robbins and Shamrock staff, and Dan Burch of MacKenzie Partners in New York. One of the top proxy wranglers in the country, Burch was critical for gathering the votes of institutional investors. A few of us would hold strategy sessions by conference call every Monday morning for months to come.

The public push to dethrone the Disney king would start with a bold, preemptive strike. Rather than wait to be ushered off the board in a few months, Roy E. Disney would resign now and call publicly for Michael Eisner to resign or retire. Stanley Gold would resign too, but that would come later.

Disney's resignation letter had to emphasize the right themes, for it would establish the outline not only for that day's story but for the whole campaign. It had to show his sharp financial concern and reflect his regret at having to resign. It also needed to go first to the Disney board and Eisner himself, so that it was real news. Otherwise, Eisner might call it a PR stunt—as I would, if I were in his shoes.

My staff ensured that copies of the letter were delivered to the board, and we had a copy delivered to Eisner's apartment in New York, where Eisner was staying that night. The letter was slipped under his door while he was watching a football game.

We were able to arrange for a four-way exclusive, setting up the story of Roy's resignation to run online in the *Wall Street Journal*, *New York Times*, *Los Angeles Times*, and *Bloomberg* on a Sunday afternoon just minutes after the letter was delivered to the board. Normally, I would go to just one media outlet—two at the most—but this story was too big. The story broke at 4:30 p.m. Eastern Time.

Roy Disney's letter was short and bittersweet, just 660 words. He accused Eisner of driving "a wedge" between Roy and his Disney colleagues and requiring them to report back to Eisner on what Roy was saying ("I find this intolerable."). He said Eisner "discussed" with the board's nominating committee leaving Roy Disney's name off the slate of directors, "effectively muzzling my voice on the board—much as you did with Andrea Van de Kamp last year. [A]fter 19 years at the helm," he charged, "you are no longer the best person to run the Walt Disney Company."

"It Is You Who Should Be Leaving, Not Me"

Roy's letter went on to specify seven failures, from "timidity" in theme-park investments to flops at ABC and Family Channel, the latter of which he said "have had, and I believe will continue to have, significant adverse impact on shareholder value.... The perception by all of our stakeholders—consumers, investors, employees, distributors and suppliers—that the company is rapacious, soul-less, and always looking for the 'quick buck', rather than long-term value which is leading to a loss of public trust," he wrote.

Then Roy concluded with the same thought he had when John Bryson told him he was getting pushed off the board: "[I]t is you who should be leaving and not me." The letter ended, "I don't know if you and the other directors can comprehend how painful it is for me and the extended Disney family to arrive at this decision," a line that would be quoted widely and sympathetically.

The next morning, Monday, December 1, the four-way scoop went Page One in print, triggering a flurry of coverage in hundreds of other outlets. Some reported that Stan Gold would stay on the Disney board (they never bothered to ask). When one reporter did ask me, I pointed out that Roy Disney and Stanley Gold were separate individuals and that Roy's letter related only to Roy. This was the truth, and I refused to comment further. It is important to point out that I never stated or asserted that Gold would stay on the Disney board. I never lie to reporters. Ever. (See my Rule 10.)

Not lying is as much a matter of good business sense as it is a matter of high morals (though it *is* a matter of morals, and I don't do it in my business or personal life). If I ever lied to a reporter and were caught (and almost every lie is exposed eventually), it would hurt the credibility of my client, ruin my credibility with that reporter—and with everyone else in contact with him at his news organization—and poison my reputation for every other client I represent. Also, it might prompt the reporter to punish my client.

Keep that in mind: *if you lie to reporters, all bets are off.* And they could crucify you.

So at Sitrick And Company we never lie. We may not answer all questions. Occasionally, actually rarely, when the case requires it we may not answer *any* questions. We may not volunteer information, but the fact is, we win by searching for facts to illuminate the truth—a truth that otherwise might go untold.

The day after we issued Roy Disney's dramatic resignation letter, we dropped the other shoe. Stanley Gold's letter of resignation was unveiled, and this one had a lot more sting. In 1,554 words of unflinching criticism of Eisner and unstinting praise of Roy Disney, the letter bashed the board's move to oust Roy as "clearly disingenuous" and "yet another attempt by this Board to squelch dissent by hiding behind the veil of 'good governance.' What a curious result." Gold cited a new rule barring board members from talking to the media or shareholders and said he could have greater success "from outside the Boardroom."

Cue the second day of worldwide coverage as reporters sensed a big conflict ahead.

For the usual proxy-fight audience of sophisticated, institutional investors and Wall Street stock analysts, Stanley Gold and Roy Disney would barnstorm the country in Roy's private jet, a Boeing 737 (a BBJ, among aircraft owners), to meet with institutional investors and pension fund officials to make their case. They also took part in conference calls set up by shareholder advisory services, and they did multiple media interviews and urged investors to show their disapproval of Eisner's reign in the shareholder vote.

Technically, this didn't mean voting "no," for there was no possibility of a "no" vote—Eisner and the directors proposed were the only choice shareholders had. But they could *withhold* their shares from being voted in favor of Eisner's reappointment, and this would, at least, show how widespread the disapproval was.

With the highest protest votes in any previous cases hitting 20 percent, we decided that if we could muster anywhere near that amount, given our late start and the huge Disney investor base, it would be a clear victory.

For two other audiences, the fervent fan base and reporters, we set up a new website, SaveDisney.com, and made it pulsate with breaking news, constant updates, direct appeals, and counter-commentary to whatever Disney did or said. To run the intensive effort, I brought in the seasoned web warrior Brian Glicklich. In his mid-forties at the time and a bit pale for a denizen of sunny Los Angeles, thanks to his spending way too many hours in cyberspace, Glicklich had worked with me in the previous year on another major issue that had attracted worldwide news.

Glicklich, who later joined my firm to head our digital and social media practice, designed SaveDisney.com to look as if it had been crafted by a Disney mom on her laptop at the kitchen table. It was bursting with bright colors and featured a font that seemed to have been typed on an old Smith Corona. (For you millennials, that's a brand of typewriter.) The organization was simple and clear, with separate, clickable tabs labeled for Disney fans, shareholders, institutional investors, and even Disney employees.

SaveDisney.com—so perfectly named for the band of ousted outsiders hurling spears at Cinderella's castle—became the go-to destination for many people watching the Disney-on-Disney fight. More than twenty-five thousand Disney devotees signed up at the site, gathering there to read the latest criticisms of their beloved company and commiserate over how much Disney had strayed from Walt's vision.

Several thousand fans also signed up online to receive "Save Disney" pins, bumper stickers, and t-shirts. They could read detailed instructions on how to vote their shares in opposition to

Michael Eisner and consider invitations to join Roy Disney for the anti-shareholder rally right before the Disney shareholder meeting.

Starting with the full text of Disney's and Gold's resignation letters, the site gave reporters easy access to documents: the latest in letters to the Disney board, letters to Michael Eisner, press releases, slide shows, news articles, and more. At one point, Terry Fahn distributed a digital press kit comprising sixteen documents. It is a Sitrickian method, if you will allow me the indulgence: *make it as easy as possible for reporters to get your information.*

People in my profession often take the opposite approach, trying to keep information from reporters—even in proxy and corporate governance contests, believe it or not. Our approach in the Disney case was whatever you need, we will help you get it. Some of the information we provided reflected our perspective, of course, but we were up front about that and above all wanted the information we disseminated to be accurate. We have learned, moreover, that providing the skinny to the reporters is a two-way street—often reporters will tell us what the other side is saying and doing, so long as they aren't violating off-the-record protection they have promised to someone else.

Three days after Roy's resignation, we released to the media his open letter bidding a fond and affectionate farewell to Disney "cast members," publishing it at the same moment on SaveDisney. com. The Walt Disney Company initially responded with a terse release asserting that Disney's and Gold's complaints were old hat and had been rejected by the board.

After the resignation letters and his farewell to employees, Roy Disney wrote an open letter to shareholders in late January, criticizing Eisner again. When the company's talks to renew a distribution deal with Pixar broke down, the SaveDisney team blamed Eisner for blowing it. According to the *L.A. Times,* "sources close to

Eisner and Apple Computer Inc. founder Jobs said the stunning split was less about the math of the deal than the equation of the personalities.... 'The relationship went sour when Michael didn't treat Jobs and the Pixar machine as a giant creative engine, he treated them as second-class citizens,' said former Disney board member Stanley Gold, who resigned last year with fellow director Roy E. Disney in a dispute with Eisner." On February fifth, we released another letter from Roy to Disney shareholders, this time inviting them to the big rally connected to the annual meeting in Philadelphia a few weeks later.

Mixing New and Old Media

Our strategy of mixing new and old media methods—disseminating information through traditional press releases and posting it on the SaveDisney.com—was working. Numerous articles in traditional media—local, national, and international—ran both in print and online throughout the campaign. The SaveDisney site got so much traffic among employees at Disney's headquarters in Burbank, California, that we had heard Michael Eisner had ordered the company's techies to shut down access to SaveDisney.com. In Stan Gold's view, this added to the new website's allure, increasing the desire of Disney staff to check out the latest at SaveDisney.com when they got home.

When Comcast made a surprise $54 billion bid for Disney on February 11, it gave Roy Disney another reason to be commenting on Eisner's failures. Even when Disney and Gold agreed with the board's rejection of the Comcast bid, their statement included criticism of Eisner (professionally, not personally). As they declared in the second paragraph of their press release, "However, the Board...is just plain wrong in continuing its lock-step support for Michael Eisner and his senior management team."

Eisner publicly remained in denial, however, with only a week and a half to go before the shareholder meeting. On the night of February 20, the Disney CEO appeared on CNN's *Larry King Live* and said, "Sometimes people disagree with you.... This will go away, I believe." Later in February, the shareholder advisory services ISS and Glass Lewis & Co. and the California pension fund CalPERS sided with Roy Disney and advised institutional investors to withhold their votes from Michael Eisner. CalPERS announced, "We have lost complete confidence in Mr. Eisner's strategic vision and leadership in creating shareholder value in the company." Similar conclusions were reached by the New Jersey State Investment Council ("Eisner has created no value for shareholders for the past seven years") and the New York State Comptroller ("I call on Disney directors...to replace Mr. Eisner as soon as possible").

All of this spawned more press releases and hundreds of news stories, as well as rounds of comment from Roy and Stan, all of it posted on SaveDisney.com.

Brian Glicklich was seeing good traffic numbers, in the thousands and climbing. Another clue that we were succeeding came when Roy's army began to hear of fans' reserving rental busses for the drive up to Philadelphia for Roy's rally on Tuesday, March 2, 2004. That event, the pinnacle of Roy's campaign, proved to be fabulously successful, generating hundreds of stories, live television coverage, and waves of excitement among the Disney faithful. More than a thousand Disney fans and shareholders showed up at the Loews Hotel for the Roy rally, which started at four in the afternoon and ended at the very Disney decent hour of six.

It was a lavish, positively giddy affair, with balloons and buttons and plush toys and speeches from Roy and Stan, with a pack of reporters and cameras tracking every moment. My thinking at the time was that this would make a great contrast against the Disney event setting up for the next day.

It seemed everyone wanted to be at Roy's rally, where the attendees were dining on sandwiches and wine. The people spilled out of the Loews ballroom and into the lobby and out onto the street. Stanley Gold had his wife and his daughter, Jennifer, an event marketer who previously had worked for the Walt Disney Company, at the Roy festival. Jennifer spotted a few of her former colleagues, PR people from Disney and ABC, who showed up with their business cards and asked to be allowed in. Gold wasn't all that surprised when I politely refused.

While Roy Disney was triumphant, Michael Eisner was somber. He was, understandably, taking all of this personally. The CEO, as James Stewart pointed out in his book *DisneyWar*, had "claimed the mantle of Walt himself," by hosting the Sunday night Disney series on ABC. He is said to have once told Michael Ovitz, before their epic falling out, that he wanted his wife on the board and hoped to set up his son, Breck Eisner, to be chairman one day. Ovitz retorted, "Michael, this isn't your family company."

For Roy E. Disney, of course, it *was* a family company. By the time of the official shareholder meeting the next day, Roy Disney was a new folk hero. Entering the meeting room at the Marriott, Roy and Stanley Gold were greeted with thunderous applause from the crowd of three thousand, some of them clad in Disney character costumes and carrying anti-Eisner pamphlets. People lined up to get Roy's autograph and pose for a photo with him.

Roy and Stanley were allotted twenty minutes to address the Disney shareholders at the annual meeting. Stanley went first and took most of the time. When Roy approached the mike, he was met with a standing ovation that seemed to go on forever. After two or three minutes, he thanked the crowd and asked everyone to please sit down. When they did, he began his speech with a request to "Mr. Eisner" not to punish him for his partner Stanley Gold's exuberance. "I hope you will allow me the full ten minutes I was promised to address my fellow shareholders," he said. Michael Eisner rose and began to demur, but given the audience reaction, decided to retreat to his seat onstage. Roy got his full ten minutes.

Terry Fahn and I, meanwhile, had set up a battery of press interviews with Roy Disney and Stanley Gold once they got to Philadelphia. It was speed dating, Sitrick-style: half a dozen one-on-one (actually two-on-one) interviews with television outlets, a dozen or so interviews with print reporters, staggered so as to do print, TV, print, TV. This would give each TV crew time to set up during the print interview. (It would have been easier to do this with a press conference, but I have already explained why we rarely do press conferences.)

This was a case where the story was so big that we could impose a condition for the interviews, albeit a modest one: the interviews had to be joint with Roy and Stan. With Gold's crisp and biting prosecutorial style and Roy's Disney name and personal popularity, these two formed the ideal yin and yang.

Surprisingly, we were able to impose this condition on one of the most powerful players in TV news: ABC's *Nightline*. Ted Koppel's producer had tried to insist that only Roy Disney appear opposite Eisner, but I pushed back, explaining this was not multiple choice. Both Disney and Gold would appear or neither would appear. Both appeared. At 11:35 p.m. Eastern Time on March 3, 2004, just hours after the Walt Disney Company's raucous shareholder meeting had ended, the theme-song trumpets of *Nightline* blared their intro, and Koppel began the live interview of his boss's boss's boss.

"It has been a very long and trying day for Michael Eisner," Koppel intoned at the show's opening. "When this day began, he was chairman of the board and CEO of the Disney Company. By this evening, you've given up one of the titles, I gather. That happened when, Michael?"

Just before nine o'clock that evening, Disney had announced that the board, "mindful of the shareholder vote today," had handed Eisner's chairman's title to director and former U.S. Senator George Mitchell, while Eisner was staying on as CEO. After a first answer, Koppel pressed: "My, I guess my question is, do you think this'll be enough to keep your critics at bay? And judging by the number of shareholders who voted against you today, you got a few critics out there."

Eisner responded that the Disney shareholders' vote was a protest against all of corporate America, a push for separating the chairman and CEO titles at all companies. Eventually, he allowed, "and there are obviously certain people that, that are not happy with me personally, I guess."

Koppel then asked Eisner to listen to his interview with Roy Disney and Stanley Gold, which he had taped earlier that afternoon after a stunning victory at the shareholders' meeting. They had started out hoping that 10 percent of the shareholder votes would be withheld from an endorsement of Michael Eisner; later they raised their hopes to maybe 20 percent. Yet the anti-Eisner vote accounted for an astounding 45 percent of all Disney shares. If the votes were counted as they would have been in a proxy contest (different rules apply in a "withhold" vote), the no-confidence vote would have been 54 percent. Among Disney employees, moreover, the anti-Eisner vote was 72 percent.

"It Is Time for New Management"

During the Koppel interview, Roy and Stan got in some good, familiar licks and made it clear that Eisner's simply handing off the chairman's title wouldn't be enough. He must step down as CEO. Stanley Gold told Koppel, "We think [the chairman and CEO titles] ought to be split, but we also think that Mr. Eisner oughta hold neither of those jobs. It is time for new management."

That was classic Gold, as blunt and unflinching as always. After the interview with Disney and Gold, Koppel asked Eisner to react. He said, "You know, they've been on this kick saying these things, these conclusions, which are completely false and fabricated, and they bring up different arguments to try to draw to the same conclusion. I don't really want to argue them point by point. Obviously, our board disagrees. We have great management. All of our operations are running well. The growth is there."

A few weeks later, on March 15, *BusinessWeek* ran a commentary by the reporters Ron Grover and Tom Lowry headlined, "Now It's Time to Say Goodbye," an allusion to the closing song of the old *Mickey Mouse Club* television show. In March 2005, a year after the Roy Disney rally, Michael Eisner announced that he would resign as CEO that coming September, to be succeeded by his number two, Robert Iger. Two months later, Iger offered Roy Disney the honorary title of director emeritus, a consulting agreement, and an office on Disney's Burbank lot. On July 8, Roy Disney accepted the offer.

Bob Iger asked for one concession: take down SaveDisney.com. Brian Glicklich stepped in to warn me and the team that this should be done gently and gradually, over a few weeks, to allow time to announce it and thank the followers and give them closure. Soon after, the website was history.

Eisner stepped down as CEO in September as planned, giving Iger an open field. In a series of stellar acquisitions, Iger talked Steve Jobs into selling Pixar to Disney and then acquired Marvel and the *Star Wars* franchise. Disney stock, in the twenty-dollar range when

Iger became CEO, hit a high of $115 by 2015, an almost six-fold rise in ten years.

Today, Gold is happy to have been wrong about Robert Iger, as he has told the CEO a few times. The Disney family held on to most of its stake, selling some shares for tax purposes when Roy passed away on December 16, 2009. Still, Gold relishes the victory and our ability to punch so far above our real weight. He is especially proud to have landed a 45 percent "no" vote against Michael Eisner, which stands as one of the biggest shareholder protests in corporate history. Stanley Gold keeps a reminder of it on the vanity plates of his 2004 Porsche Cayenne SUV: 45PRCNT.

Chapter 5

Challenging 20/20

After counseling more than a thousand clients and being involved with tens of thousands of stories, I have learned that there are no absolutes in my business—particularly in the crisis-management side of my business. No rule applies to every case or at all times, not even Sitrick's Ten Rules for Engagement. There is one rule, however, that comes pretty close: *Thou shalt not attack reporters*. Make it about the facts.

The urge to shoot the messenger dates back at least 2,500 years to Sophocles and his play *Antigone*, and Shakespeare warned against it in *Henry IV, Part 2*. People who have been criticized have been trying to shoot the messenger—the media—ever since: politicians embroiled in scandal, CEOs fighting to hold on to their jobs, companies caught cutting the wrong corners, celebrities. I have seen this strategy deployed many times, almost always with bad results.

Make no mistake: if a reporter has been a paid consultant to a hedge fund shorting your company's stock, if he is a member of an organization that is criticizing your company in his story, or if he owns a stake in your competitor, you have every right to bring this up with the reporter and, if necessary, go to his editor. But in all my years of doing this kind of work, I have seen this happen only once or twice. More often—though, again, in the minority of cases—a reporter just gets it wrong. When that happens, we bring the error to his or her attention, argue our case, and most of the time ask for a correction or a clarification. If necessary, we will appeal to his or her editor or even, as a last resort (always letting the reporter know we are doing so), have the company's lawyers write the media company's legal counsel, but we never make it personal. We stick to the facts. (More on that later.)

Although punching back at reporters personally may feel satisfying in the moment, it almost always is the wrong response. It sends the message that you can't argue the facts so you call the reporter names. This approach is not going to accomplish anything except to make the reporter more hostile.

Then there is the risk that *if you make it personal, the reporter could make it even more so.* Reporters are human beings, and like all of us, they have feelings. While they may try to separate their feelings from their reporting, they may not be able to do so. As I said in my first book, *Spin*, give me a set of facts, and without changing any of them I will give you four different stories ranging from hostile to glowing. It's one thing to attack reporters' work, it's another to attack their integrity, especially when your attack is not based on facts.

Yet many in the PR business fall into one of two extreme categories: those who are too quick to pick a fight, and those who are too afraid to fight at all. They fail their boss or client with either approach. In the first category, PR pros, hoping to impress their clients, respond to unfavorable press or even inquiries by attacking the motives, skill, and honesty of reporters. In the second group, PR people are afraid to push back at all against reporters for fear of souring relations with them.

As I write, I have been involved with a sharp-eyed writer for *Forbes* on behalf of a client whom the writer doesn't trust. It's clear this writer wants to be harshly critical. The client wants me to scream and yell at him. Am I doing that? No, I am taking the facts the writer gives me and knocking them down, one at a time. *Fight with facts.* A respected reporter once told me that an experienced PR person had demanded he take down a story he had written about a client of hers. "Why?" the reporter asked. "Are there inaccuracies, misstatements of fact?" "No," the PR person replied, "my client doesn't like it." The journalist told me he just hung up on her without saying another word.

The fallout from a reporter-bashing strategy can be damaging. By the time my firm shows up, the client can be in an all-out war with, say, the *Wall Street Journal*, played out every day in front of more than two million readers in print and online. The PR people start out refusing to comment entirely (violating Rule 9 of my Ten Rules), then they begin to respond testily, only to get quoted saying defensive or threatening things like, "That question is slanderous," when, in fact, it was not.

Then the PR staffers escalate their complaints to the reporter's editor, then to the editor's bosses, not refuting the facts but personally attacking the reporter's integrity and professionalism. Asked for specifics, they can't provide anything meaningful. Simultaneously, they set up a website repeating the same comments they made to the editor, including the attacks on the reporter's professionalism and integrity. In one case, where my client's PR team had gone on the offensive against a reporter at a major national publication, when I met with his editor's editor whom I know well, she told me, "All they did was call him names, they didn't challenge a single fact." In short, it made things worse.

In my practice, I have seen this conflict spiral out of control quickly, and the company, instead of working to correct the inaccuracies of a story, gets consumed with arguing about the bias of the reporter. When I ask what they base their charges of bias on, they respond that the stories are negative. But what is the evidence of the reporter's or editor's bias? Their answer: the stories are negative!

Sometimes I arrive at a client's office and the PR advisors there will tell me something like I should be confronting the top editor and demanding that she "do her job." Really? And what is this supposed to accomplish, other than making her angry? This strategy, which is doomed to failure, is a perfect example of why I have been saying for years: *most PR people are incompetent*—at least in dealing with high-stakes media situations.

I witnessed the effects of alienating a reporter and her editor shortly after I ventured out to form my own firm in 1989. Roy Disney's and Stanley Gold's Shamrock Holdings, making an unsolicited bid to acquire Polaroid, was taking a beating in the press both nationally and in Polaroid's hometown of Boston. "They're calling me 'Roy the Raider,'" Disney told me at the time. Brought on board to develop a communications strategy and deal with the media, I offered the reporter covering the story for the *Boston Globe* an exclusive interview with Stanley Gold, Shamrock's CEO, who would tell her why he wanted the company and what his plans for it were. She lit into me in response, yelling at me and demanding an interview with Stanley Gold. Once she had calmed down, I reminded her that was what I offered at the onset of the call. "We'll even come to your office to do it," I said.

I learned from the reporter that Shamrock's other outside PR people had complained to this reporter's editors about her coverage and demanded that she be removed from the story. Her editors had complied, only to reconsider and put her back on it. Of course she was upset with my client! We won her over by treating her as a professional and, most importantly, giving her what she wanted—an interview with Stanley Gold, in the *Globe*'s offices, no less. Stanley was vintage Stanley: the story was a ten on a scale of ten and, magically, the paper's ongoing coverage dramatically improved.

Fighting Back Without Making It Personal

As you probably know by now, I do not believe in making it personal, even when I feel the media has stepped over the line. I believe, in fact, that it is counterproductive.

The case that follows will demonstrate how you can fight back without making it personal. If you stay focused on the facts, you can protect your business and your reputation when the media comes calling with a "hit piece."

Metabolife, whose herbal weight-loss supplement drew regulatory scrutiny in the late 1990s, came into the gun-sights of ABC's *20/20*, which was preparing a sensationalistic piece suggesting that the product was endangering lives. My partners and I discovered that the producers not only had the facts wrong, but had committed what we believed were numerous breaches of journalistic ethics. After going over their heads (and telling them we were doing so) and getting no relief, we decided we had no choice but to call the public's attention to the unethical practices of *20/20*, making the reporting tactics of ABC News a subject as central to the story as the program's focus on Metabolife—if not more so. More than that, we would set a precedent for crisis response using the Internet and the multimedia capabilities of what was then grandly called the World Wide Web.

I had sensed early on that in the Internet age, every company could be a media company, with its own channel to reach its particular audience. In response to various questions about our client and its products, we had sent the *20/20* producers thousands of pages of documents supporting the efficacy and safety of our client's product, Metabolife 356, countering their assertions with an arsenal of facts. To no avail.

Rather than wait for *20/20* to air a damaging story and respond only later, we preempted it—and shocked the media world—by posting, online, the entire unedited video of the *20/20* interview with the Metabolife CEO *before* ABC itself could air the story. And we made sure the world knew why we were doing this. We wanted ABC News to do what we believed it should have done from the onset: to include the relevant facts in its story. And as you will see, we were enormously successful.

By the time *20/20* went to air, the producers, after weeks of refusing to bend at all, balanced the story with several key concessions that Sitrick And Company had fought for fiercely. In the end, we provoked a media backlash that shifted the story from one theme—was Metabolife 356's key ingredient, ephedra, dangerous—to another—was ABC News fair? Did *20/20* unfairly tarnish a brand that was helping people lose weight?

We relied in particular on five of my ten Rules for Engagement: Rule 1: First, get the facts.

Rule 3: Act preemptively.

Rule 6: Social media are often a means to an end.

Rule 7: If you don't tell your story, someone else will tell it for you.

Rule 8: Put your opponent on the Wheel of Pain.

My firm had previously tangled with ABC News in December 1996, on behalf of Food Lion. Four years earlier, *Primetime Live* had aired a twenty-minute "exposé" of unsafe food-handling practices at the grocery store chain. Just before open arguments were to begin in the resulting lawsuit, Food Lion hired Sitrick And Company.

I have recounted this story in *Spin*. Two ABC producers who lied about their job records in applying to work at a Food Lion store secretly filmed their fellow employees. Food Lion sued for misrepresentation and fraud, the statute of limitations having already run for libel.

In the trial's discovery phase, Food Lion lawyers had uncovered tape from the cutting-room floor that contradicted the truncated snippets the program had used in telling the story. The segment had aired video of one worker questioning the freshness of some chicken breasts but omitted that her manager told her to throw them out, and she did. The segment also showed workers slipping on a supposedly grimy floor, yet the outtakes revealed that they were slipping on soap bubbles, not grime. I wrote in *Spin*,

> We would seize the momentum from ABC by redefining the issue. When the network insisted that Food Lion's lawsuit was an attack on all journalism, we'd simply ask reporters, "Hey, would your editor let you get away with the stuff those guys did?" Invariably, the answer was no.

ABC lost the case, and the jury awarded Food Lion $5.5 million in punitive damages for fraud, trespass, and "disloyalty." The stunning award would be reduced by the trial judge and all but wiped out on appeal, but ABC lost decisively in what in some ways is the more important court—the court of public opinion. Even other leading media voices objected to ABC News' techniques. "By pre-empting the situation—specifically, by acting aggressively to change the nature of the debate by focusing on the facts—we had prevailed over a much more powerful opponent," as I put it in *Spin*.

Sitrick And Company had started working for Metabolife before the producers at *20/20* drew a target on the company. At the time, Metabolife's bigger concern was a crackdown by the Food and Drug Administration.

A year before we were retained, the FDA had issued a warning about the Chinese herb ma huang, or ephedra, the main ingredient in the company's sole product, Metabolife 356. Now the FDA was proposing a ban on products containing eight milligrams or more of the herbal stimulant and stricter labeling for anything containing less. These regulations would wipe out Metabolife's business.

Metabolife's founder and CEO had started the company with a fifteen-thousand-dollar loan, selling 4,752 bottles of Metabolife 356 in its first year. He had devised the supplement, based on traditional Chinese medicine, to help his cancer-stricken father. Three years later, Metabolife sold more than nine million bottles, and by its fourth year in business, the company was on track to sell twenty-two million bottles, or two billion tablets, and rack up $900 million in revenue. It was sold in more than 1,200 retail locations and by more than fifty thousand independent sellers.

That roaring success caught the attention of the FDA. Back when ephedra was merely an obscure product sold in indie health-food stores, no one in the FDA cared much. Metabolife came onto the FDA's radar screen only after it had fifty thousand independent reps selling it and millions of people consuming the herbal remedy daily, racking up hundreds of millions of dollars in annual sales. By 1999, when Sitrick And Company entered the case, Metabolife 356 had been on the market for four years with billions of servings consumed safely in the U.S.

Counting other products containing this natural herbal extract, ephedra had been used for decades by millions of people in the United States and for centuries in China. The FDA based the proposed ban on eight hundred adverse event reports (AERs) for all types of ephedra products sold by a wide range of makers over a four-year period, but that was a clinically insignificant number given the many millions of people consuming ephedra in various products. More than 70 percent of those reports, moreover, had no medical records, which is why the U.S. General Accounting Office (since renamed the Government Accountability Office) would later say the FDA lacked sufficient medical evidence to support its proposed ban of ephedrine.

Tony Knight, a partner in the firm and a former twenty-five-year veteran journalist with extensive knowledge about the supplement industry, reviewed the FDA's approach and viewed it as questionable.

For example, the FDA had not evaluated the AERS to ensure they were valid and medically reliable. There was no way to be certain that a health event was related to the supplement that was taken. In many reports, there was evidence that the health event was unrelated to the supplement. The AERs included cases where a gunshot suicide, a drunk driving auto fatality, and a store clerk shot and killed in a robbery were listed as ephedra deaths. Purported injuries included medically impossible claims that ephedra caused multiple sclerosis or goiter.

The FDA used just thirteen adverse event reports as the basis for proposing ephedra limits, but the treating physicians involved with three of the thirteen adverse events said there was no connection between the event and the dietary supplement in question.

The industry brought all of those highly relevant and compelling facts to light, but the media had a field day, reporting over and over again that the FDA had received more than 800 AERs that included heart attack, seizure, stroke, and death.

News reports that the FDA is investigating a company's product can do millions of dollars of damage instantly to a brand, scaring off customers and, in the case of a public company, turning off investors. Most seriously of all, the publicity can set off a swarm of trial lawyers looking for clients for class-action lawsuits molded to the FDA's concerns. This last battlefront was almost guaranteed to open in the Metabolife flap.

The FDA, we felt at the time, might be targeting Metabolife as part of an effort to extend its regulatory reach to the herbal industry. The FDA had lost a bid to kill the law passed by Congress requiring it to develop a new and separate regulatory framework for dietary supplements. Rather than develop such a framework, some observers said, the agency was out to show Congress it had made a mistake. Ephedra and Metabolife were target number one.

Yet there was no upside to pointing out this hidden agenda. When the FDA is at your door, you have to answer one question: is your product safe? If it isn't, nothing else matters. No one cares that the FDA was trying to expand its turf by making an example of Metabolife.

Metabolife came to us hoping to mount a public campaign to counter the one the FDA was waging against Metabolife. The agency was touring cities in peak weight-loss season (in January, after the holidays, and May, as spring unfolds, and June with the advent of bikini weather), setting up a hotline to collect complaints about the supplement and briefing local reporters on the dangers of ephedra. Each visit by the FDA prompted the local press, especially TV reporters, to deluge Metabolife with calls, producing a raft of stories about the supplement's safety.

The FDA's barnstorming struck Tony Knight and me as unreliable at best: how could callers to telephone hotlines be trusted to accurately report what they had taken and to know what the medical effects were without having seen a doctor? Was there *any* vetting of these complaints for accuracy? To us the entire effort seemed flimsy and unverified.

At the same time, Metabolife's CEO explained to us that he actually had sought the FDA's oversight of the industry, proposing a set of rules early on in an attempt to win over the agency.

Getting the Facts to Mount a Defense

I dispatched Tony Knight to review medical studies, company materials, trial data, press accounts, and more so we could refute the FDA's allegations. Tony is one of the best researchers I have ever worked with, and I knew that he would quickly know more about this subject than most so-called experts. His work enabled us to assemble a fact-based campaign based on unassailable science and history.

We showed that various physicians over many years had said ephedra was safe and that millions of people had been ingesting the herb for thousands of years in China. Millions more people had taken an over-the-counter synthetic pharmaceutical, ephedrine, a concentrated form of the active ingredient found in the plant, in much larger doses than the FDA had approved. Our research also showed that far more patients were sent to the emergency room because of aspirin than because of ephedra.

We also collected customer testimonials, which was easy because so many people found the product effective for weight loss. When we responded to media inquiries with customer interviews and a doctor's statement that Metabolife 356 was reasonably safe at recommended doses and when used as directed, we neutralized much of the attack on the product.

Yet we were fighting what seemed to be an unending battle. At first we were responding to one story a week, then a few stories per week in various places, and eventually we were dealing with two or three stories per day. One of the toughest was a three-part series aired on ABC's Boston affiliate, WCVB-TV. We had gone back and forth for weeks with the reporter, who also had her own consumer-affairs show on the local cable system. We gave her research papers, independent trial results, and other data to counter the FDA's anonymous, anecdotal hotline reports. The series, however, opened with assertions by a physician, George Blackburn, that Metabolife could cause death. We struck back on day two of her report with a fiercely worded press release denouncing the doctor's "grossly misleading and irresponsible" statement, which had "grossly distorted the medical facts."

Our client promptly sued the station, its owner, a Hearst Corporation subsidiary, the reporter, and Dr. Blackburn, charging each of them with defamation, slander, trade libel, and intentional and negligent interference with "prospective economic advantage." The lawsuit pointed out that Dr. Blackburn was on the payroll of a Metabolife competitor and had taken a grant from the maker of a rival diet product. These conflicts of interest should have disqualified Dr. Blackburn from appearing in the story, or at least should have been disclosed.

Just ten days after Metabolife sued ABC's Boston affiliate, 20/20 began looking into the product, its interest piqued by the local station's report and the lawsuit, as ABC officials later told the media. Metabolife's CEO thought he smelled retaliation.

The producers at 20/20 were difficult from the start. They claimed to be doing a story on all ephedra products, not a story targeting Metabolife in particular. We asked what other companies they were talking with and who else was being featured. They wouldn't tell us. We suspected that there were no other companies, but it was clear that they were going to do a story with or without our participation, and to me that's not a contest. It is my belief that you are almost always better off engaging (that doesn't necessarily mean providing your client for an interview), at least until you understand what the story will say.

After a fair amount of back-and-forth with *20/20's* producers on the scope of their story and the information they were seeking, they demanded an interview with Metabolife's CEO. I asked if they were going to air an interview with a physician to talk about health and safety concerns about the product. They said yes. I replied if they were talking about health issues, they should speak with our client's chief medical officer. They said no, they wanted our CEO. I told them I was not going to have a business executive debate a medical doctor on health and safety issues. If they had an MD, then we must have an MD, the company's chief medical officer. After some resistance on their part, they agreed that the CEO and the company's chief medical officer would appear together in the interview, with the physician addressing any medical issues that came up.

We spent months providing information and materials to *20/20*. We answered the producers' questions and provided them with several boxes of independent research demonstrating the safety of ephedra, the health benefits of even modest weight loss, and extensive third-party studies on the safety and efficacy of pharmaceutical ephedrine. We sent them a list of doctors who had recommended Metabolife to their patients. We pointed out that the General Accounting Office had just issued a report critical of the FDA's handling of the AERs in its ephedra crackdown.

The GAO said the FDA had "not evaluated the reports to be valid and medically reliable." (In non-bureaucrat-speak this means they evaluated the reports to be not valid or medically reliable.) In its tally of supposedly ephedra-related deaths, the FDA had included a suicide by gunshot, an auto accident, and a murder merely because all three victims had recently taken an ephedra product. The FDA also included "medically impossible claims that ephedra caused multiple sclerosis or goiter," the report revealed.

In all, the agency had used only thirteen valid AERs as the basis for proposing limits on ephedrine doses. In three of these cases, the treating physicians saw no connection to any dietary supplement. The FDA didn't even try to determine if, in fact, those thirteen adverse events were caused by supplements containing ephedrine alkaloids.

In releasing the GAO report, the ranking Democrat on the House Committee on Science said, "I would suggest that FDA withdraw the proposed rule, do their job right and see whether we can come up with a rule that everyone can support grounded in real science and reliable data."

Dueling Cameras

Undeterred by the GAO report, the *20/20* producers continued to pursue the Metabolife story. They wanted to set a date to interview Metabolife's CEO and, however reluctantly, they had agreed to include the company's chief medical officer. I advised the CEO that he should grant the interview (with the physician). The CEO wanted to videotape the interview to show it to distributors and employees. We hired our own videographer. We gave *20/20* our video feed and the show's crew provided us with an audio feed.

To this dueling-cameras setting, the Metabolife CEO added a nice touch: he insisted the interview with *20/20* be taped at a friendly location—the gymnasium of his high school alma mater. The idea had a homey, appealing quality. Reporters, in their lust for a great story, can forget a company is just a bunch of real people with real ambitions and real feelings; this would remind them and the viewers of that.

And so on September 9, the 20/20 producers set up their cameras in the high school gym, while hundreds of students and Metabolife employees streamed in and filled the bleachers, ready to cheer on their hometown hero. It felt and looked like a pep rally.

The interview was as confrontational as I feared it might be. A correspondent known for his anti-business reports (he used to do "shame on you" segments about customer rip-offs) put the Metabolife CEO on the defensive, at one point dramatically revealing that 20/20 had talked to a doctor who had raised serious questions about the safety of Metabolife, saying the product could kill you. Nevertheless, the CEO held his own, coming across as calm and likeable under fire and citing research showing his product was safe and effective when used as directed.

In the ensuing weeks, I became alarmed by the behavior of the 20/20 producers and felt we might have to take counter-measures. Two weeks before the story was set for broadcast, the segment producer asked Metabolife to respond to the claims of a woman on a website run by a trial lawyer looking for plaintiffs. The patient claimed she had suffered a seizure as a result of taking Metabolife 356, but the producer admitted she had seen no medical records, that no lawsuit had been filed against the company, and that no complaint had been filed with the FDA or with Metabolife. I couldn't believe such a flimsy case might be cited on the air—it was irresponsible on its face, in my view.

Then Tony Knight turned up shocking information about the physician the ABC correspondent cited as saying that "the product could kill you" and whom *20/20* was going to feature as an "expert witness" on the broadcast. Turns out he had been the lead author of a paper reporting positive results in a small clinical trial that Metabolife had funded at one of Harvard University's teaching hospitals. Though this physician, from St. Luke's Hospital in New York City, hadn't done any of the main research, he was a published author, and using his name enhanced the paper's chances of acceptance by a medical journal. And as recently as four months before the *20/20* report was to run, this doctor had said of ephedra in the *Washington Post*, "It definitely works," adding that Metabolife was safe when used as directed and that he wouldn't hesitate to recommend it to most patients. So why was this doctor now getting ready to trash my client on *20/20*? Tony found out that he was on the board of science advisors for Slim-Fast, a Metabolife competitor. A star witness of *20/20*'s story had a clear conflict of interest.

When we confronted the producers with this discovery, they said they didn't think it would affect his objectivity or opinion and saw no reason to disclose this information to the audience. I was flabbergasted. It was clear we were facing a "hit piece," and we had to take drastic action.

With my two partners on the case—Tony Knight and Lew Phelps—I called my brother David, a top intellectual property lawyer, and asked him if we owned the rights to the video footage Metabolife had taken. If we hired the videographer, if *20/20* exchanged its audio feed for our video feed, and if *20/20* knew we were filming, then yes, we owned it. Knowing that Metabolife's outside lawyers were on the conservative side, I told David I needed a legal opinion. He asked when. I said in forty-eight hours. He told me that was impossible. "I'm calling Mom," I responded. He chuckled and said he would do it.

Thinking Outside the Box

Tony, Lew, and I then got Metabolife's CEO and its outside lawyer, a former federal prosecutor, on the line, and within moments I was telling the room: why don't we put the entire seventy-minute video of the interview on the Internet—before *20/20* can get its story on the air? It has to be unedited and have the time stamp running. "Before you say anything," I told the outside lawyer, "my brother is an experienced intellectual property lawyer, and we will have a legal opinion in forty-eight hours saying we own the rights to the videotape."

I explained that we would include links to the supporting documentation that we had provided to ABC News—all the studies, data, and independent reports showing Metabolife is safe, even a link to the doctor's statement in the *Washington Post* and his photo on the Slim-Fast website. Then I suggested that we take out a full-page ad in the *New York Times* exposing ABC News' violation of journalistic standards to its peers. I told the team that the day before the ad ran, I would contact the *Wall Street Journal*—a "Lead Steer"—to generate nationwide coverage of our campaign.

This will make it harder for *20/20* to distort or ignore certain facts, I explained to the group; the world will be able to see what was cut and what was kept. It will pressure the producers to be honest and transparent by drawing attention to their techniques. Of course, it also will show that our product is safe and effective, but by making the methods of *20/20* the focus, we can preempt their story with our own.

The company's lawyers initially didn't exactly love the idea, one of them predicting it would prompt ABC to punish us. I responded that I wasn't sure how it could get much worse. What are they going to do, put a hit on us? I was confident this would force the producers to change their story. After the *Journal* story ran, we would send the ad and press release to every TV critic for every newspaper in the country, and the people at *20/20* would have to go out of their way to at least *appear* to be fair.

The Metabolife CEO wholeheartedly agreed with me, and his willingness to fight ABC was a testimony to his belief in the safety of his product. After all, we would have to post the entire unedited interview online—warts and all—for everyone to see. I felt it was critical that we not edit the tape at all. The public needed to know that Metabolife was playing it straight, as opposed to the truncated version they would see on *20/20*.

As we began to implement our plan, I awoke in the middle of the night with another idea—let's try to buy a commercial midway during the *20/20* airing of the Metabolife story with a silent, scrolling message asking viewers to go to our website to vote on whether the story they had seen thus far was fair. The nightstand next to my bed holds a notepad and pen for these momentary epiphanies, and I scribbled down this idea and tried to go back to sleep.

I knew this could work for us in either of two ways. If ABC refused to run the commercial, we'd have a story on the rejection, and if ABC accepted the ad, so much the better. We'd reach an audience of millions with our message and generate still more news coverage of our fight against *20/20*.

A Multi-Media Campaign

And so it was. We launched a new website (newsinterview.com) and ran full-page ads in the *Times* and the *New York Post*. The stark, unadorned ad led with an all-caps headline:

SEE THE COMPLETE UNEDITED FOOTAGE OF
AN INTERVIEW BY ABC-TV'S "20/20" BEFORE
THE SHOW AIRS

The copy explained why Metabolife resorted to this move ("So when the segment is aired by ABC you can compare what is actually broadcast to the full interview and other important information posted on the web," and "so that you can evaluate the experts '20/20' relies upon in its story... "). The ad also fully mapped out the criticizing doctor's conflict of interest and called out a second doctor with similar conflicts, concluding, "Metabolife supports vigorous debate and public scrutiny but it should be open and honest. Because of Metabolife's concern that the '20/20' story may not report the facts accurately, it has posted the entire, unedited interview on the web."

We put out the press release on our big reveal at one o'clock in the morning. The ad ran but only after giving a heads-up exclusive to the *Wall Street Journal*, which would run it online before our news release was issued and publish it in print that morning on the front page of the second section under the headline "Diet-Pill Maker Battles Report on Web Before it Airs on TV."

The *Journal* article sparked hundreds of follow-up stories mainly questioning the fairness of the *20/20* story, not the safety of the supplement. The story spread across the country—the *New York Times*, *Time* magazine, two major stories in *Newsweek*, coverage in nearly every major newspaper across the country. Fox, CNN, and PBS covered it extensively. The three major broadcast networks stayed away, however.

We also aired commercials on 1,500 radio stations, urging listeners to check out our website. The $1.5 million ad spend sparked multiples of that in news coverage, as hundreds of publications covered the story of our fight. In the opening days, the website drew 1.1 million hits, way better than we had expected.

Just over a week later, *20/20* aired its story on Metabolife. I watched at my home in Los Angeles, hosting a few colleagues, family members, and reporters so we could learn, in real time, how the story ended up. Barbara Walters opened the program, saying,

I'm glad you could join us, because tonight we have the report that's been causing all kinds of talk. A four-month investigation into the diet herbal supplement called Metabolife. Maybe you take it, or maybe you know someone who does, because so many of us want to lose weight, and this seems like a miracle pill. But, boy, is Metabolife controversial. So you won't want to miss what our investigation uncovered.

Cut to video of the Metabolife CEO's home crowd in the high school gym.

To my delight, the story started off with fast bites from two young women praising the product and saying they lost ten or fifteen pounds by taking Metabolife. This, after the *20/20* producers had rebuffed our entreaties to interview people who had used the product successfully.

Then came two doctors critical of Metabolife, the second one being the physician previously quoted in the *Washington Post* as saying it was safe and he wouldn't hesitate giving it to his patients. Now he said, "We did not say it was safe. These products may be safe in some people, but not all people...." Well, yes, as can be said for all medications and supplements, right? There was no mention of his statement that it could "kill you" or that he was a Slim-Fast advisor.

The segment included a sound bite from Dr. Robert Stark, whom we had urged the show to consult, though they had refused to do so before our ad and the subsequent media onslaught. Dr. Stark said, "This is as safe as—as any other herb or—or dietary products." There followed a strong statement by Metabolife's medical director: "We've got over four years of experience with our product, millions of people taking billions of servings. If there was a significant health problem, I think we'd know it."

A Stunning Admission

The correspondent even pointed out that despite the FDA's criticism of Metabolife, "another government agency [namely, the GAO] has questioned the reliability of those [adverse event] reports and the FDA's handling of them." Then came this stunning admission: "Because the agency is still investigating and hasn't released complete information, there's no way to say how many adverse events involve Metabolife. Further, *no link has been proven between the health problems and the supplements*" (emphasis added). That was as close to exoneration as we could get, I felt.

At the end, the correspondent told viewers, "Last week, in an extraordinary and unprecedented move, Metabolife, which had taped my interview with Metabolife's CEO, took all seventy minutes of it and put it on the Internet." He continued, "The company took out full-page ads in newspapers, alerting people to the website. The ads also point out that the researcher (the doctor who said the product could kill you), is a 'trustee of the Slim-Fast Nutrition Institute. Slim-Fast being a competitor....'" This was precisely the disclosure we had urged the program to make and which the producers had previously refused to include. At my house, the celebration was on.

ABC News executives have said we had no effect on the program. Of course not! After refusing to include people who had successfully used the product, it was a coincidence that they decided to include them after our video, the various news stories, and ad ran. After refusing to disclose that the doctor they had chosen as the star critic of the product had a conflict of interest, it was also a coincidence that they ended up making such a disclosure. After refusing to include any physicians or researchers who had found the product safe and effective, again it was just a coincidence they included one in the broadcast. And what about Metabolife sales? In fact, sales of Metabolife increased after the broadcast. Why? Because the facts, as we told them, were on our side.

Another coup came five days later, when PBS' *Newshour with Jim Lehrer* covered the Metabolife controversy—that is to say, the reporting practices at *20/20*. Metabolife's CEO appeared, not to debate some doctor about FDA policy or Metabolife safety, but to joust over journalistic ethics with the then-president of ABC News.

In the case of *20/20* versus Metabolife, we were able to reshape the story and balance it substantially, getting the producers to include the facts that we had insisted from the onset fairness dictated they *should* make. Yet these concessions came only after great toil and sweat and controversy. We were sure never to make our criticism personal, we never named the producers involved and, instead, focused our attacks on the facts or lack of same. Nor have I named the producers or the correspondent here.

———

Though we had pretty much completed our assignment for Metabolife shortly after the *20/20* show aired in 1999, we continued to work for the company on-and-off for the next couple of years. Roughly five years later, in 2004, the FDA reimposed a ban on ephedra supplements for weight loss. Although over-the-counter drugs with higher doses of concentrated ephedrine were allowed, the FDA said long-term consumption of ephedra for weight loss was not justified based on the known side effects. A federal judge threw out the ruling in 2005. In 2006, the ban was ultimately upheld by the U.S. Court of Appeals.

Metabolife filed bankruptcy in 2005, in the face of a deluge of lawsuits filed by plaintiffs' lawyers. In 2008, Metabolife's founder, would plead guilty to lying to the FDA in a letter the company had sent to the agency years earlier; the letter stated in part that the company had "*never received a notice from a consumer that any serious adverse health event has occurred because of the ingestion*" of the ephedra product. Metabolife maintained that the complaints, received on a company hotline, were not evidence that the product caused serious side effects because the complaints were never substantiated. The company's attorney said the prosecutors "concocted a hypertechnical violation by taking statements to a regulatory agency out of context."

The company's founder served six months in jail, got out, and wrote a book saying he didn't know about the letter until a couple of years after it went to the FDA—and stating that scientific evidence proved that Metabolife was safe and effective when used as directed. He pointed out that the amount of ephedrine, and the utilization of another active ingredient, caffeine, in these FDA approved pharmaceutical products, far exceed the levels the FDA deemed as unsafe in Metabolife. The book's title: *The Metabolife Story: The Rape of Cinderella.*

I believe the company's founder when he says he did not know of the letter until years after it was sent to the FDA.

Our challenge to ABC, irrespective of what ultimately happened to the company, was that they fairly report all of the facts: the independent studies that showed the safety of the product, as well as the views of critics they were planning to include—and that if they had critics who were receiving compensation from a competitor of our client they disclose this fact to their viewers; we asked that they include a tiny sampling of the millions of people who had safely and effectively used the product, as well as those who may have had a bad experience with the product. It was telling that they were not able find a single person who had a bad experience. The fact is, as our client said in his book, independent studies proved that his product was safe and effective when used as directed.   And millions and millions of people had used the product over many many years without an incident.

The ABC broadcast reflected all of the above.

Chapter 6

Taking On Short Sellers

When crisis cases play out in the media for all to see, if you have the right relationships with the right journalists, you can learn a lot about what's coming, enabling you to preempt, respond, and counter. It's different, however, when you take on short sellers—the mysterious, often anonymous, band of traders, hedge funds, and analysts who make their living by targeting a company and, more often than not, its executives in a bid to take down its stock price, sometimes by almost any means necessary.

Trying to identify them can be like trying to grab a ghost. When you take on the "shorts," the rules often are bent or broken by the other side. Some of them are unabashedly *un*ethical, and because they recognize no standards of behavior, you don't know what they will do next. It is as if they don't let the facts get in the way of a good story—no, wait, that is *precisely* how some of them operate.

101

In fact, some short sellers will *invent* facts, planting rumors in the media and on the street that they know damn well are not true to batter the price of a stock they have shorted. They have been known to misrepresent themselves, impersonating reporters, government officials, and company executives to extract information. Worst of all, they operate with the utter impunity of anonymity, letting them lodge even the most scandalous charges without being held accountable.

Yet some in the media, including top-grade publications, are only too happy to make use of tips from short sellers with an agenda and parrot their storyline in articles directly generated by the shorts. The web, which now is a major outlet in and of itself, has spawned thousands of online chatrooms for stock gossip and provided a megaphone for blogger websites, including those that are long on bold opinions, invective, and scurrilous assertions without showing any regard for the ethics and standards that have governed journalism for decades. Twitter posts add to the turmoil, with some thinly traded stocks vulnerable to wild fluctuations in response to silly speculation. Then, if the story is right or your luck is bad, mainstream, top-line media will pick up on social media stories and do their own stories. There can be hundreds of tweets and Facebook posts, but they won't have anywhere near the impact of a major story in *Barron's*, the *Wall Street Journal*, the *Financial Times*, or the *New York Times* on the price of a company's stock. (Hence my Rule 7: *Social media are often a means to an end*. Even now, traditional mass-media franchises still have a much bigger effect on Wall Street and bringing about change.)

When short sellers start rattling your company's cage, therefore, you *must* respond responsibly, quickly, copiously, and persistently. Rule 1 of Sitrick's Ten Rules for Engagement is that confining yourself to "no comment" *sometimes* can be PR malpractice. When you go to war against short sellers, "no comment" can be disastrous.

Since this may be the only response possible if you don't have the facts, it is crucial to get the facts as soon as possible. Otherwise, you're a sitting duck for both the shorts and the media. An editor I knew at *Barron's*, a Vietnam veteran, used to say whenever a company he was writing about refused to cooperate, "That's fine with me, because they've just declared themselves to be in the free-fire zone." Shorts love "no comment" for the same reason. So do I when we are on offense.

Trying to strike back at short sellers requires getting hold of the right facts, but also being able to document them, whether with an audited financial statement, testimony or validation from the right expert, a new study, or some other form of proof. It also requires research on the opposition to figure out who is throwing the spears and what his angle or motivation is. Then the strategic communications counselor must be able to get this information to the right reporters at the right outlets to shield your client's reputation and stock price and mount a counteroffensive of your own.

To be clear, a lot of PR people will argue that because a short seller holds a large short position in the company's stock, the reporter should not use what he or she says. When I am confronted with this comeback, my response is that, while it is important that the reporter know about the short seller's position so he can take it into account when vetting the information, the only thing that matters is whether the information is true. If what he is saying is true, he can be a convicted felon. In a court of law the accused is innocent until proved guilty, but in the court of public opinion, he is often assumed guilty until proved innocent. This is especially true when the short is a regular source of information for the reporter or his publication.

Before we go further, let me offer a quick definition. To sell a stock short is to bet on its decline. The short seller sells "borrowed" shares, which he doesn't own, pocketing the proceeds for the time being, with the promise to return the borrowed shares later—presumably, after the stock price has fallen and the short seller can buy the replacement shares at a much cheaper price than when he sold the borrowed shares to start the trade.

If you short Apple stock at, say, $125, and it falls to one hundred, you could "cover the short" by buying shares at one hundred dollars, paying them back to your broker, and pocketing the twenty-five-dollars-per-share difference. If, instead, Apple rises to two hundred dollars, you could get crushed in a "short squeeze," having to replace the shorted shares by acquiring them at prices far higher than what your borrowed shares fetched when you first sold them.

To be sure, nothing is inherently wrong with short selling. It is an entirely legal practice that allows investors to hedge their upside bets, helping the market to determine the right price for a stock and making markets more liquid and adaptable. The problem is that some short sellers try to knock down a company's stock price by planting damaging and false rumors. As you might suspect by now, I have a problem with that. Lying is wrong, and when you tell lies to manipulate stock prices, you may be breaking the law. As for other short sellers who didn't launch the lie but pile on and trade on the rumors, if they too disseminate information they know to be untrue, they could be breaking the law as well. And they should be stopped.

When short sellers wage an attack, more is at stake than a company's stock price. Irresponsible and false rumors can seriously damage relations with lenders and vendors, forcing a company to pay higher interest rates on new debt and accept less favorable terms from suppliers. Speculation about solvency or a regulatory investigation can derail deals and spook customers, partners, and employees. And a stock's fall can gain momentum as investors decide it doesn't matter whether the rumors are false because this stock is headed down anyway.

Perception Becomes Reality

Perception becomes reality. A company can end up in trouble because of rumors that it *may* be in trouble or key constituents think it is in trouble. The valuation of a company may depend less on its actual performance and more on how investors *feel* about it—whether they trust and have confidence in management, and whether they like what they see.

Short sellers operating outside ethical bounds therefore play a con game that relies on undermining the confidence other investors have in a business. It is the strategic communications advisor's daunting mission to restore that confidence at the worst time by proving that the rumors are wrong—assuming, of course, that they *are* wrong. A word to the wise, then, when you must wage combat with short sellers: sometimes, the facts *don't* speak for themselves. Short sellers thrive in companies with complicated businesses, which by their very nature can result in a vacuum of understandable facts. They also thrive when companies don't respond to allegations, filling an information void with speculation, rumor, conjecture, forecasting, guesses, and, in some of the toughest cases I have handled, outright, intentional, bald-faced lies. The best way to fight an onslaught of non-facts is with relentless use of the real facts.

I'll say it again: *the facts* don't *speak for themselves.* The truth of that insight was reinforced a while back when I met the CEO of an internationally respected company that had come under attack by a fairly large group of short sellers. A man of understated skill and integrity, he faced a pack of jackals who were spreading the lie that his company was on the brink of financial collapse.

The company, though it had been under attack for more than a year, had ignored the innuendo and false rumors, deeming them so incredible as to be unworthy of response. The CEO, like many chief executives when their company comes under fire, had chosen to keep a low profile, declining press interviews and letting the financial gains speak for themselves, an approach his PR advisors had endorsed. Now the CEO had lost faith in this passive strategy. "We were ignoring this. We can't ignore this anymore," he told me in our first face-to-face meeting in his offices. "We thought the facts would speak for themselves."

"I'm sorry, but in cases like this they don't," I responded. "Unless somebody corrects it, the wrong facts can go on forever."

For this CEO, whose identity cannot be revealed here, the company's lawyers and we were able to neutralize the short sellers by demonstrating that they had been lying. The stock price reacted positively. Once we were able to get out the real facts about the company and its performance, the market responded by sending the company's stock back to its pre-attack levels. As the business continued to improve, the stock reacted accordingly. Today, the company is thriving and so is its stock price.

In many short seller raids, traders go to desperate lengths to try to damage the target, providing false tips to government investigators, alleging wrongdoing to the company's bankers, accountants, and customers, and convincing reporters to write stories based on the shorts' version of the facts. Keep that last method in mind: *reporters are on the front lines of many short seller campaigns, and often you must focus your countermoves on their efforts.* It's an interesting circle of life: bankers, customers, rating agencies, analysts, and investors are influenced by what they read in the media; on the other hand, what reporters write in the media is influenced by those they consider credible sources, which include bankers, customers, rating agencies, analysts, investors, and short sellers.

In one instance, the first attack surfaced in a blistering *New York Times* article. In another, it was an analyst's report, which was then quoted in a major financial magazine. In a third case, the sniping came in local newspapers, first criticizing the company and then the board.

I have been fortunate that with very, very few exceptions, the CEOs and companies I have represented have played by the rules and within the law. While I have represented them, all have played by the rules and within the law. Nevertheless, I have seen many cases in which it took shockingly little evidence, concocted by a group of anonymous short sellers, to jolt a major public company and unjustifiably tarnish the otherwise impeccable reputation of its CEO. And that's why I have formulated Rule 7: *If you don't tell your story, someone else will tell it for you.*

In a short seller attack, traders will spread a damaging story in the vacuum left by the company's silence. The firm's inside and outside PR advisors often advise the firm that responding to the criticism will just make it worse. Sometimes the PR people field an inquiry themselves and never even tell their client, deciding on their own to ignore it. In one case, a reporter for a major business publication told us that the PR people kept promising an interview only to postpone it several times and then say it wasn't happening. When I asked the client about it, he told me no one in the company even knew the reporter was requesting an interview. Yet now the reporter was angry and believed the company was "jerking her around."

Clients must keep in mind that what their agency does on their behalf is attributed to them, even if they know nothing about it. If a PR agency is rude to a reporter, slamming doors on his fingers, refusing to comment, failing to return his calls, it is as if the company itself is doing those things.

In combatting short sellers for clients over the past several decades, I have found that the more complicated a business is, the more attractive a target it is for the shorts. Few analysts and very few reporters or investors understand the intricacies of these complicated businesses, whether they are in financial services or pharmaceuticals or technology. This narrow band of understanding allows a lot of wiggle room in interpretation, and short sellers like that. If a short puts forth a plausible interpretation of a company's health or prospects, most reporters—and even some analysts—are incapable of evaluating it, though the good ones will check with a second source.

Short sellers also like a thinly traded stock, the price of which can be pushed around more easily because the daily "float"—the supply of company shares available for trading hands among buyers and sellers—is so small. Such stock is susceptible to volatility and manipulation. The other side of that coin is that if the company's stock were to rebound sharply, the shorts would get squeezed, their losses multiplying with each rise in the company's shares while they struggle to acquire enough shares on the open market to cover their souring bets. And the more stock they buy on the open market, the higher the price goes. In fact, I have seen many cases where setting the story straight fueled a sharp rise in the company's stock price, inflicting great pain on our client's adversaries. Critics of short seller tactics might view this as just deserts.

In waging battle against short sellers, it is important to understand the basis of their story and then disprove it with specific *facts*. That is how you turn a story. It isn't magic, it's a matter of identifying the key points and demonstrating that what the reporter has been told is wrong, communicating the real facts comprehensibly and convincingly.

While I cannot get into many of the specifics of how we proceed in telling our clients' stories, I will say that we provide riveting details, evidence, that expose the falsehoods. To gather the facts, we sometimes have to conduct our own forensic probe. This is where former top journalists and litigators come in handy.

One of the reasons reporters are so good at this job (assuming you find the right ones) is that they know how to gather and evaluate information, how to dig down to the facts. The same is true of good litigators.

In one of the cases we worked on together, one of my partners, who had been a *Wall Street Journal* reporter before joining my firm, began by inspecting ten years of financial statements with help from a client's senior financial analysts, trying to unearth the problems that sparked doubt among short sellers while also sifting out the figures that could contradict them. In another case involving two major pharmaceutical companies, we had to educate ourselves not only about the companies and their CEO but about the science itself. In yet another case, another partner who had been a reporter and editor with the *Wall Street Journal*, *Forbes*, and *Bloomberg* and I did the same. I think you get the idea.

After learning about the company, we review the analysts' reports and media coverage, identify the errors, and set about correcting the record. Working with our clients' lawyers, we help a company beat back the shorts and restore shareholder value—in some cases at a substantial multiple of the stock's lows. The truth will prevail if you put the proper amount of effort into telling it in the right way to the right constituents.

A Matter of Life and Death

A company's reputation for a stable balance sheet and the trustworthiness and wisdom of its leadership are among its greatest assets. Short sellers seem to gravitate toward a target whose reputation for integrity is a key asset for attack. Drug companies, for example, must be trusted for their clinical trial results, patient safety, and commitment to medical ethics. When short sellers attack, it can be a matter of life or death.

In 2002 the shorts started circling around an innovative drug company, the publicly held American Pharmaceutical Partners of Schaumburg, Illinois, and Los Angeles. APP, as it was known, and its privately held affiliate, American BioScience of Los Angeles, were in the final stages of testing a potential blockbuster cancer drug called Abraxane.

For all the promise of this new drug, some short sellers took aim at derailing it, peddling the self-serving story that APP had overhyped the promise, that its clinical trials were rigged, and that it had too cozy a relationship with American BioScience, the parent that had spun it off and taken it public the year before. The shorts did whatever they could to sow doubt about the drug, even though this threatened to delay FDA approval and endanger the lives of cancer patients.

The late stages of experimental drug trials, which are filled with uncertainty, provide an ideal environment for short sellers. Since drugs can pass phase I and phase II trials, sending a company's stock price higher in anticipation of approval, only to fail phase III and be denied FDA approval, the trials invite speculation and sometimes outright misrepresentation. A drug maker's stock price can swing wildly at the slightest hint of what the results might be, and short sellers can surf the gaps between these highs and lows.

In raising doubts about Abraxane, the traders drew a bead on a second target as well: the two companies' founder, CEO, and controlling shareholder, a brilliant, bold, and extraordinarily accomplished surgeon, researcher, and inventor named Patrick Soon-Shiong, whom they tried to isolate and impugn.

Dr. Soon-Shiong had already been fired and sued at an earlier company he had founded because he refused to continue work on a procedure that would put patients' lives at risk. He hired my firm after a story appeared in the *New York Times* in March 2002 accusing APP of having an improper business relationship with Premier, Inc., a powerful hospital distributor that owned a stake in APP. Premier had investments in twenty medical firms, half of which did business with the firm, posing possible conflicts of interest, the *Times* asserted. From there, the short sellers moved on to impugning first Dr. Soon-Shiong personally and then the drug Abraxane, which increases the potency and reduces the adverse side-effects of a common cancer drug, Taxol. (Taxol lost patent protection in 2000 and is known generically as paclitaxel.)

I needed to know all the facts down to the molecular level to be able to talk about why Abraxane was a breakthrough. Dr. Soon-Shiong explained that with traditional delivery methods of cancer medication, only a small percentage of the drug actually reaches the tumor. This inefficiency is the result of administering the drug in a "shotgun" approach throughout the body and the human immune system's tendency to attack cancer drugs as soon as they enter the body, sensing an invader and reducing their potency by half or more. Dr. Soon-Shiong wanted to avoid this counterattack by sneaking the medicine past the immune system's sentries.

Tumors feed themselves by taking nutrients from the blood cells. All solid tumors contain secreted protein acidic and are rich in cysteine, or SPARC, Dr. Soon-Shiong told me. SPARC is the vehicle that draws the white blood cells into the tumor so it can survive and grow. What if, he wondered, we could trick the tumor into thinking it was feeding itself, when instead it was killing itself? He believed he could do this by using nanotechnology to shrink the cancer medication to a thousandth of the size of a blood cell, hide millions of molecules of this cancer medication inside submicroscopic balls made with a coating of a human protein (albumin), and inject it into the patient's bloodstream. The tumor might blithely ingest the tiny, undetectable medicine balls, and instead of feeding itself would kill itself. Because the balls were coated with albumin, a protein found in egg whites, each one would act like a Trojan horse, traversing the bloodstream unmolested. This might let the Taxol travel to its destination without setting off alarms in the immune system.

There is an added benefit, Dr. Soon-Shiong told me. Taxol usually must be delivered in a chemical solvent known as Cremophor. Patients, to battle the deleterious effects of the Cremophor, must load up in advance on steroids, which have their own side effects. The Cremophor is so toxic and caustic that it melts through IV tubing, requiring special glass tubes to administer it. The Abraxane approach would eliminate the need for the solvent, the special equipment, and the steroid treatments, Dr. Soon-Shiong had told analysts, investors, and medical colleagues. Thus, Abraxane offered a possible triple advantage: more potency, fewer and milder side effects, and easier and faster delivery.

If this new molecular delivery system worked, APP, which would make and deliver the drug, and American BioScience, which owned the drug, designed it, and now was in late-stage trials to test it, had plans to produce an array of cancer drugs, saving or extending the lives of hundreds of thousands of patients and, in the process, reaping billions of dollars in sales.

Raising Doubts, Questioning Integrity

But short sellers were doing all they could to raise doubts about Abraxane and Dr. Soon-Shiong himself, questioning the integrity of the clinical trials and accusing him of all kinds of things, including putting his own interests before those of his minority shareholders.

American BioScience, the research and development arm, was formed in the early 1990s, and in 1996 APP was founded with an initial focus on U.S. marketing and distribution of generic pharmaceutical products manufactured by others. In June 1998, APP acquired Fujisawa USA's generic injectable pharmaceutical business, including manufacturing facilities in Melrose Park, Illinois, and Grand Island, New York, and a research and development facility in Melrose Park. (Dr. Soon-Shiong held a more than 80 percent stake in both companies.)

APP did a booming business selling generic injectable drugs, and in November 2001, it announced a deal to acquire the North American rights to Abraxane (still in trials) from its 65 percent owner and progenitor, American BioScience. APP agreed to pay American BioScience $60 million up front plus $25 million later and a split of future profits. A month later, Dr. Soon-Shiong staged an initial public offering of APP shares on the Nasdaq stock market, raising $134 million. And the month after that, in January 2002, APP handed the required $60 million upfront payment to American BioScience.

Some critics charged that he was self-dealing, draining away tens of millions of dollars that APP had just raised from outsiders in the IPO, and diverting the cash to his privately held firm, American BioScience. APP emphasized that an outside consultant had given the deal a positive fairness opinion and that all four of the company's outside directors had approved the terms to ensure all shareholders would fare as well as Patrick Soon-Shiong would.

By early 2003, short interest in APP had soared to 17.5 million shares, roughly half of all the company's shares that traded on the Nasdaq. All that selling in the stock depressed the company's share price to a low of less than six dollars in the first half of the year. Typical of the media coverage tilting against Patrick Soon-Shiong and APP was a story in TheStreet.com in March 2003 that began, "The most intriguing question about American Pharmaceutical Partners (APPX: Nasdaq) is who will benefit most from the business: Chairman and CEO Dr. Patrick Soon-Shiong or its outside shareholders?"

Actually, one might argue that the "most intriguing question" was what new cancer-fighting drugs might be unleashed if Abraxane was found to extend patients' lives in trials then underway. Instead, the story went on to discuss Dr. Soon-Shiong's control of both companies and their business relationship:

> That is one of the reasons why short sellers have targeted American Pharmaceutical, which they see as simply a cash machine for Soon-Shiong and American BioScience. To these critics, who have borrowed against 47% of the freely traded shares, everything about this arrangement favors Soon-Shiong leaving outside shareholders holding a very short straw.

The story did point out (in the bottom half) that APP executives "insist all the details concerning the deep and interlocking relationships...are disclosed" and noted that the company was "engaged in a rigorous practice of full public disclosure" and that its auditors and regulators had not raised any concerns. It then quoted my partner on the case, Lew Phelps, as the company spokesman, saying: "None of this is kept secret from investors, and no one is holding a gun to their heads making them invest in our company."

The short sellers kept fanning the flames of the rumor that these dealings between APP and American BioScience hadn't been disclosed at all, even though this was flatly false. On Wall Street, failing to *disclose* some controversial matter can get you in even more trouble than the controversy itself, so this can be an attack entry point for the shorts.

Then one afternoon I got a call from Dr. Soon-Shiong saying that a reporter from the *Wall Street Journal*'s "Heard on the Street" column was writing something for the next day. "My IR (investor relations) firm said we shouldn't respond," he told me. "What are they calling about?" I asked. "I don't know," he said. I suggested I call and ask. "You can always say no comment, once we find out," I said, knowing that this almost never happens once the client hears the questions. "Let's at least make an informed decision."

I got the issues the reporter was asking about. He was claiming that several key items had not been disclosed. I discussed it with Dr. Soon-Shiong. "They absolutely have been," he said. They're in our current 10Q."

"Then let's get on the phone and point them out to him," I said. And we did just that.

Dr. Soon-Shiong said he was nearby and would walk over to my offices, based in Century City at the time. I promptly got the reporter on the phone to go over the assertions he planned to include in his story—likely fed to him by the shorts. The first item, Dr. Soon-Shiong said, is on page *x*, line *y*, of the 10Q. "See it?" I would say, and read it to the reporter. By the fourth example, he said, "I got it, and I will never use that person as a source again," adding that there would be no story.

In September 2003, the company put out a press release hailing promising early results for Abraxane over Taxol in the ongoing trial but saying the details and data wouldn't be released until a cancer drug conference in December. This delay, despite the outstanding results, encouraged the short sellers' fearmongering, and they knocked down the share price of APP stock accordingly, reducing it by one-third of its former value.

You can play whack-a-mole indefinitely and struggle to keep up with the rumors planted by the shorts, but it can be a frustrating game. We needed to get out in front of them, to tell our own story in our way. To do that, I knew we needed to pick the right Lead Steer, a media outlet that, if we delivered the evidence, wouldn't be afraid to take a contrarian view and devote effort and space to telling Patrick Soon-Shiong's side of the story. Ideally, it would be an outlet that other media would be likely to follow.

Forbes magazine, in this case, was the right fit. Contrarian by design, it zigged where other reporters zagged, celebrating what its managing editor at the time called "heroes of capitalism, and the triumphs and travails on the path to creating new wealth." So I invited the managing editor to a private lunch with Rudy Giuliani, the former New York mayor and a possible Republican presidential contender. Giuliani was consulting to Dr. Soon-Shiong at the time. I told the editor at the outset that the purpose of the meeting was for him to sit down with the doctor and hear what he had to say. If he agreed that there was a good, contrarian story there, he should assign someone to write it.

The lunch went well. There were only three of us there, and the *Forbes* editor was the only journalist at the table. (I avoid group sessions with journalists, preferring to offer an exclusive or a special opportunity to one journalist at a time.) Quickly grasping the importance and the sizzle of the Soon-Shiong story, he assigned the profile to a young staff writer, shepherding it into the magazine's October 6, 2003 issue (which appeared online and on newsstands two weeks earlier than the publish date).

That editor was none other than Dennis Kneale, my collaborator on this book. He and his reporter put together a heroic tale of an innovative scientist-entrepreneur crusading to save lives (and create new wealth) while battling hordes of short sellers. The story was worthy of Horatio Alger: born in South Africa to Chinese parents who had fled China in World War II. Graduated from medical school near the top of his class, one of the first nonwhite surgical residents to join a major hospital in Johannesburg, earning a thousand dollars a month (half the pay of white doctors). Joined the faculty of UCLA medical school in 1983, and two years later, at age thirty-four, performed the school's first pancreas transplant, saving the life of a diabetic woman.

A Unique Insight

The *Forbes* article described how Dr. Soon-Shiong, searching for less invasive treatments, pursued an emerging technique that, rather than replace the pancreas entirely, sought to inject the existing organ with an extra dose of islet cells, which produce insulin inside the pancreas. Then came his unique insight: one could protect the islet cells from attack by the body's immune system by "hiding" them inside capsules made from a seaweed-based gel.

Dr. Soon-Shiong formed a new company, VivoRX, to pursue this work, joined by the drug-maker Mylan. Then he formed a second company for himself, VivoRX Pharmaceutical, to research the broader notion of shrouding other cancer drugs inside a "biologically active" capsule to rev up potency without triggering the immune system.

In 1998, Dr. Soon-Shiong refused to continue the procedure after he discovered it could put patients at serious risk, and VivoRX fired him. Cleared of any wrongdoing by an independent arbiter who reviewed seventeen thousand documents in the case, as the *Forbes* story pointed out, he went on to pursue his research at his second company, which he renamed American BioScience. While the earlier diabetes research withered after he left (he had a noncompete agreement in diabetes research), his new efforts to develop Abraxane showed enormous promise. Once again, he set up a new, separate company, this one to produce and distribute drugs from other makers: American Pharmaceutical Partners, APP, which he took public in December 2001.

The *Forbes* profile had a great "why now?" angle: soon the results would be released for final phase III trials of Patrick Soon-Shiong's new cancer drug. The headline was perfect: "Vindication." Three months later the company released trial results, which were promising and impressive.

"New Drug Said to Improve Delivery of Cancer Medication," ran the headline in the *New York Times* on December 6, 2003. The story announced that in the trial of 460 women with metastatic breast cancer, Abraxane had reduced tumors in 33 percent of them, compared with 19 percent for the old Taxol delivery with solvent and the steroid therapy. Those on Abraxane were able to get 50 percent more paclitaxel than those on Taxol, and in just half an hour compared with a three-hour infusion for Taxol patients. Abraxane, just as Dr. Soon-Shiong had hoped, didn't require the steroid treatments that must accompany Taxol, and only 9 percent of women on the new drug had a severe reduction in infection-fighting white blood cells, compared with 22 percent of women on Taxol.

Shares of APP popped up nicely on the news, and by the end of 2003 the company's short interest had fallen from seventeen million shares to ten million, the share price climbing from six dollars early in the year to twenty. Soon, however, the short sellers were back, chipping away at the results. "New doubts raised by trial methods in cancer drug study," the *Los Angeles Business Journal* reported on January 5, 2004, adding:

> The stock initially surged on the news, but since then it
> has dropped back down as short sellers, who have been
> gunning for the company and its controversial chief

executive, L.A.-based Patrick Soon-Shiong, seized on questions about the study's methodology and the drug's potential to gain Food and Drug Administration approval.

The shorts complained that three-quarters of the trial patient base consisted of women in Russia, questioning whether the results could be trusted. Taxol showed less effectiveness in the Russian patients than elsewhere, which could make Abraxane look better than it is, they asserted. The article quoted a report by a Wall Street analyst who was a former FDA medical reviewer and a critic of this trial's design: "We still believe the odds favor non-approval with the phase 1, 2 and 3 data in hand for Abraxane at this time."

By September 2004, the shorts had succeeded in rousing the interest of regulators, and the *Wall Street Journal* disclosed that the Securities and Exchange Commission was conducting a preliminary inquiry into disclosures made by American Pharmaceutical Partners regarding Abraxane. In particular, the SEC was said to be looking at whether APP misled investors regarding whether Abraxane would require steroid treatments. (Nothing ever came of this.)

In January 2005 came the proof of what Patrick Soon-Shiong knew to be true. Much to the short sellers' dismay, the FDA approved Abraxane for breast-cancer patients who had not been helped by first-line treatments. This made Abraxane a second-line treatment, which has a smaller market, but it was only the beginning. Shares of the company jumped 47 percent in a single day, a triumph that Dr. Soon-Shiong commemorated with paperweights displaying APP's stock chart from that day. Shares of APP more than doubled from their low in late 2004, approaching the thirty-dollar mark a few months after Abraxane won FDA approval. The short interest in the company, meanwhile, plummeted from ten million shares to five million and falling. This battle was all but over.

By the end of 2005, Dr. Soon-Shiong moved to quell the controversy over his control of the two companies, publicly-held APP and privately-held American BioScience, by merging them, APP acquiring its former parent for $4.1 billion in APP stock. This handed more than three billion dollars in stock to Dr. Soon-Shiong with his 80 percent stake in American BioScience, sparking a new round of short seller accusations of self-dealing and sweetheart terms.

The merged company, renamed Abraxis BioScience, soon had seventy-four trials underway for Abraxane, testing it against various cancer targets. With Abraxane on the market, the financial firepower of Dr. Soon-Shiong's breakthrough—revving up an off-patent cancer drug with a new delivery system that unlocked more of its power and eased its side effects—became clear.

Then in 2007, Patrick Soon-Shiong split his company in two—again—forming separate, publicly held concerns: Abraxis BioScience, Inc., which held the Abraxane business and the protein-nanocoating technology, and APP (for Abraxis Pharmaceutical Products), which had the injectables business. Dr. Soon-Shiong owned 80+ percent of both Abraxis BioScience and APP. He made this move because he felt the market wasn't fully valuing the two parts of the company, and he proved to be right: the combo had a total market value of $3.5 billion just before the split, and less than a year later the total value of the two separate companies combined was at six billion dollars.

Abraxane won approval as a second-line defense in Europe in 2008, and eventually the drug won FDA clearance as a first-line treatment for breast cancer and for some cases of melanoma and pancreatic cancer, with promising trials for lung cancer, small-cell carcinoma, and still other targets underway. In September 2008, as shares of APP were at seventeen dollars and change and near their high, the company sold itself to a German healthcare giant for twenty-three dollars a share, plus a contingent value right that could deliver up to an additional $980 million, or six dollars per share in cash, for a total consideration of $5.6 billion. Investors who had purchased APP stock in the IPO back in 2001 had reaped a seven-fold return on their investment in seven years. If you had invested ten thousand dollars in APP stock at the original IPO, by the time APP was sold seven years later, your investment would have grown to more than $72,000. The S&P 500 stock index went up only 13 percent in the same seven-year period.

That rich return, moreover, was for only half of what Dr. Soon-Shiong created. Then on June 30, 2010, the other half got bought, too, Abraxis BioScience (now a billion-dollar-a-year business thanks to Abraxane's later approval to treat pancreatic cancer) selling itself to Celgene for $3.6 billion. Add that to the earlier payoff, and a ten-thousand-dollar investment in the original APP back at the beginning (2001) had soared to $97,400, up almost ten times in less than nine years. The S&P 500 index of big-company stocks, in the same period, enduring two bubble-bursts (the dotcom meltdown in 2000–2001 and the global meltdown in 2008–2009), had risen only 4.2 percent.

Billions for Companies Once Derided

All those billions, for companies that once were derided by short sellers as headed for failure and bankruptcy, thanks to the brilliance, creativity, and, perhaps most of all, the perseverance and persistence of a single innovator, an American immigrant named Patrick Soon-Shiong. With a net worth north of $12 billion, he is the richest doctor in the world. He is also one of the most compassionate men I have ever met, the personification of the caring doctor you used to see in TV dramas.

Dr. Soon-Shiong acquired Magic Johnson's 4.5 percent stake in the Los Angeles Lakers basketball team in 2010, and in 2016 he made a far bigger splash by paying $70 million for a 13 percent stake in the Tribune Company (now Tronc), the owner of the *Los Angeles Times* and *Chicago Tribune*, to rescue it from the unwanted embrace of Gannett. For this, much to his dismay but not to my surprise, he drew vastly more coverage in the media than he gets for trying to develop drugs to cure cancer. He continues working on his innovations with stealth delivery systems for cancer and diabetes (having circled back to where he began his research), and continues to use me as a kind of consigliere.

Some short sellers may have made some profits here and there by shorting the stock of American Pharma, covering their bets and shorting it again on the rebound, but others got clobbered by the stock's rise, losing millions of dollars. A few of them may have been bankrupted. And all of these short sellers likely would have made far more money by betting in Patrick Soon-Shiong's favor rather than rallying against him.

For all the billions of dollars his innovations generated, how-ever, the even higher value created by Patrick Soon-Shiong is that his cancer drugs now are shrinking tumors, easing therapy and side effects, and improving and saving the lives of thousands of patients. For example, Abraxane been used to treat other types of cancer, achieving complete remission in pancreatic cancer. Dr. Soon-Shiong has invested more than a billion dollars in his newest company, Nantworks, which is dedicated to improving the quality of human life. As should be expected, he has made tremendous inroads. He is someone I am honored to call my friend and my client, and it has been a privilege to work alongside him, both as strategic public relations counsel and as a member of his various boards of directors including those of APP, Abraxis BioScience, and one of his two new public companies, NantHealth. If you are a cancer patient, or if you love someone who is, you owe a debt of gratitude to Patrick

Soon-Shiong and those like him. The value of his work is incalculable. At the risk of using what has become an overused term, it is priceless.

Chapter 7

Saving Celebrities

Do celebrities commit the same sins as we mere mortals and unfairly draw the world's attention for the commonplace? Or do they break the rules on such a grand scale that they get the infamy they deserve?

The answer would be...yes.

Fame and celebrity never have been more easily and instantly attainable, thanks to the rise of 24/7 celebrity coverage, TMZ, YouTube, and the net. And thanks to those same forces, fame and celebrity have never been so dangerous. In a world of 2.6 billion camera-equipped smartphones, instant web access, and the live feeds on Facebook, Periscope, and Snapchat, a celebrity's life is a scandal waiting to happen.

And when scandal erupts, a number of celebrities have called our firm for advice. (Our work for many of them remains invisible.) Although Sitrick And Company focuses on strategic communications counsel for leading companies and corporate titans as well as some of the hottest "unicorn" upstarts, we also have a thriving practice advising stars in entertainment, sports, and the media.

Our client roster is filled with names seen in boldface on TMZ and in the gossip columns of the *New York Post*. It has included Paris Hilton, Yankee slugger Alex "A-Rod" Rodriguez, former Dolphins lineman Richie Incognito, basketball great Kobe Bryant, Mötley Crüe's Tommy Lee, Chris Brown, actress Halle Berry, radio host Rush Limbaugh, and the Michael Jackson estate. (As a Google search would show, our role in advising all of these clients has been disclosed previously by our being quoted as spokesmen or issuing statements on their behalf.)

That last case, in the aftermath of the tragic death of the King of Pop, inserted my firm into one of the biggest celebrity stories in decades. Led by the creative genius of lawyer John Branca and legendary music executive John McClain, co-executors of the Jackson estate, we were able to restore stability and rebuild the Michael Jackson brand so that his three children would be assured of their father's support long after his premature demise. It stands as one of the most successful celebrity brand rehabs in history.

Some of the most famous people in the world, revered by millions, come to my firm at some of the most difficult times in their lives. Despite the assumption in some quarters that these stars are spoiled and unrepentant, most of the celebrities I have advised are modest and contrite. They want to make it better, and my partners and I do what we can to help them do that.

When I give speeches, I am fond of saying my firm's clients have run the gamut from Thomas H. Lee to Tommy Lee, and while I always hope this line will elicit a few laughs, it is a bit of a comedic risk. Those who know Thomas H. Lee the private-equity magnate may not know Tommy Lee the heavy metal musician, and vice versa. The millennials in the audience might not know who *either* man is!

The blurring of the line between business and celebrity has resulted in our representing clients from both worlds. Is Sir Richard Branson a business figure or a celebrity? What about Elon Musk of Tesla, who has been a client of our firm?

It is difficult to generalize about managing celebrity scandal. The personalities and situations and details are unique to each case. No one approach can work for most cases, let alone all of them, and yet...*of course* some inferences can be drawn from the scores of celebrity cases I have handled. My aim is to synthesize these cases into an overarching way to think about managing and fixing celebrity crises.

When celebrities stumble into controversy, two things help me rehabilitate their reputations. First, Americans love celebrities. They are our royalty, as many people have said. And second, Americans love a great comeback. They will forgive you if your infraction is not too grave and you do the right thing in the aftermath, although I am not a big believer in mournful, Jimmy Swaggart-style apologies. Okay, you're sorry—but those are just words. *What are you doing to fix it?* And then there is the issue of nuance: as I told one very high profile individual, *America will forgive an illness, but not a sickness.* (You can use your imagination to determine what that means.) For celebrity crisis cases, my Rule 5 is critical: Focus on the fix.

Other factors can make it especially difficult to defuse the crises of the rich and famous. This is a schadenfreude-prone era. Jealousy has made bringing down big celebrities a sport. Moreover, the celebrity news cycle isn't just 24/7 nowadays—it is every couple of minutes, a couple of dozen times per hour, every hour around the clock and around the world. Now it is the *consumption* of celebrity news that goes on non-stop 24/7 on billions of smartphones, tablets, and flat-screens, feeding an appetite for dish that is global and insatiable.

Celebrities know that their claim to fame could be wiped out in a few tweets. Get caught using the wrong word in a video shot by some fan with an iPhone and your career can be impaired in a microsecond, even if you were joking and there is no evidence that you are, say, racist. (One very high profile case comes to mind.) This only adds to their insecurity and their vulnerability by the time they come to us…oftentimes later than they should have.

Therefore, if you want to find a way to fix a problem, you must proceed quickly but with caution, making certain to find out, up front, whether the client did what he or she is accused of doing and has any additional skeletons waiting to tumble out of the closet. Which means: *You must be sure to ask your client, "Is it true? Is there anything else we need to worry about?"* This is Job No. 1 not just in celebrity cases, but in all crisis situations. I don't lie for clients, and I won't assert their innocence unless they have explicitly assured me of same (and their assurance has to be plausible). This is in their interest as much as it is in mine. Lies make a bad problem worse.

When a man strikes a woman, no matter what the circumstances, there is almost no explanation that will mitigate the fallout. Period. In situations like this, when it comes down to "he said, she said," "he" inevitably loses. Having said that, in most cases, there *is* no excuse. Sometimes there are mitigating circumstances—a wife or girlfriend struck him, say in the head, with a phone or a stiletto heel, and he was pushing away from her in self-defense. Still, we don't try to make any excuses. After all, whom is the public going to believe?

The Wheel of Pain

I have handled cases on both sides of this lamentable divide. In one case, a rock star who was accused of beating and drugging his soon-to-be ex-wife refused to even discuss, let alone sign, his divorce settlement. My suggestion: let's put him and his record label where they deserve to be—on the Wheel of Pain.

The Wheel of Pain, as I explained in my first book, is a tactic that should be employed only when absolutely necessary—and even then only when you are absolutely certain of your facts. But when those conditions are satisfied, it can bring almost instantaneous results. Like all the others in this book, it is designed to change someone's mind. The difference is in this case, the "someone" happens to be the public or the press and ultimately the adversary himself.

Here, what we were doing was basically putting the bad acts of this rock star, which previously had been kept private or confined to court papers, out there for the world to see.

So, after getting the lawyer's and client's permission, we granted an exclusive interview to a major celebrity magazine in which my client revealed how the rock star had her living in fear, how he had drugged her to the point that she fell to the floor and was gasping for breath, how he had beaten her up and smashed her belongings (allegations she had made in court). Then we suggested to the reporter for this celebrity magazine that she call the star's record label and ask for a response for the story she was writing. It worked startlingly swiftly. Prior to the article's publication, the celebrity and the executives at his record label were ignoring calls from my client's lawyer. Within a few weeks after it was published, my client had her divorce settlement signed, sealed, and delivered.

In another case, one I cannot say much about, a young woman got drunk and ended up in a violent argument with her famous boyfriend (my client), attacking him in a jealous rage while he was driving. He shoved her away, photos of her injuries were "leaked," and charges were filed. But none of these details ever became public. Heartfelt apology, counseling, a one-on-one interview and no jail time, and his career was restored.

We have always been fascinated by the lives of the famous, but these days far more media outlets, traditional and online, feed that fascination, stoking and extending the coverage of any given scandal and going to new extremes in how much they will reveal—and just how personal and intrusive they will get. Mishaps and small-time embarrassments that ended up on the cutting-room floor when the gossip columns had limited space now show up everywhere online, where space is infinite.

As the appetite for gossip has grown, journalists' definition of "newsworthy" has expanded. They are more relaxed in their decisions about what is a plausible rumor worth repeating versus what gets ruled out as irresponsible aspersion and, in the case of a handful of blogs, less mindful of an obligation to seek comment before running a story that will hurt someone.

Today, celebrity scandal is good business if you are TMZ or even the *New York Times*. There is a difference in what news the two media organizations consider "fit to print," but both of them make sure that what is posted or printed is both vetted and "lawyered" where necessary. But scandal can be very bad business if you are the celebrity—in business, Hollywood, or sports—at the center of a breaking crisis. As I tell clients, it's one thing when something is done in the shadows of darkness, but when a misdeed is brought out into the daylight, it's something else altogether. A drunk-driving arrest can reduce your next movie paycheck by a few million dollars and knock even more value off your celebrity brand in the long term. If it is high-profile enough, it can cost an executive his or her job.

Think about it: some four thousand people are arrested in the United States for driving under the influence of alcohol or drugs *every single day*. That's scary, reprehensible, and sad, but it is so commonplace that most of the time it isn't newsworthy. Yet when it involves someone famous, suddenly it is major news. When it involves someone famous, viewers and readers are riveted by it, and the media run as many stories on it as they can to lure a larger audience and, in the longer run, sell more advertising at higher prices.

There's a basic truth I keep in mind as I devise a strategy for celebrity cases: *this isn't about the public's need to know—this is about business.* With the right strategy, you can use this approach to your advantage, recognizing the value of granting access and exclusive interviews. Yet most people in the celebrity PR business do the opposite: they duck, cover, and stay quiet, hoping it will go away. There are three things to keep in mind in a celebrity crisis:

- The bigger or more salacious the problem, or the bigger the "star," the more negative is the publicity that will follow.
- Odds are it will not go away—at least, not anytime soon—and in the world we live in, these things can stay online forever.
- Assertions can be exaggerated or completely false, especially in court filings. But, if they are in court filings, the media will feel they are fair game, even if you say you have evidence that the allegations are false. While most responsible media will print your denial, it rarely will garner as much space as the allegation. That's because the lawsuit is news. What you say is a response to the news. Plus, what you say orally or in an email is not protected from a defamation standpoint, but what you say in a court filing has something called litigation privilege. Our legal system insulates the filer from libel charges—in

>making even the most irresponsible, false, and dam-
>aging allegations—so long as the charges are made
>in court proceedings. (This applies to the man on the
>street as well as the man on the screen.) And the
>media can simply report, "In a lawsuit filed today,
>person x said...."

In talking about celebrity crisis and media coverage, we can't ignore one of the newer arrivals and now one of the most powerful outlets of the celebrity machine: TMZ. The website and TV show, the creations of Harvey Levin, a University of Chicago–trained lawyer, are often the scourge of celebrities, taking a page from the Mike Wallace-*60 Minutes* handbook and ambushing them as they emerge from an airport, hotel, limo, or restaurant.

Yet a word to the wise for any celebrity or any executive approaching his own kind of celebrity status: *you ignore TMZ at your peril.* Some people dismiss it, but they are wrong to do so. As a story posted on *BuzzFeed* News on July 24, 2014, pointed out,

>TMZ has been responsible for breaking the biggest celeb-
>rity scandals of the last 10 years: effectively ending a
>30-year career (Mel Gibson), tarnishing golf's most
>sacred idol (Tiger Woods), and puncturing the pristine
>image of celebrity royalty (Solange Knowles attacking
>Jay Z). But it isn't just celebs: In 2009, TMZ caught a
>bank spending millions of taxpayer bailout funds on a
>lavish party (Northern Trust), and, via spin-off TMZS-
>ports, instigated the $2 billion sale of an NBA team by
>applying the same surveillance to former Clippers owner
>(Donald Sterling), once reserved for the Hollywood stars
>and socialites.

I recently worked with a prominent Washington, DC, lawyer who, to my amazement, had never even heard of TMZ. While I will get flack for saying this, in my years of dealing with TMZ, I have found Harvey and his people to be consistently careful to ensure that what they publish is accurate.

Do I always like what they publish about my clients? No, of course not, but overall I have found them to be fair. And TMZ doesn't traffic only in the negative. This isn't to say that negative stories cannot be helpful, if one is on the attack. While TMZ is probably the best known of the online media outlets in its realm, there are scores of others, including Radar.com and online versions of what are referred to as "traditional" media, including People. com, which isn't as daring.

Last year a prominent client came under a blistering attack in a book that was widely picked up in the media. Research showed that, despite the author's holier-than-thou attitude, he himself had a history of spousal abuse, racism, and anti-Semitism. So we presented evidence of this record to a highly viewed online outlet, its lawyers vetted it, and these facts were all over the Internet over the weekend—before the publicity campaign began for the book. Suddenly my client's chief accuser now was the focus of a torrent of new accusations.

Pre-Empting the News

Making a pre-emptive strike in the so-called gossip media also can be useful when you need to pre-empt bad news by releasing it yourself (admittedly not something that is endorsed by many in my profession) or getting out the "bad news" first and ensuring that countering facts also are included in the story. A client of mine, a very rich and well-known woman, was going through a highly publicized bad divorce with her prominent husband, and although they had split up, she feared he was going to leak word to the media that she had taken up with one of their low-level employees. This was factually accurate and unquestionably would have attracted media coverage, especially with the spin her ex's PR folks would have put on the story. What to do?

We pre-empted the story. I placed a call to an editor I knew, providing him with information about the background and "pedigree" of the boyfriend and telling him when and where his cameras could get a shot of my client with her new beau. They weren't well known enough to be recognizable to the photographers, so I told the editor I would be sitting at the restaurant table with them, have your photographers check out my company website to see my photo so they will know where to point their cameras. "Just be sure you shoot me from the back," I said. They complied. When the photos ran, you could see a crescent of the back of my head in the foreground; and now, any tinge of scandal had been neutralized by the facts, as opposed to hyperbole on the part of the ex.

In another case, I had a famous basketball player who was just emerging from surgery and getting inaccurate and unfavorable coverage about his future in the NBA. He wanted to grant an exclusive interview to a particular reporter at ESPN to set things straight, but that would upset every other basketball reporter who covered him and had asked for an interview, as I pointed out to the star. But if, say, the New York Post or TMZ or ESPN were to ambush him, getting the first, on-the-spot interview, no beat reporter would be scooped by a rival and nobody would be upset. Then my guy could circle back for the follow-up with the beat reporter at ESPN or anyone else. So I called an editor at one of these media outlets and told him where the hoops star would be at two o'clock the following afternoon. And there, as fate would have it, he was "ambushed."

For all the buzz about how the Internet has made traditional media obsolete, traditional media still can trump the online outposts. At the risk of being repetitive, you ignore the old-guard media to your detriment. Yes, TMZ has been responsible for breaking numerous stories, but the *New York Post*, the *New York Times*, *Los Angeles Times*, and other mainstream media have their own impressive lists. While big stories might break online, the biggest consequences are usually felt after a story has appeared in more traditional media.

This isn't to minimize the impact of the new media. The fact is, stories of consequence, whether in sports, entertainment, or even business, that break first on, say, TMZ, almost always get picked up and repeated by mainstream media, often by the most prestigious of traditional media. This in itself is a testament to the power of online outlets. Still, while online outlets' reporting on infractions can prompt inquiries and consternation and perhaps the same ultimate consequences as if the stories had appeared first in the *Los Angeles Times* or *New York Times*, the impact of those stories' appearing in such august media almost guarantees those consequences.

Journalists may be friendly to you—they may even be good friends of yours—but that doesn't mean they won't do a negative story on you or your clients when it is warranted. They will listen to what you have to say, but they have a job to do. I have valued relationships with many reporters and editors, counting them among my friends, but I wouldn't ask them, or expect them, not to do their jobs. Here are two key points: (1) It's all about the facts, and (2) I rarely make demands of reporters; when warranted, I make requests.

Demands are reserved for breaches of journalistic ethics, refusal to include our comment if my client is a defendant in litigation or the subject of a critical story, or something like that. Even then I show respect, and if the journalist refuses, I don't raise my voice. I explain why I think it's unfair, and if they refuse, I tell them I am going to go to their editor. I tell them not as a threat, but as a courtesy. PR people in Hollywood and Washington are known to make demands on the media, sometimes in a demeaning way. I never have seen this "strategy," if you can call it that, work out very well.

TMZ was the first to break the news of Michael Jackson's sudden death, just eighteen minutes after doctors at Ronald Reagan UCLA Medical Center in Los Angeles had pronounced him dead. TMZ's flash headline: "Michael Jackson passed away today at the age of 50." The *Los Angeles Times* got out confirmation seven minutes later. The fabulously talented entertainer, who lived an unorthodox and much-scrutinized personal life, had been given an overdose of propofol, a hospital anesthetic, on top of lorazepam and midzalom.

The Michael Jackson case blew up into the biggest story around the world for weeks and months afterward. One of my partners on the case, Jim Bates, still recalls the first sign of crisis that day: a gaggle of TV helicopters hovering over Jackson's home, ten miles from our offices (then in Century City in LA). Ten minutes later, choppers were hovering over the hospital where Jackson would be declared dead.

John Branca called me within hours of learning he would be the Michael Jackson estate's co-executor and asked if we would represent the estate. I was in Hawaii, attending the wedding of a friend's son. The following Monday morning, Jim Bates got a call from Branca. Bates and Branca knew each other from when Jim was a reporter and editor at the *Los Angeles Times*. As an article in *Vanity Fair* later noted: "By the time the will and a related trust agreement arrived at the courthouse, (John) Branca...already had retained the services of...Mike Sitrick—described by the website Gawker as the 'Ninja Master of the Dark Art of Spin.'"

Around the same time, another player in the Jackson saga contacted another partner at my firm, Terry Fahn. The call came from a representative of AEG, sponsor of the planned Michael Jackson comeback tour for which Jackson was in rehearsals when he died. We went to work for the Jackson estate.

The Michael Jackson Estate

At the time of the singer's death, the estate was half a billion dollars in debt and wobbling, financially. Jackson's reputation had been through the wringer, even after he was acquitted of allegations of child molestation in 2005. His finances, frankly, were a mess. He had been described as a millionaire who lived like a billionaire. Jackson had been forced to cede control of his world-famous Neverland ranch after defaulting on a note, and he was so stretched that at the time of his demise he was $1,800 behind on the phone bill and nine thousand dollars behind on his water and electric bill—and he still owed $341,000 to his lawyer in the child-abuse defense.

To bring in new income, fast, Jackson had set a deal with AEG, a giant concert promoter and venue owner, to play fifty sold-out concerts in a row, all of them at the O2 arena in London. He was in Los Angeles in rehearsals at AEG's Staples Center for that run when he died—cutting off the new income stream and putting his estate's finances in even deeper trouble.

Yet if the estate were to start selling off assets to raise money to cover expenses, it would reduce the potential for creating recurring revenue that could continue supporting Michael Jackson's three children. His oldest, Michael Joseph Jackson Jr. (known as Prince), was twelve years old when the King of Pop died. His second-born, daughter Paris Michael Katherine Jackson, was eleven, and his youngest, Prince Michael Jackson II, was seven. The youngest was called "Blanket," and he came to global fame as an infant, when Jackson held him over a hotel balcony in Paris to acknowledge hordes of fans below.

Michael Jackson had been wise and fortunate to name Branca and John McClain, a music producer who had been a close friend of Michael Jackson since their childhood, co-executors of his will. McClain is a co-founder of the innovative and street-wise record label Interscope, and he orchestrated the dazzling rise of Jackson's sister Janet.

John Branca, a long-time partner of the powerhouse law firm Ziffren Brittenham, is one of the most successful and creative lawyers in the music business, a legend who has represented more than thirty members of the Rock and Roll Hall of Fame, from the Elvis Presley estate to the Beach Boys, the Doors, the Rolling Stones, Carlos Santana, the Bee Gees, Fleetwood Mac, Elton John, Crosby Stills Nash & Young, the Eagles' Don Henley, and more.

Branca had represented Michael Jackson since the days of *Thriller*, released in 1983 and the best-selling album of all time. He wisely had advised Jackson to buy the Beatles' music catalog in 1985. That purchase, combined with Jackson's own trove of songs, would form the foundation of the fortune left to his children. Jackson had been best man at Branca's wedding, bringing along Bubbles, the chimpanzee he had dressed in a tiny tuxedo. The singer and his advisor had broken off relations and reconciled three times, the third time coming just weeks before Jackson died. Even during their times apart, and despite Jackson's filing three wills in succession to reflect changes with each new child, Jackson always had stuck with Branca and McClain as co-executors.

John Branca and John McClain were the leaders of what they would come to call Team Jackson, flanked by litigator Howard Weitzman, who was named one of the top fifteen lawyers in the country by *The National Law Journal*, and dealmaker Joel Katz, attorney Zia Modabber, probate attorneys Paul Gordon Hoffman and Jeryll Cohen, as well as Karen Langford (Branca's right hand or left hand, whichever you like), Jeff Jampol, music publicist Diana Baron, and (from Sitrick And Company) Jim Bates, Terry Fahn, and me. At my firm, our day-to-day mission, led by Jim Bates, was to help Branca and McClain rebuild the Jackson brand, which was critical to the success of the estate, as well as reinforce the credibility and legitimacy of the new management, which in the early days was under attack. This included attacks on the authenticity of Jackson's last will and testament and a flurry of inaccurate rumors.

True: Jackson's three children would be cared for by his mother, Katherine, or by the singer Diana Ross if his mother were unavailable. *Not true*: Jackson's remains were to be buried at Neverland. We had to see that the truth was reported so that the estate could get on with its main job of building the success of the Michael Jackson estate for the well-being of his kids.

The co-executors, Branca and McClain, moved swiftly to stabilize the estate's finances, fend off a barrage of sometimes bizarre charges and lawsuits, and strike a multitude of new deals bringing hundreds of millions of dollars in revenue for Michael's heirs. The success is due in large part to John Branca, one of the smartest and shrewdest strategists in the music business whom I have had the pleasure of calling my client.

Along the way, Team Jackson was able to rebut criticism of the executors to a remarkable degree and refocus attention on the artistry of Michael Jackson, helping his celebrity estate become one of the most successful in history and achieving what *60 Minutes* called "the most remarkable financial and image resurrection in pop culture history."

Countering Rumors, Court Challenges

From the get-go, Team Jackson had to contend with confusing rumors, court challenges, and an assortment of oddball characters and hangers-on in the wake of Jackson's death. Enter litigator Howard Weitzman. Howard was and is the estate's right hand, serving as counsel to the executors in every sense of the word. His clients have included every major motion picture studio, talent agencies William Morris, ICM, and CAA, and many high-profile clients including John DeLorean, Michael Jackson, Marlon Brando, Morgan Freeman, and Arnold Schwarzenegger.

Early on, Michael's mother sought to remove Branca and McClain as co-executors. Under the will, she stood to receive 40 percent of her son's wealth and custody of his three children, with their 40 percent share, with her stake passing on to the kids after her death. She eventually dropped her challenge. Jackson's estranged dad, Joe Jackson, was complaining loudly about receiving nothing from his son's estate, but a judge ruled he had no standing to sue. A few years later, moreover, he would come around to praise the work of Branca and McClain.

Then five of Michael's eight siblings leaked to the media a letter demanding that Branca and McClain resign. It was strictly a PR move. None of them had been named in Michael's will, and none had standing in probate court. The five were Randy, Janet, Rebbie, and two members of the original Jackson Five, Jermaine and Tito (who quickly asked that his name be removed). The other two surviving members of the Jackson Five, Jackie and Marlon, didn't sign the letter, nor did the remaining Jackson sibling, La Toya. Along the way, a fight erupted at the family mansion in which one Jackson ripped off the shirt worn by another, and the police were called. Howard Weitzman and Mrs. Jackson's attorney worked things out, but in the meantime, all of this generated more headlines across hundreds of websites.

At another point, the family matriarch went missing for several days. Young Paris tweeted messages asking about her whereabouts, but Katherine turned out to be resting at a resort with a couple of her grown children. All of these pulses created waves of media coverage, and we had to ensure that the Michael Jackson estate's main priorities—to stabilize and build the finances and ensure income for the three Jackson children—weren't threatened by any new developments.

Meanwhile, at various points such headline-generating figures as Al Sharpton and Jesse Jackson were in the mix, not to mention a mysterious man named Thome Tohme. Three years after Jackson's death, Kim Masters wrote in the *Hollywood Reporter*, "…as his luster began to fade, the vultures began to circle, leaving the executors of his estate in legal battles with crazies, creditors and, now, the shadowy guru at the King of Pop's side in his final days."

Tohme, who claimed to hold a medical degree and to be an ambassador-at-large from Senegal (neither of which could be verified by reporters at the time), was close to Jackson in his final year before being fired a few months before Jackson died. Tohme was claiming credit for a Jackson rebound and demanding compensation. The estate sued him for enriching himself, while he countersued in an effort to get money.

Overall, the estate would employ twenty different law firms fending off the challenges or filing actions of their own on the estate's behalf. One woman sued the Jackson estate for $50 million, claiming the singer had been stalking her for years and continued to do so even after he died. Another lawsuit sought a trillion dollars, alleging that Michael Jackson had stolen the plaintiff's secret formula for a herpes cure. A third case, filed by a convicted criminal, sought a billion dollars and alleged the plaintiff had had an affair with Jackson in the 1970s which inspired his albums *Thriller* and *Bad*. There was also a three-million-dollar lawsuit filed by a local man who opposed spending taxpayer dollars on police needed to control the huge number of fans spilling into downtown Los Angeles for Michael Jackson's memorial service at Staples Center, which was broadcast worldwide. It was tossed out of court.

The estate also had to fend off claims from a promoter, Howard Mann, who had purchased a number of Jackson's personal items in a bankruptcy proceeding a few years earlier and now saw stunning upside in a museum tour. Mann had "cut his teeth in the titillation trade," as one story in the *Los Angeles Times* put it, describing him as having dabbled in a startup for online gambling, featuring female porn stars as topless dealers, and a naked women's wrestling league.

In the months after Jackson's death, Mann had approached Katherine Jackson, offering her "hundreds of thousands of dollars" in return for her cooperation, he told the paper. The snag: Mrs. Jackson had no legal authority over the name, copyright, trademark, and intellectual property rights pertaining to Michael Jackson. All of that was under the control of the Jackson estate, which viewed Howard Mann's plans as an infringement. Branca turned to the estate's attorney Howard Weitzman of Kinsella Weitzman to go to court to stop the threat. Weitzman told the media, referring to Howard Mann, "His day is coming. The estate will take appropriate legal action."

Branca and McClain were in a difficult and rather sensitive position. They didn't want to show any disrespect for Michael

Jackson's mom, yet had to make it clear, in their dealings with the media, that the Jackson estate was in charge to avoid confusion in deals they were making for the benefit of the estate. Ultimately, the courts would side with the estate.

Branca and Team Jackson also had to fend off the Heal the World Foundation, which was a barely extant charity claiming to represent Michael Jackson. It popped up two days after his death, when a woman who had never met Michael, according to media reports, claimed to have won his okay to start a charity with the same name as one that he had let go dormant years earlier. It was funded in part by one Howard Mann.

Our side had to handle this gently, so we put out a statement emphasizing that this new foundation had, as an Associated Press story reported, "done little fundraising or charitable giving" and that it had "no relation to Michael Jackson's charity that touched so many lives before becoming inactive several years before Michael's death." If the Jackson estate didn't move against Heal the World, "others would be profiting from IP that rightfully belongs to Michael's children." Ultimately, lawyers for Katherine Jackson and the executors would broker a deal putting the Heal the World Foundation under control of the estate.

During Jim Bates' tenure at Sitrick And Company, he has developed an expertise in entertainment, representing producers, studios, and celebrities and their estates. A former deputy entertainment editor at the *Los Angeles Times*, he has worked on dozens of entertainment cases while at Sitrick, from the estates of Michael Jackson and author Philip K. Dick to wrestler Hulk Hogan, producer Sean "Diddy" Combs, music producer Dr. Luke, the Screen Actors Guild, videogame giant Activision Blizzard, and the producers of *The Wolf of Wall Street* and the producer of *Thomas the Tank Engine*.

The biggest change Jim has seen over the years is rapid-fire pace of gossip items. It used to require a major new step to spark a follow-up story on some celebrity's strife. Now every quarter-turn is worthy of an entire spate of stories, every response can generate a news item, and any follow-up response to that first response does the same. A star's fleeting tweet becomes an entire story, sparking a flurry of other tweets that emanate like ripples from a pebble dropped into a pond.

Moreover, the accessibility of the net hands a megaphone to nobodies. Many people writing about celebrities have no sources at all, no contact with the famous or their representatives. They just retread and tweet every unsubstantiated rumor reported, even if it originated with a single website. Nevertheless, we have to deal with them. The public doesn't necessarily differentiate between them and credible sources, and the appetite for celebrity news is so voracious that a report itself becomes the news event, regardless of the source. So we must respond with a counter-story on more fronts than ever before.

One of our first moves in the Jackson case was to quell the rumors regarding the will, though we didn't take our usual tack of offering exclusive details to one Lead Steer reporter. Instead, we filed the will with the court, putting its entire contents in the public domain—and then, moments later, we sent out a copy of the entire contents of the will to every reporter covering the Jackson estate, so that they could get access to the real thing without having to visit a website, much less go to the courthouse to sift through probate records.

We wanted to show that the bizarre rumors were false, and that the will was legitimate and made perfect sense. The will stated clearly that Jackson's assets were to go entirely to his three children. They would be cared for by Michael's mother, who would be taken care of during her lifetime, and a portion of the assets would go to charity.

A Game-Changing Idea

One of Branca's and McClain's truly game-changing ideas came just days after Jackson died. The entertainer, renowned for his diligent preparation and striving for perfection, had his rehearsals filmed so he could review the progress, like an NFL coach looking at game films. As soon as Branca and McClain screened the footage, they knew: this could make a movie, a documentary tribute to Michael Jackson, the Performer. To direct the film, they tapped choreographer Kenny Ortega, already known as the architect of the Disney Channel's enormously successful (and aptly titled) *High School Musical* franchise. Just four months later came the premiere of *This Is It*.

It revealed Jackson as a meticulous, concerned, full-on artist, demanding and exacting and, even though it was just a rehearsal, as riveting a performer as he had ever been. It reminded everyone of what we had admired most about Michael Jackson, and it crowded out the controversial imagery that had dogged him in the last years of his career.

It remains the top-grossing documentary of all time in worldwide box office, raking in more than $260 million. Additional sales to television channels and home video also were strong, adding up to over $500 million in total revenue driven by the film. All told, *This Is It* brought $200 million into the Jackson estate.

At the end of the film, as the credits roll, you will see the names of the key players on Branca and McClain's team, including Jim Bates, Terry Fahn, and me. A typical Branca and McClain touch, and it meant a lot to all of us who had worked so hard to achieve the Jackson estate's goals.

At Branca's direction, and to the delight of all of us on Team Jackson, the film's smash reception led to one touring show and one Las Vegas-based production based on Jackson's musical oeuvre, played against the artistry of the acrobats in Cirque de Soleil.

This produced another revenue stream and further rehabilitated the musician's brand. Later, the estate signed Jackson's longtime music partners at Sony to a $250 million deal to release seven new albums over the next decade, in one of the biggest music deals in industry history.

Early on in the Michael Jackson case, Branca realized that an important constituency had to be cultivated and cared for: Jackson's millions of adoring fans. It struck him that the fan base fully looked to the Jackson estate to take the lead in restoring the name of Michael Jackson. To build ties to the fan base and mobilize it, Branca brought in extra help in the person of Jeff Jampol, a longtime talent manager and advisor. Jampol manages the estates of Janis Joplin, the Doors' Jim Morrison, Tupac Shakur, the Ramones, Rick James, and quite a few more, keeping their income streams flowing by releasing new records, merchandising lines, and live theater tours. This requires maintaining close relations with longtime fans and cultivating new ones, and now he would turn to doing the same for the Jackson estate.

A "fan base" is a burden and an asset that few corporations— the Walt Disney Company being an exception—have to worry about. But in celebrity cases, you ignore fans at the expense of your client. For Branca and Team Jackson, we were able to harness fan outrage to derail a lurid, unauthorized cable TV documentary that we felt would be bad for the Jackson estate. In Europe, the Discovery Channel had begun promoting a tabloid program purported to be a re-enactment of Michael Jackson's autopsy. One ad featured a hospital gurney bearing a shrouded corpse with one hand exposed— wearing Jackson's trademark glittery glove. In poor taste, at best.

A letter from co-executors Branca and McClain chastising Discovery executives for a program that was in "shockingly bad taste," was "leaked somehow" to the fan base, and the story blew up...in a good way. The cable titan couldn't afford fan controversy just then, given that it was close to launching the new Oprah channel, OWN. Two days later, Discovery shelved the autopsy program; it never appeared.

Overall, the rehabilitation of the Michael Jackson brand and his estate was a huge success thanks to the efforts of John Branca and his co-executor, John McClain, and the other members of Team Jackson.

With the spate of new deals, the Michael Jackson estate cut its half-billion-dollar debt in half and generated almost half a billion dollars in fresh income in the first three years after Jackson passed away. As a crowning move, in March 2016, Branca and the estate agreed to sell to Sony Corporation Michael Jackson's 50 percent stake in Sony ATV Publishing, which he had owned since 1985. The price tag: $750 million. In this Internet era, which has destroyed much of the value in the music recording business, that is an astounding number.

Jackson, in the deal Branca had negotiated, had paid $41.5 million for the Beatles' Apple catalog in 1985, or about $93 million in today's dollars. Now the Jackson estate was selling it for $750 million, an eightfold return over thirty years. The stock market's inflation-adjusted returns were up *five-fold* in the same period. Jackson's copyrights thus performed 60 percent better than stocks, which are considered the best long-term investment of all.

The estate was giving up the copyrights and publishing income for three million songs, from "New York, New York," "All You Need is Love," and "You've Got a Friend" to the theme song from *Mission: Impossible*. Yet the estate was able to hold on to other music assets, including Jackson's master recordings and publishing rights to all of the songs he wrote, such as "Beat It" and "Billie Jean," and a 10 percent stake in Sony's EMI Publishing worth well over $200 million.

The latest Sony deal allowed the estate to extinguish that last $250 million in debt, which had been owed to Sony from a loan Jackson had taken out to fix his faltering finances years earlier. It continues on solid footing, protecting the Jackson assets and the brand's integrity.

Restoring a brand's integrity can be a difficult feat to pull off for any celebrity under fire. It is important to recognize that a story often has eight sides to it, not just one or two, and often, somewhere beneath all the turmoil and accusations, is the real agenda—making money. Another motive often at work is revenge. A onetime insider and hanger-on, say, who left a celeb's circle and is miffed to be on the outs. Nobody talking to the media is under oath, so plenty of people feel free to lie.

News—True or Not—Can Spread Before You Have a Chance to Respond

One of the biggest risks of celebrity scandal today is that the news—even when it is untrue—gets out incredibly quickly and spreads so rapidly on the web before anyone has had a chance to respond. While the reporter who broke the *first* story exposing something salacious might have given the target a chance to comment, that same target may not have been available for comment to other reporters on, say, a Saturday night at eight o'clock. Regardless of whether the subject of the story does get a chance to comment in the first story, dozens of other media outlets will often blithely pick up the story without seeking any further comment themselves. Thus, dozens and dozens of stories can go out with allegations that are not true but with no comment from the other side or with a comment that is incorrectly or misleadingly reported.

For the follow-up stories, the speed of news on the web can trump any obligation to hold off until the target of a story can respond.

Making the charge itself, then, can be tantamount to convicting the celebrity. Unfairly, allegations alone can kill a career, even when they are untrue. Sometimes this means you must try to pull off a near-impossible feat: *to kill a story outright, before it runs.*

A "blind" case in point: some years ago, I got a call from the head of a film company, who was in the middle of producing a motion picture starring a beloved American actor then in his seventies. A damaging story was about to run in the *Globe*, he told me. "The *Boston Globe*?" I asked. No, the tabloid *Globe*, the grocery-stand celebrity *Globe*. It was about to report that the actor had advanced prostate cancer and had only months to live. The actor said the story wasn't true, but he could say good-bye to any more acting jobs if this false account got published. "Here's the name and telephone number of the reporter who called," my caller said.

The Downside of "No Comment"

So I called up the reporter and introduce myself. "We have it on good authority that your client has advanced prostate cancer and has only months to live," he said. How do you know? Have you seen his medical reports? "No," the reporter replies, "but we saw him walking out of his oncologist's office building, and the doctor there specializes in the worst cases of prostate cancer." "Can you give me the address?" I asked. "Sure," he said. So I called my client. It turned out that he was walking out of his internist's office, which was in the same building. I called the reporter back and told him.

Now, here's the thing: if I had insisted on leaving it at "no comment," as some of the most respected PR advisors in this game are wont to do, this story would have run. The actor's career would have been hurt, and he would have spent the next year denying he was dying. Instead, I got the facts. The *Globe*, I am happy to report, killed the story. It was all over in a weekend, and I had won another lifelong client.

This is the ideal: to make the problem go away so quietly and quickly as to make my services, at least in the crisis area, no longer necessary.

Still, killing a story where it lies, before it runs and despite all the expense, time, and effort some reporter has put into it, is a rare and difficult achievement. Most of the time it is impossible. The pre-emptive kill requires an arsenal of hard, incontrovertible facts—but, also, it requires good journalists who want to get it right. You will see both elements at center stage in the chapter that follows, on our efforts on behalf of a defense contractor that was in the gun-sights of a major TV news magazine.

Chapter 8

Killing Stories

For half a century, when producers of television news magazines have come calling on businesses, businesses have almost always quaked in fear. CEOs have heart palpitations, their PR advisors grip their smartphones and try not to let their nerves show, and company lawyers usually begin sending letters in an attempt to kill the story before anyone even knows what the story will say.

60 Minutes is the granddaddy of the bunch, followed by a panoply of contenders, such as *20/20*, *48 Hours*, *PrimeTime*, and *Dateline*. To be sure, these programs have celebrated plenty of business heroes, from Amazon's Jeff Bezos to sage billionaire investor Warren Buffett to Microsoft co-founder Bill Gates. They also have vindicated the falsely accused, such as the Duke University lacrosse players wrongly accused of rape and several of our clients, including the late Pattie Dunn, former chairman of Hewlett-Packard; Eugene

Melnyk, founder and chairman of Biovail; and Dr. Patrick Soon-Shiong, founder and chairman of American Pharmaceutical Partners and Abraxis BioScience and, more recently, NantWorks.

Pattie Dunn was indicted, having been wrongly accused of "pretexting" and spying on her board (all charges were dropped, see chapter three). Melnyk and Soon-Shiong and their companies were attacked and accused of a whole host of horribles by short sellers (their charges also shown to be false; see chapter six). But despite these stories and others like them, TV news magazine shows are better known for exposing the dark underbelly of business and government. Wall Street rip-offs, defense contractor scams, auto company recalls, bad hospitals, con artists, CEOs guilty of misdeeds—these stories populate their rogues' gallery on display.

Reporters have a well-worn saying, "Tough but fair," and, while some might disagree, that pretty much has been my experience in dealing with the primetime news magazines.

Rarely ever can you hope for what some say is the impossible: to get these programs (or any major news organization, for that matter) to retreat from a story on your client and never put it online, in print, or on the air. We were able to achieve this feat for our client, a defense contractor that I'll refer to by the pseudonym Training Sciences International, or TSI. The case involved a story set to air on one of this country's major network news magazines—just weeks before the publicly traded company was set to be acquired for more than a billion dollars. But after the producers, their bosses, and their lawyers reviewed the case we put together demonstrating that the premises and facts of the planned piece were wrong, they killed the story—a rare occurrence, indeed.

But while I take great pride in the work we did in putting together evidence proving that the information the producers had assembled was wrong, the real credit goes to the professionals at that organization and the journalistic standards they upheld. It demonstrated that they were truly concerned about getting it right, as opposed to just getting it on the air.

Storytelling is the major stock-in-trade at my firm, not to mention story *selling*, but sometimes we have to play defense, and that can include correcting reporters' errors by assembling a set of contradictory facts that demonstrate what the reporter has is wrong. (In fact, a line in my bio states, "Although many of his cases have dominated the headlines, perhaps even more telling are the cases which are never heard about—where Mr. Sitrick and his firm are brought in to keep their clients out of the press and off the web, a much more difficult task.") Sometimes the case you build can be so convincing as to kill the story entirely, though this is rare. As you try to counter to demonstrate what the producer or reporter has is wrong, these three steps forward may help:

- Review the information the reporter has and determine what is accurate and what is not
- If inaccurate, find out what the correct information is
- Present the "facts" to the reporter in a manner that demonstrates what he or she has is false

This is how my firm came to be involved in a story that threatened to do horrible damage to a company, its shareholders, and its employees. The story the TV news magazine was doing was aimed at TSI and its training program for uniformed personnel in the Middle East. The story would have been scandalous, to be sure: more than a billion dollars in U.S. taxpayer funds spent over eight years to train more than a hundred thousand new members, only to end up with what the media came to characterize as a band of misfits and klutzes. Mismanagement of funds, expense account violations, billing for time not worked, allegations of incompetence, homophobia and racism, reports of drunken late-night parties, and turf battles between the State Department and the Department of Defense. These were just some of the allegations.

Sitrick And Company had already had been hired by TSI to handle various strategic communications tasks; no crisis had yet descended. Then TSI executives started hearing from sources in one country who warned them that a camera crew from a major television news magazine had been seen locally, there to shoot footage of U.S. installations, interview locals, and contact current and former employees about TSI's training program. Worse, word was that the news magazine team had visited this country *twice*, meaning the investment of time and resources was high. This was a big story.

The More Time Invested, the Harder It Is to Kill a Story

The deeper a TV show gets into reporting a story, the more time and money it has invested in doing that story and the slimmer your chances of influencing it, let alone killing it. (This generally applies to print media, as well. Yet another reason to engage early, if at all possible.) By the time we got involved in the TSI case, the news magazine crew was already two months into it. We were getting to this situation late.

TSI's chairman called me after learning that the news magazine program was drawing a bead on the company. His management was disinclined to talk to the producers, but this, I advised him, was a decision that should be made only after we knew what they intended to report.

Before you can decide whether to "take the stand" and sit down in front of cameras (or for an interview with a print reporter, for that matter), you should try to ascertain what the story is about, what information they have and where the information came from, and whether the sources they are using are credible. You should not agree to sit down for an interview until you know what the other side is looking for—otherwise you are walking down a long, dark alley with no idea of who or what might be lying in wait.

There are a few ways to do this. You can ask the reporter what he is working on and what he has. You can ask the reporter for a list of questions he wants to ask. You can sit down with the reporter entirely off the record. This means nothing said in the session can be discussed with anyone outside their news organization, nor can it be used on-air, online, or in print unless you allow it.

Generally, I do this in phases. I begin by calling the reporter. During that call, I ask what he is working on, how far along he is in the reporting process, and what is the source of his information, if he can tell me. Usually his sources are unnamed, and he refuses, of course, to disclose those names. Chatting with a reporter provides a spontaneity and give-and-take that neither side can get via email. Depending on the outcome of that chat, we may move forward with the interview or we may move to another level of fact-gathering.

In a situation like the one we were facing with this news magazine, the producer was unwilling to share any of the details of what he found in his reporting. Time was a particularly critical factor, given how far along the news organization was in its reporting, to say nothing of the pending acquisition. From what senior executives had heard from those contacted by the program's producers, while they only had bits and pieces, they knew it was going to be bad.

TSI executives were wary of having even an off-the-record exchange with the program's producers. I told them that I had worked with this show's people many times before, and they always had kept their word. If they agreed it would be off-the-record and nothing could be used, that would be the case. The worst outcome is you find out what the producers have, and you can prepare for it, even if you decide against cooperating with them. But I knew that in most cases, once clients hear, off the record, what the story is about and what parts the producers are getting wrong, the clients feel compelled to correct it.

And trying to correct the story—before it airs or gets published— is almost always the most effective way to mitigate potential damage. You don't win in boxing by *taking* punches but by *throwing* punches. Muhammed Ali beat George Forman with rope-a-dope, but if he didn't hit back, in the end, he never would have won, right?

As soon as we heard about the news magazine's foray into TSI territory, we got our client's permission to engage with the show's producers, asking them to tell us what they were doing and what information they had about our client. After sharing this information with our client and the lawyers, I called back the producer, saying that before TSI would consider the request to make the CEO available for an on-camera interview, we needed to have an off-the-record meeting so that my client could better understand the story and what allegations were being made.

This really isn't all that uncommon a request in situations like this, but the producer said, flatly, "We don't sit down for off-the-record meetings."

"Of course you do," I said.

Producer: "No we don't."

I told the producer I had held off-the-record briefings with other producers for his show various times in the past and named two producers senior to him, in case he wanted to consult them about it. He would not relent. He was young, aggressive, and on the rise at his program, and I had been assured he also was smart and hardworking. The call ended, and I was left to run the calculations: What to do?

This is where everything could have fallen apart. If you react harshly, if you get the lawyers involved (wrong move at this point), it could fall into a dark hole or the program could air before you get resolution. If you take it personally, get your back up and say fine, forget it, I won't talk at all, that story runs on the network program anyway. It will be told by people other than you, likely the wrong people as far as you are concerned, and then, when you complain about inaccuracies and imbalance, the producers will say you had your chance to tell your side of the story and you chose not to.

And the producers would be right, though that still doesn't excuse inaccuracies. But the damage is done.

"Do You Feel Lucky?"

Yet I have seen other PR people, when the pressure is on and crisis is descending, make this mistake. An offending story triggers a call from the company communications chief to the reporter's boss, so the PR exec can berate the editor or senior producer and yell at him for failing on the job. This may make the PR handler feel better, it may even impress his boss, but now the PR person has made two new enemies, the reporter *and* the reporter's boss, and most importantly, still hasn't succeeded in correcting the record.

As I have said before, reporters will tell you this doesn't affect their coverage of the story. And while I believe most reporters are professional enough to let the facts dictate what they write or what they say on the air, what about the things on the margin? What about tone of voice? Nuances, subtleties—they can make a huge difference in a story. Reporters are human beings and have feelings like the rest of us, and to ignore this is to risk offense. So the question for PR people who take this approach is, as Dirty Harry might say, "Do you feel lucky?"

In the TSI case, what was my real, immediate objective? It was to get the program's producers to sit down with us off the record and share what they had so the client could decide whether to participate in the process. Berating a recalcitrant producer wouldn't achieve this. (Not that I even considered doing that. That is never an approach I take, for a variety of reasons, including the one stated above.) Solution: find another way to accomplish your objective.

And so I placed a call to a top executive at that same program, who has worked with me on many stories over the years. (This executive, a twenty-year veteran of the network, is one of the smartest, toughest journalists I have ever worked with. Not for one moment would this veteran compromise journalistic integrity for our friendship, nor would I ever ask. We both know this.) Soon after, the meeting was set, with this senior executive sitting in and the producer meeting my client off the record.

The meeting took place at Sitrick And Company's offices in New York, and in some ways it went as one might expect. The people on my side of the table—the TSI CEO, a lawyer, and a few others, listening intently as the producer uncloaked a list of serious allegations he had collected from unnamed *former* TSI employees and others. One good sign: several of the allegations dated four years, some as far back as ten years (we later discovered), related by disgruntled ex-employees who hadn't worked for TSI in several years.

The producers offered to tape an interview right away, but we demurred. We wanted to make sure our answers were based on facts, and they had hit us with a tsunami of allegations, many of which went beyond the firsthand knowledge of anyone in the room. We needed time to research what they had told us to determine if it was true. Crafting an arsenal of accurate, well-researched answers requires time, effort, and attention. You can't and shouldn't do this job on the fly, especially during an interview, let alone an on-camera interview. It would be media suicide. You must be prepared, ready to answer every question.

That said, the TSI executives represented the company well, explaining they were the company's new management and had put into place new policies and procedures. They said they would look into the allegations the producers had recited and would get back to them.

While gathering the facts and preparing a response, we were hit with a grenade. A month or so after our off-the-record meeting, a high-profile investigative website published an exposé excoriating our client. It is a litany of horrors: crooked uniformed men who supply ammunition to the Taliban, hundreds of millions of dollars in training invoices that were approved but poorly accounted for, and high attrition. Hundreds of thousands of locals had been trained since the program's start several years earlier, but fewer than 20 percent were still serving. TSI wasn't mentioned until the eighth paragraph but then was referenced repeatedly for the rest of the story.

The investigative story had landed without our ever having been aware it was in process, let alone that it was set for publication. In fact, the first we learned that anyone else was working on something about TSI was when we read the story. The story quoted several unnamed ex-TSI people saying horribly critical things that appeared to have happened just "yesterday" (figuratively, not literally). Never mind whether they had left the company long before or had been fired for cause or were suing the company and had an axe to grind, all of which would prove to be true about a meaningful number of the sources talking to the producers for the program.

The company later denied a multitude of assertions in the story, but it was too late. For journalists, the charges were so juicy that the same gaffe was repeated over and over, even though it no longer applied. The website story sparked a congressional investigation, and a few weeks later, after a hearing, it was ready for primetime: a network news anchor opened with a joke about billions of tax-payer dollars spent to instruct trainees to be lousy shots.

That was bad enough, but for us the implications were serious on another front. This just seemed to reinforce what some sources had told the producers for the TV news magazine. Adding to the complexity was the growing interest in the TSI story as President Obama pushed plans to accelerate a U.S. withdrawal that would remove most troops within the next year. TSI was one of the largest contractors in the Middle East, at a time when contractors provided roughly half of all the personnel deployed there, racking up huge spending but insulating the U.S. government from criticism that it was putting too many military lives at risk. By late 2010, for example, the United States had 145,000 troops in Iraq and Afghanistan—plus 187,000 contractors doing jobs that otherwise would have required more than doubling the deployment of troops.

Thousands Trained, Most of Them Illiterate

At TSI, dozens of contract employees had lost their lives working in support roles for U.S. troops in the Middle Eastern region. Against this backdrop, the police-training mission suddenly had moved to center stage. TSI, contracting with the federal government, had trained thousands of recruits, the overwhelming percentage of whom were illiterate, a not-inconsequential percentage testing positive for hashish, and most of them never having driven a car, sat in a class-room, or used a toothbrush or modern plumbing.

All of that controversy had put the TV news magazine in even hotter pursuit of the TSI story, so we had to re-engage with the producer. I needed to know more about what the show had. So I gave the producer a call and asked him to send me a list of questions by email so that I could show them to TSI brass and we could get started on researching the answers.

Producer: "We don't send questions by email." Pause. "Even if my show does, I don't." Again with this? To be sure, TV producers can be torn between two competing goals: they want good answers, and providing questions up front can ensure that, yet they want the drama, on camera, of spontaneity and surprise—the "gotcha" moments that are a trademark for some TV magazine programs.

I wasn't going to argue with him, though. The purpose wasn't to provoke him. I wanted to get as much information about the story from him as I could. And so I told him okay, fine, tell me the questions and I will write them down and run them by you, and I started scribbling furiously as he began rattling them off.

Later, someone on my staff pointed out that few CEOs of a firm our size would deign to sit down and take hand-scrawled notes over the phone from a reporter or producer. But you have to seize the moment and subjugate your ego, even when you think you are in the right. And most importantly, you need to get as much infor-mation as you can about what they want to say.

And so I wrote down all the questions from the producer, typed them up, and emailed the list right back to him, asking for any fixes he might spot before I forwarded them to my client. The producer responded in detail, and I forwarded the list to TSI executives. This went on for several weeks. To expedite, the producer would send me questions, I would get the answers from the client and then receive follow-ups or new questions and "facts" to check.

After seeing the first series of questions and how inaccurate the assumptions were on which they were based, I proposed we get a media lawyer involved, just in case things went awry. Companies usually wait until *after* the story runs, when the damage has been done, to hire a libel lawyer, or they have him start sending threatening letters in advance, even when there is nothing but assumptions about what might be in the story upon which to base the threats. I felt that bringing on an expert in this area ahead of time, to consult and advise, would allow us to move quickly if we needed to.

For the TSI case, I recommended Anthony Michael Glassman of Glassman, Browning, Saltsman & Jacobs in Beverly Hills. Tony and his partner, Rebecca Kaufman, and I had worked together on complex cases several times before.

A former federal prosecutor, Glassman has spent more than forty years advising clients on defamation, libel, privacy and First Amendment cases, sometimes suing and sometimes defending. He has argued in hundreds of trials, defending the tabloid *Globe* against suits brought by Clint Eastwood, Tom Selleck, and Rod Stewart, and defending *Playboy* from actions filed by Charlize Theron, Vanna White, and Daryl Hannah. He has defended Hugh Hefner and sued Larry Flynt, handling both cases successfully. And he and Rebecca successfully have sued print media and television news magazines, including one that defamed an African-American minister, another client of ours.

I always have worked well with lawyers, in part, I believe, because our approaches are so similar, based on deep-dive research, relentless fact-finding, and an ability to weave all of that into a good story. Despite some dramatic moments, much of what I do, and much of what my partners do, is painstaking, fiendishly focused on fine points and minuscule details, and technical to an extreme.

The facts matter, and the fine points of the facts can matter even more. It isn't enough just to tell a reporter, "Did not!" You must prove it, provide convincing and overwhelming evidence to the contrary. In a court of law, you are presumed innocent. It is up to the plaintiffs or prosecutors to prove you are guilty beyond a reasonable doubt, but in the court of public opinion the reverse is true: *you are guilty until proven innocent.* It is up to you, the accused, to prove your innocence beyond a reasonable doubt.

For the next three months, a flood of so-called facts and allegations were revealed to us by the television news magazine's producers, and we responded to nearly every one in writing with information proving, in virtually every instance, that their information was wrong.

We also were concerned that, even though we had evidence that the allegations were false, the airing of these scandalous charges would provoke national coverage and investigations by the Justice Department, State Department, and Defense Department, to say nothing of congressional hearings. It wouldn't matter if months or years later the allegations were found to be untrue. The damage would be done. The livelihoods of thousands of hardworking people also were on the line.

A Declaration of Defense

Just weeks before the scheduled airing of the program came the culmination of the TSI case: our declaration of defense, delivered in a long, fact-packed letter to the senior producer who oversaw the television news program. It was signed by me and based on exhaustive research by a handful of my partners, client staff, and me. The letter ran nine pages and offered responses to eleven separate allegations and a list of four suggested independent sources.

My opening paragraph said that TSI "has significant concerns that much of the information you have obtained in your reporting is unsubstantiated, inaccurate, out-of-date, and/or biased and therefore, it has equal concerns that the story that you are working on will not be fair or accurate." We pointed out that the program hadn't identified, to us, any TSI worker, former or current, who had served in the company's Mideast operations in the last three years; that it relied on two ex-employees who had left three years prior and cited events that occurred four or more years earlier; that one source had never worked in the Middle East and was fired for poor performance and was suing the company.

Doubling down, the letter continued:

> How could these individuals...possibly provide accurate or reliable information about what is going on with. . . training in [one country] two years ago, last year or today?...The Company and I feel that these issues raise a major question: how can you or [your network] give any credence to what people say about [TSI's] activities or performance in [the Mideast]—sensationalistic as it may be—if none of the people who are willing to go on camera...have served in or even been in [the country] within the last several years?

We further impugned the story's anonymous sources in this footnote: "It is very easy to make false accusations and statements when you can hide under the cloak of anonymity and not be held responsible for what you say. Perhaps a current employee might have a reason to request anonymity, but not a former employee, unless he or she is not willing to stand behind what they say."

We countered almost every charge cited by the news organization with a direct denial and a few paragraphs of proof of *why* the allegations were false. One of the most incendiary charges involved a disturbing incident that played out one drunken night at a TSI site "in country." A white Southerner confronted a black Northerner who was upset at seeing a Confederate flag sticker in the local canteen. The black trainer was so rattled by the confrontation that he slept that night with his pistol at his side, according to his testimony in a lawsuit filed against TSI.

TSI had investigated the matter thoroughly—and had taken action swiftly and decisively. In our response, we pointed out the incident occurred years earlier and explained, "The Company investigated these allegations and took appropriate disciplinary action. Three employees were terminated, including the Regional Coordinator at the site. Five additional employees received written reprimands. It is important to note that this matter occurred four years ago and was promptly and appropriately addressed. No similar incidents have occurred to the Company's knowledge...[Y] ou have not found any evidence of a recurrence or more recent allegations."

In my closer, I invoked that first off-the-record meeting a few months earlier:

> From our first meeting in February, for which [TSI's] CEO, other members of the executive team, and I traveled to New York to provide you with background on the program, we have sought to provide you accurate substantive information to enable you to produce an objective and creditable story.
>
> Given your reputation and my experience with your news organization, to say nothing of the reputation of the program, [TSI] and I have every expectation that you will thoroughly examine the accuracy of the assertions you are considering to ensure that you are reporting only

accurate facts and unbiased views in this story. We are
pleased to continue to help provide you with the information you need.

Later that evening I followed up with an email to the TSI story's
producer after learning that he was tracking allegations of possible
time-sheet fraud yet hadn't deigned to tell us about it. "This is not
only inaccurate, but disturbing in that you never raised these issues
with us," I wrote.

The same day my letter went out, a second letter, more ominous
in tone and written by Tony Glassman, our defamation lawyer, was
delivered to a general counsel of the network. Glassman's letter
tracked most of the same points but added:

Taken as a whole, these allegations individually and col-
lectively could well, expressly or by implication, falsely
defame and disparage my client and cause enormous
damage to its reputation.

Glassman warned that for this television news program to "give
credence" to such questionable sources "would violate both journalistic and legal standards. As noted by the Supreme Court, even
a public figure may prevail in a defamation action...."

Five days later, Glassman followed up with a second letter,
thirteen pages long and riddled with repeated explicit denials, complete with the facts backing them up, citations of libel case law, and
excerpts from, as well as an attached copy of, the back-and-forth
email traffic between the producer and me. And, near the very end,
this:

In light of the record summarized above I trust that the
network will not move forward with these demonstrably

false and enormously defamatory and damaging charges.
...I am confident that [your news organization] will
continue to adhere to controlling journalistic and legal
precedent and will be guided accordingly.

And then it was over, the story's quiet demise coming suddenly
and quickly, after so many months of painstaking research and
debate. In a brief exchange by email with the producer a few days
after our letters went out, he told me only that the story was being
held for now, to be revisited the following TV season.

The story on TSI never aired. When TSI's general counsel realized it was dead, he wrote me an email: "Mike, thank you. You
saved the company...literally."

Chapter 9

Personal Crises

A wealthy investor gets sued by his longtime, part-time lover, who reveals a battery of shocking details of their private liaisons for all to see, including his colleagues and his wife and children. In a feud between two billionaires, charges fly of racism, the hiring of hitmen, and the planting of a pack of cocaine in an attempt to spark an arrest. At a prominent medical clinic, a married, ostensibly heterosexual doctor admits he fondled a male patient on the examination table. On two separate occasions.

Elsewhere, in a clash between a billionaire and a centimillionaire over issues in their gated community of vacation homes, the billionaire is alleged to have smeared his adversary with fabricated accusations of child molestation, among other dirty tricks. And in yet another case, the grown daughter of a wealthy family threatens to tell the world that she and her brother had incest in their teenage years unless her family pays her more than a million dollars.

I have represented one of the parties in each of these predicaments—as well as a famous male athlete caught in compromising photos, and a prominent executive accused of violating securities laws and dropping drugs in customers' drinks. (All charges ultimately were dropped.) Dare I mention one of the more bizarre tales, in which a wealthy man carried on an online, real-time video-sex affair with a woman who, unbeknownst to him, was a quadruple amputee? She also turned out to be married. All he ever saw on-screen was her head and shoulders. She threatened to publicize their sexting escapades unless he paid her a considerable sum of money. We were able to make it go away—without his having to pay her one dollar.

Families of any income level can face accusations of salacious, tawdry, or perverse behavior, but when sensational charges are directed at the rich and famous, they often spark lawsuits and make for titillating headlines that leave the media and public hungry for details. Thanks to social media, the line between what really took place and what is fabricated is getting thinner. Merely being *accused* of doing something unseemly can become the equivalent of having actually done it in the public eye. Publicity compounds the problem—and that is where I enter the picture.

Cases involving deeply personal issues require acute sensitivity, not to mention extreme confidentiality. The level of embarrassment for a client can be especially high in these headline-grabbing situations, which need to be handled with great care and skill. Containing and stomping out an inventive *lie* can be difficult now that people can gossip across an online "backyard fence" that stretches around the entire globe. And lies—really bad ones—can be inserted in the middle of the truth, lending them a veneer of credibility. This happens all too often today in litigation, especially in divorce cases. Personal crises can hurt not only the principals, but also the companies where they're employed and their families and friends.

Combating this kind of false information can be incredibly difficult. In the disputes about what is real and what is made up, what was consensual and what was forced, what was beneficial and what was exploitive, making these critical distinctions can trigger a backlash if not handled just right. The risk is particularly high in cases of "he said, she said."

Family Feud

That was the predicament facing a prominent family when, late one afternoon, the voice of Stephanie Bruscoli, my longtime executive assistant, came over my intercom: "There is an attorney on the line. He wants to speak with you about retaining our firm to help one of his clients. He says he was referred by a mutual friend."

I, of course, picked up the phone, as most of my cases come by referral.

The attorney told me he represented the daughter and grandson of a prominent family whose patriarch (his clients' father and grandfather, respectively) is known throughout the United States and, indeed, much of the world. Unfortunately, said the attorney, he was not yet at liberty to disclose the name. (To make it easier to tell this story, though, I'll call the patriarch "George," his daughter "Mary," and Mary's son "Tom.")

"That's okay," I said. "What's the situation? How can I help?"

The lawyer said Tom, who had a successful business, and his mother had been threatened that unless they paid Tom's sister (Mary's daughter—I'll call her "Jill") one million dollars, Jill would file a false and defamatory lawsuit claiming that when she was an adolescent, her brother sexually abused and exploited her multiple times. In Jill's explicit and detailed draft complaint, moreover, she identified herself not only by her surname but her middle name, which was her grandfather's name, ensuring that the suit would get national attention and hurt her grandfather as well as her mother and brother.

"Specifically what is she alleging?" I asked the attorney.

"She is alleging that while she was an adolescent, she and her brother had sexual intercourse, and that their mother not only knew about it but permitted and encouraged it," the lawyer said. "I have spoken with my clients, and both Mary and Tom say that this is patently false. Moreover, they tell me that Jill had made this claim in anger against her brother before and recanted it, apologizing before others." He said Jill had also made a claim of child sex abuse against another family member but under oath had recanted that allegation.

The attorney told me that Jill had lived a troubled life. For two decades her mother had paid for her housing, mental health counseling, and substance-abuse counseling. She had once pleaded guilty to stealing from her mother, and earlier had stolen her brother's car.

If we were retained, the lawyer would want me to provide advice and counsel to Mary and Tom and prepare a statement and press release in case the lawsuit was filed. "That's fine," I said, "but all that will do is set up a 'he said, she said' situation. I think we need to do more, if we can." I had in mind something that didn't fall within the traditional description of public relations but would help immensely with our case. "I'm not a lawyer," I said, "but this sounds an awful lot like extortion or at least civil extortion to me."

It wouldn't have been the first time I had seen someone attempt to use the threat of a lawsuit to extort a settlement, although this case was especially egregious. The U.S. legal system, for better or worse, allows anyone to file a lawsuit and stuff it with inflammatory allegations, which the media dutifully amplify. Never mind that frivolous lawsuits are often tossed out or watered down by judges— the damage is already done, as plaintiffs' attorneys well know. You can deny an accusation, but it lives on. Having reported that a case was filed, the media rarely report when it goes away.

"I had thought of that," the attorney said. "What are you thinking?"

"I believe we should take a two-prong approach. One might not be admissible in a court of law, but it will be powerful evidence in the court of public opinion. I'm talking about a polygraph test. You can retain an expert through your law firm and give Tom a test. Assuming he passes, we can use it with media and his clients to demonstrate that the assertions are false. I recognize that these things aren't perfect, and sometimes the person taking the test fails even if he is telling the truth. But as you know better than I, there's no risk, since the results will be privileged and confidential."

"I like this," the lawyer said. He said he would talk to his clients.

Some days later, the lawyer retained our firm and disclosed our new clients' names, as well as Mary's maiden name, which would have been instantly recognizable on the media-centric East Coast. This lawsuit would indeed get national attention. The salacious accusations alone would generate headlines; the well-known name would have pushed it over the top.

The attorney put me on the phone with his clients, and we discussed the case and strategy in detail. Over the next few weeks we had numerous other conversations about the messaging, strategy, tactics, and timing. I tried to be upfront about the risks. I always explain the risks and benefits so clients don't feel blindsided or deceived and so they can make an informed decision. Few people, apart from celebrities, are accustomed to the intense glare of the media, especially in a sordid case that invites scrutiny by strangers. But in the age of social media, anyone can pass judgment and render an opinion, irrespective of whether he knows what he's talking about.

Because the filing of Jill's lawsuit would undoubtedly attract attention among the frenetic New York media, as well as nationally, I recommended we inform one media outlet in New York and one in the clients' hometown about the story. They agreed.

The attorney and clients decided to file a preemptive lawsuit against Jill. The risk, of course, is that it attracts attention you didn't want in the first place. But if you let the other side carry through with their threat, you're on defense from the start, trying to prove a negative. If you can go on the offensive, you set the terms of engagement. You have to consider how likely your opponent is to file a suit and whether you are willing to take that chance.

My concern in this case was that letting Jill go first would leave us with a "he said, she said" case. The lie detector test would give us an advantage, but the media would have a ten- or twenty-page lawsuit to write about but only a three- or four-sentence statement from us. That means that in a thousand-word article, we might have fifty words in the third or fourth paragraph, if we were lucky. I thought letting Jill file first was too big a risk, and it turned out our clients and their lawyer thought so too. So we decided to strike first.

We came up with a statement for Tom to use in his firm and one to use with his customers and worked on answers to questions he might receive from employees, clients, and friends. These mock Q&A sessions can prepare a client for the worst. I often ask one of the former reporters in my firm to put on his ink-stained-wretch hat and compose questions he might ask if he were still in the media, along with suggested answers. I tell him don't sugarcoat it—the client should know in advance how to deal with anything thrown their way. The question you're not prepared for is the question you'll be asked.

We also wrote a press release. The purpose was to summarize our complaint—so a reporter could see at a glance what it was about—and to provide a statement from the family. While a

litigation press release is largely shaped by the underlying complaint, I want to get the attention of reporters, who don't want to
slog through a lot of impenetrable legalese. I try to give them a
reason to write the story and guide them with a compelling narrative that will help them get it right.

The attorney retained a polygraph expert, and Tom took and
passed a lie detector test.

Shortly thereafter, my clients filed a lawsuit against Jill alleging
civil extortion and infliction of emotional distress. The introduction of a complaint sets the stage for the facts that follow. The
lawyer wrote a strong and compelling argument, combining solid
facts with measured outrage. I consider the introduction so important that I often assist in "punching up" the lawyer's draft to ensure
the right elements are highlighted and summarized. If done right,
the reporters will often lift the introduction as the lead-in to their
own stories, or at least quote it.

The complaint began:

> Plaintiffs bring this action after defendant, through her
> lawyer, threatened to in effect unleash a public smear
> campaign against plaintiffs by making salacious false
> allegations public through the filing of a lawsuit charg-
> ing one of the Plaintiffs, her brother,...with "child sex
> abuse" when they were both minors, and the other
> Plaintiff, her mother,...with knowledge of this false
> alleged conduct, unless plaintiffs paid defendant over a
> million dollars. Plaintiffs deny these allegations because
> they are false.

The New York newspaper that carried the story wrote along
the lines of our complaint. Jill was "allegedly threatening to
besmirch the family name in an effort to extract $1 million from

her mother and brother, a new lawsuit reveals." The story called it a "sordid $1 million extortion scheme" and "alleged get-rich-quick scheme," among other colorful descriptions. To be sure, the newspaper also aired the details of Jill's bogus accusations. But by getting ahead of the story, we were able to introduce and defuse the allegations on our own terms.

Most importantly, the story prominently noted that Tom "recently passed a polygraph test tied to his sister's allegations."

The other side's contribution? Nothing. Jill's "lawyer declined to comment." The local paper where Jill lived and where the complaint was filed provided even more detail, describing "a pitched family feud that includes allegations of extortion, sexual abuse and emotional distress," and reporting that Mary's and Tom's lawsuit "claims the daughter is trying to 'unleash a public smear campaign' against the family." This story also mentioned that Tom had "passed a recent polygraph test during which he denied abusing his sister," and cited specifics of the sister's prior troubles. Once again, Jill's attorney "declined comment on the lawsuit."

Concurrent with the filing of the lawsuit, Tom emailed the prepared statements to his staff and clients and also called key clients. The reaction was appropriate: clients, employees, and friends alike told Tom and Mary how sorry they were that they had to endure this.

Perception equaled reality: they were the victims here, not the villains. It helped that they had one hell of a lawyer. Jill never filed her lawsuit.

When the Truth Hurts

Sometimes, unfortunately, the sordid accusations are true.

One day I received a telephone call from someone I had never met, the CEO of a well-known chain of medical facilities. After introducing himself, he went right into the subject matter of the call. I'm not one for small talk myself, so I welcomed his getting to the point.

"I really need your help," he said, with more than a little urgency in his voice. "One of our top surgeons has been charged by the state medical board with inappropriately touching a patient during an exam."

"Is there proof of this?" I asked. I'm not judgmental in these cases. I just want the facts. My job isn't to render a verdict about human behavior, it's to mitigate the damage.

"The doctor admitted it in a settlement he made with the patient and to the medical board," he said. And the patient had a video of the act on his smart phone.

Okay, I thought. Guess he did it. And it sounds like the patient set up the doctor—but that won't excuse the doc's behavior or make the story go away.

"What do you mean he inappropriately touched a patient," I said. "How and where?"

"He touched his genitals and then masturbated the patient," the CEO answered. "And not on one occasion, but during two separate visits."

"What did the doctor say when you confronted him?" I asked.

"He said he is heterosexual. He's been married for twenty years and has two children. He had never done anything like that before."

"Okay, fine. But how did he explain what happened?"

"He said he has no idea why he did that. He doesn't know what came over him."

My partner Sallie Hofmeister was in my office meeting with me on another client matter when the call came in, and so I drafted her to help me on this case. We told him we wanted to see the medical board's complaint and would call him back.

Shortly after hanging up, I got a call, coincidentally, from an old friend who knew this doctor. Small world.

"You've got to help him, Mike," he said. "I know him and his family. He is devastated. He doesn't know what he is going to do. He's never done anything like this before. He is married and has two wonderful children."

I responded that I was sorry, but I couldn't help him. I had already been retained by the medical facility. "Look," I said, "neither they nor we want to hurt him, and we have no intention of doing so, but we have to protect the reputation of the facility."

Minutes later, the doctor himself called me, his voice cracking slightly. I told him the same thing I told our mutual friend but added, "You should check yourself into counseling so you can understand why you did what you did and so you can tell your patients you have done so. And you need to put into place measures to ensure that this can never happen again."

"Like what?" he interrupted.

"Like making sure that you are never in an examination room alone with a patient; like having a nurse in every examination room when you are with a patient."

Sallie and I then began our research on the client's facility. First, we went online to look at and familiarize ourselves with the medical board complaint, just as a reporter would do. Then we began a review of the facility. We wanted to see if they had a spotless record. We wanted to ensure there were no complaints against any of their other doctors that the media could use to construct a larger story. Fortunately, everything checked out.

We did this immediately because with the complaint online, it was only a matter of time before reporters got wind of it. Accusations like this would bubble up to the national media in no time.

We called the client back and told him that he needed to take a series of immediate actions. First, he should communicate with the doctors and staff. They already knew through the grapevine what had happened, but it was important they know that the facility had terminated the doctor and the steps that were being taken to ensure that this would never occur again. Internal transparency is critical in these situations to avoid panic among employees, who might be nervous about their jobs or worried about damage to their reputation. It is also critical because word has a way of spreading. Since they could be asked about the incident by patients and others, it was important that they know how the facility was responding. What actually happened is not as important as assuring everyone that it won't happen again.

We shared some suggestions, which the CEO said he would implement. Sallie, with her reporter's instinct for leaving no question unturned, asked if there was anything else he could tell us that might be of use. He casually mentioned that the incident happened while the doctor was moonlighting at an unaffiliated facility. This would prove critical in turning the story away from our client's facility.

We told our client that his outside lawyer should call the medical board's lawyers and explain that the incident occurred in *another* facility. It was not fair or accurate to have the name of our client's facility on the cover of the complaint, and it was not fair or accurate to fail to make this fact clear in the body of the complaint. The medical board's lawyer agreed.

When the media got wind of this complaint—obviously not from us—Sallie pointed out to the reporter that while it was true the doctor was on the staff of our client's facility, the incident happened while he was moonlighting at another facility, as the medical board complaint itself noted. For the sake of fairness and accuracy, she insisted, that fact should be reflected in the story.

The media reported it that way, and our client came through this incident with its reputation deservedly intact. In fact, in much of the coverage, our client's name was not even mentioned. As for the doctor, he too took our advice, got counseling, implemented the procedures we suggested, and is still in practice today.

Head Them Off at the Pass

Less sordid but just as potentially damaging was another situation I handled where an employer faced the potential of collateral damage because a partner was the subject of a pending negative story.

The call came on an otherwise pleasant spring Saturday from an attorney I had worked with previously. The client was an investment banking firm, a partner of which had been nominated for a high-ranking position in the new administration. His congressional confirmation hearings were a few days away, and a national news organization was investigating his alleged ties to a man behind a Ponzi scheme—a man who had committed suicide as investigators were closing in on him. The partner was also said to have worked on deals with and served on the board of a company in an industry that he would oversee in his government role.

I called my partner Seth Lubove and asked him to work with me on the case. As noted elsewhere in this book, Seth is one of the best researchers I have ever worked with. He is able to uncover critical information that is key to our representation of our clients. He has great news instincts and a grasp of an uncanny variety of topics. A former reporter and editor, Seth provided valuable guidance in this case on the ethical guidelines subscribed to by news organizations, which we were able to use to protect a client from an unfair report or a lack of transparency about a journalist's story.

The attorney set up a conference call with another partner of the client, who explained that the reporters were trying to make a connection between the Ponzi schemer, the administration nominee, and the investment bank. "We don't want to get our name dragged through the mud," he said.

The client said there was no direct connection between the firm and the Ponzi scheme, but the reporters were calling around to the firm's customers and asking pointed questions about the relationship. At least three of the firm's clients reached out to the partner and said the reporters were focusing on the Ponzi scheme. Until this point, the firm never received any communications from the reporters.

With the confirmation hearings looming, I said we should immediately contact one of the reporters and find out what exactly they were working on. "We need to speak to the reporter and tell him that fairness dictates you provide us with any questions or information you have so we can adequately respond," I said. "We need to flush him out."

Reporters can be coy about what they're working on, counting on the element of surprise to catch you off guard or force you to comment on short notice. The first time you hear of a story might be when a reporter calls, and in the worst case he says you have thirty minutes to respond. Or you may hear that "something is in the works" when a former employee or vendor is contacted by the reporter, before the subject of the story is even aware of it. It's a common technique, especially among so-called investigative reporters. When it happens, I often get in touch with the reporter and politely ask how may we assist. It won't make him any less aggressive, but at least I have time to engage and provide thoughtful comments.

The partner we were talking to thought the reporter's calling around to customers amounted to "character assassination," a common feeling when one's business practices are subjected to the tender mercies of the media. I said we would tell the reporter we were surprised the firm hadn't received the courtesy of a call, since it was a primary subject of the story.

The investment bank had had some indirect business dealings with the Ponzi schemer but in completely legitimate transactions that were unrelated to the Ponzi scheme, and the partner who was nominated to a government position had had nothing to do with any of those deals. And even then, the deals were done solely through a third party, not directly. Members of the investment bank had met the Ponzi schemer all of one time, at a conference, and were unaware of his side scam.

When the reporters finally sent their questions, the story became much clearer: not only was the nominee tainted by conflicts of interest and associated with a (now dead) Ponzi schemer, but the firm—our client—was incompetent.

Left unanswered, these accusations could have caused irreparable damage to the nominee and the firm. As I have said, there are times when "no comment" will suffice, but they are few and far between. This clearly wasn't one of them. After getting the facts, I encouraged the client to respond forcefully and factually in writing to all of the allegations, refuting them with the strength of our detailed answers. Although the questions were addressed to the partner who was up for nomination, the bank answered on his behalf, since many of the queries concerned the firm and its business practices.

The reporter, for instance, demanded a response to the statement that "client companies listed on your disclosure forms are down between roughly 50% and 99% since the time of [the firm's] first deal with them until now." We responded that their assertion was "a misleading, selective, and inaccurate portrayal," and that the firm had far more successes than failures. "Overall results are not reflected by a handful of investments, selectively singled out," we said, providing multiple examples of successful investments and the returns.

The reporter also asked about the nominee's and the firm's "relationship" to the Ponzi schemer. The response was assertive and unambiguous: neither the firm nor the nominee "had any knowledge of or interactions with this entity, and it is false and defamatory to suggest or imply that [the client or nominee] had any knowledge or involvement in alleged illegal activities conducted by" the person behind the Ponzi scheme.

Other questions asked about the nominee's compensation and his "involvement" in companies that had suffered "large stock losses." Again, after getting the facts, I counseled full and factual disclosure. The reporters' follow-up questions were along the same lines, getting into details about prior transactions and the alleged connection to the Ponzi scheme.

For good measure, I made sure one of the top editors of the news organization was copied on our responses along with the reporters, ensuring that the boss was in the loop. While editors are usually deferential to their reporters and will defend them to outsiders—presuming they're even aware of a story in the first place—copying the editor ensures that they see the answers that the reporter is getting. If there is a dispute about context or how the reporter has characterized those answers, the editor has the original answer and context from the onset. Reporters don't like it when you go over their head, which is why I either show a copy to them or tell them in advance that I plan to speak to their editor.

The story did not appear prior to the nominee's hearings, and he was confirmed with little debate. When it was finally published a few weeks later, it reflected the facts and was far less accusatory than first represented. The reporters had done their job fairly, and neither the nominee nor his prior firm suffered from unfair or unfavorable publicity.

Chapter 10

Restoring Reputation

W ill Rogers said, "It takes a lifetime to build a good reputation, but you can lose it in a minute."

That is precisely what happened to the man hailed as the "Bond King" by the media, William H. Gross, the cofounder and longtime public face of Pacific Investment Management Company—Pimco—and the onetime overseer of the biggest mutual bond fund in the world, with almost $300 billion in assets under management at its peak. Despite an impeccable investment record that spanned decades, Gross took a hit to his reputation when his chief investing partner and heir apparent abruptly quit at the start of 2014 and Gross was wrongly blamed for it. Within months Bill Gross, who had been fawned over by the media almost his entire career, was the subject of derision and sarcasm in the press, which published inaccurate accounts of him.

Gross resigned from Pimco a year later, and when he moved to sue his former partners in the fall of 2015, Patricia L. Glaser, of Glaser Weil Fink Howard Avchen & Shapiro, brought in Sitrick And Company to handle media and assist in setting the record straight for this investing titan.

Bill Gross was a much-followed oracle in the multi-trillion-dollar global bond markets, and after the restoration of his reputation, he is once more. A fixture on CNBC and elsewhere for years, he is known for prognostications that can move the markets. When he speaks on television in his distinctive, chalky voice, investors listen, and many of them trade on his opinionated proclamations. After the global economic collapse in late 2008 and 2009, he established a post-meltdown meme known as "the New Normal," which predicted an era of low interest rates, low growth, and diminished possibilities that would characterize the tepid economic recovery.

Gross grew up in San Francisco, earned a psychology degree at Duke, and served in the Navy during the Vietnam War. Blessed with a golden gut and sharp mathematical and analytical skills, he started out in the highest-risk "investing" of all—gambling—playing blackjack in the casinos of Las Vegas. He parlayed two hundred dollars into ten thousand and got so good at counting cards that some casinos banned him.

He co-founded Pimco in 1971 as the investment arm of Pacific Life Insurance Company, starting out with all of twelve million dollars in client funds. Gross built Pimco as a brand characterized by patient, long-term investing with an emphasis on bonds and low risk, while achieving returns at or near the double digits typically only seen in riskier equities markets. Assets under management had risen to $70 billion by 1994, when Pacific Life spun off parts of Pimco to Gross and his team and the public markets. By 1999, Pimco took in over $9 billion in new investor money for the year, triple the sum it had taken in just two years earlier.

Allianz bought Pimco in 2000, and Bill Gross stayed on, guiding it to torrid growth. When stocks crashed that year, investors rushed to safety and bought into Bill's beloved bond fund. Pimco took in over $12 billion in new money in 2001 and more than twice that sum in 2002. Billions more poured into Gross's fund after the worldwide crisis of 2008–2009.

Bill Gross built a stellar, world-class investment record, outperforming his rivals consistently for years. Under his watch, the Pimco Total Return Fund beat the returns of its peers by an average of an extra 1.56 percentage points per year, every year for ten years up to 2013. That is roughly three to four billion dollars per year in extra investment profits, every year for a decade. Extraordinary.

For his impressive returns from 2000 through 2009, Morningstar, the fund-ratings bible, named him the Fixed Income Manager of the Decade in 2010, having also named him Fixed Income Manager of the Year in 1998, 2000, and 2007. As Pimco's total assets under management neared $2 trillion, its annual revenue from management fees exceeded $12 billion a year.

In the insular and strait-laced world of fixed-income investing, Gross's move to sue Pimco would have been news in and of itself, though probably just for a day. What was contained in that lawsuit, however, made it into something much bigger—a story with "legs."

When Patty Glaser, his lead lawyer, called me in September 2015 to ask that we sign on for the case, which she would file in a few weeks, I was happy to oblige. Patty and I have worked together on dozens of cases over the past twenty-five years or so, and on a few occasions we have been on opposite sides. She is not just recognized by the Hollywood and business media as one of the top litigators in the country, but by legal publications as well: *Chambers and Partners,* which identifies and ranks the most outstanding law firms and lawyers in over 180 jurisdictions throughout the world, describes her as a "trial icon," and Martindale-Hubbell recognizes her as an AV Preeminent Rated Lawyer—the highest category awarded, indicating that a lawyer's peers regard him or her at the highest level of professional excellence.

No Time for Pleasantries

After getting Patty's call on a Saturday morning, one of the first things I did was call the firm partner I wanted to join me on this case: Seth Lubove. A former reporter and editor with the *Wall Street Journal*, *Forbes* magazine, and *Bloomberg News* with thirty years of journalism experience, Seth knows the financial markets and which players to watch, and he loves a story that goes against the grain. He helped put himself through college in the late 1970s by serving in the U.S. Marine Corps Reserves, as a grunt behind an M60 machine gun, eschewing officer training because he wanted to know what the real thing was like. His nickname in the firm— given to him by me—is "Sarge." Seth still emits traces of that military bearing as he works, all day long and often into the night, at his stand-up desk.

It was a Saturday morning in September, Seth was out with his wife, and they were just embarking on a bike ride down to Venice Beach, his cell phone resting in the basket of her bicycle. "Your phone's ringing," she told him, and he stopped dead in the street and scooped it up to take my call. Embarrassing as this is to admit, I wasted little time with pleasantries, telling him, "We're representing Bill Gross, who's getting ready to sue Pimco."

Seth, who covered fixed-income investing among other topics in sixteen years at *Forbes* and seven and a half years at *Bloomberg*, knew instantly just how huge were the implications of this lawsuit. It meant the Bill Gross story was only beginning, that he was not going away quietly—he was going to fight. As Seth resumed his bike ride down to Venice Beach, he could barely feel the pedals, his mind racing with the possibilities.

———

In the financial world, your reputation is everything—your reputation for high integrity, truthfulness, smarts, and market savvy. In this richest of business realms, even an obscure, arcane dispute can put billions of dollars at risk. Sometimes the stakes can run even higher than that: they can be a matter of freedom, and even life or death. In 2015, a client came to my firm asking for our help in shining a light on and, he hoped, rectifying a terrible travesty that was the result of a lawsuit against one of the wealthiest and most powerful businessmen in South America. This client's associates were part of a small investor group that was asking a court to recognize the legitimacy of a $75 million private share purchase from several years earlier that now was valued at more than $2 billion. A decision in the group's favor could produce a huge windfall and even bring a change of control at one of the largest conglomerates in South America.

But the bigger problem was that the investor group's head, an eighty-year-old man who was battling cancer, had been languishing in prison for almost a year, jailed without trial for allegedly violating a court order in connection with the lawsuit. The client believed court officials had taken bribes to keep the investor head imprisoned as a means of intimidation. We felt that making his plight more broadly known might win his release.

So Tom Becker, head of our New York office and a former reporter for Dow Jones and *Bloomberg*, began reaching out to contacts in the international media and to a writer at the *Financial Times*. Becker gave the FT an inside look at the case, at the same time suggesting to other journalists that they call law enforcement officials, elected representatives, and even the defendants in the lawsuit. They asked questions about the prison sentence, what kind of care the man was receiving, and when and whether he ever would get a trial.

One month later, the *Financial Times* published a story on the dispute, including the fact that the investor group's head was in prison without a trial. A month later the man was allowed to go home and receive the medical care he needed while awaiting trial. His associates believed that the release saved his life. His legal fight against the South American conglomerate continues.

In the case of Bill Gross and Pimco, no one was behind bars, but the reputation he had earned from a lifetime of outstanding work was at risk. In his four decades at Pimco, Bill Gross came to personify the brand, but along the way he made room for a second star at the firm: Mohamed El-Erian. Having joined the firm in 1999, El-Erian left to run the multibillion-dollar Harvard University endowment for a year, returning in 2007 to serve as co-chief investment officer with Gross with the expectation of eventually succeeding him. Theirs was an uneasy alliance, which became further strained after the financial meltdown. As one journalist later put it, Gross is a "former blackjack player and a trader at heart. El-Erian is an economist with a more methodical approach." Bill prized bonds, while Mohamed focused on hedge fund-style investments with higher risks, potentially higher returns, and higher fees for Pimco. This divergence in their views would cause a rift in their relationship.

Bill Gross's bond fund remained the flagship of Pimco, but in 2011, the fund had an off year, underperforming the benchmark

Barclays U.S. Aggregate Bond Index. The Total Return Fund finished 2013 down 1.9 percent, the first losing year for Gross since 1999, although it still beat the benchmark Barclays index, which fell 2.02 percent. The fund's investors pulled out $41 billion in the year.

Although Gross, in what would be his final three years at Pimco, racked up returns almost double those of the benchmark bond-market index, he came under fire in the press, a stinging first. Each criticism, once stated, seemed to spark another, and the critics grew bolder as the months wore on.

Then in January 2014 came a shocker—Mohamed El-Erian's sudden, surprise resignation, followed by Pimco's explanation that he was leaving to spend more time with his family and write a book. The press pretty much played it straight, reprinting El-Erian's provided statement: "I have been extremely honored and fortunate to work alongside Bill Gross, who is one of the very best investors in the world." Bill Gross put out a tweet on Twitter that drew widespread uptake: "I'm ready to go for another 40 years!"

Pinning the Blame

Then, seemingly out of nowhere came a story in the *Financial Times* that broke insider details of El-Erian's departure, laying the blame at Gross's feet. The other shoe dropped a month later, on page one of the *Wall Street Journal*, stomping on the pristine reputation of Bill Gross. Headline: "Inside the Showdown Atop Pimco, the World's Biggest Bond Firm." Deck: "After clashing with Pimco co-founder Bill Gross, CEO Mohamed El-Erian decided to leave the fund giant."

The story largely pinned the blame for El-Erian's abrupt departure on Gross, citing infighting between him and Mohamed and a litany of uncomplimentary characterizations. In *Journal* parlance, it is known as a "reconstruction," because it pieces together various accounts in the aftermath of a huge, dramatic event to tell it from the inside out. The story opened with a scene from a few months earlier, in which Bill Gross and Mohamed El-Erian "squared off in front of more than a dozen colleagues amid disagreements about Mr. Gross's conduct...." It then quoted Gross as telling El-Erian, "I have a 41-year track record of investing excellence. What do *you* have?"

"I'm tired of cleaning up your s—," El-Erian responded, citing "conduct by Mr. Gross that he felt was hurting Pimco...."

The *Journal* reported that Gross's decisions had "confused" employees, that he "doesn't like employees speaking with him or making eye contact, especially in the morning," and that he "prefers silence and at times reprimands those who break it, even if they're discussing investments...." He was said to chide employees for failing to number the pages of their presentations and to rankle at any dissent once he had set an investment strategy. The paper also quoted one former trader, on the record and by name, as saying Gross "grew tired and wary of those closest to him" once they rose in power, turning each veteran's former "halo" into "a crown of thorns where interactions with Bill would turn adversarial, short, and unpleasant."

The story continued, "Late last year, in front of a number of traders, Mr. Gross said, 'if only Mohamed would let me, I could run all the $2 trillion myself.... I'm Secretariat. Why would you bet on anyone other than Secretariat?'" Gross's response in the *Journal* reconstruction was primarily a prepared statement citing forty years of "superior results for our clients" and saying, "I ask of others only what I demand of myself: hard work, dedication and intense focus on putting our clients first."

That *Journal* story was "the crusher," as Bill Gross himself later put it, and the fallout was swift and widespread. A few dozen other publications and websites ran fast "folos" picking up the *Journal* story. The same day the story ran, the co-author of the *Journal*'s story, Gregory Zuckerman, went on CNBC to talk about it, and Bill himself, frustrated, called in to CNBC a while later to complain on the air about the *Journal* takedown.

CNBC anchor Brian Sullivan told viewers, "Bill, thank you very much for joining us. I'm assuming you're calling in to react to what you heard from Greg Zuckerman. Or maybe yell at us." Bill returned serve nicely: "No, I am not, Brian. I respect Greg. We've been good friends for ten or fifteen years, but, like the old radio announcer Paul Harvey said, it's time for the rest of the story. I think he only had half of it." He went on to say the *Journal* reporter "gave us a chance last night to go over some of the facts, and we disputed some of them," and labels the story "far overblown."

Gross told CNBC he isn't a "morning person," and he needs five cups of coffee to wake up, but he says he isn't all that strict—he even instituted an authorized "conga line" at eight in the morning on some days to loosen up the atmosphere. Gross also revealed that El-Erian had resigned after helping set a plan to share power among six newly named sector CIOs. "Mohamed left because he told us that he wasn't the man to carry out his own plan," Gross said on air.

Once the *Journal* story had run, the anti-Gross meme spread. A few weeks later, a member of the board of trustees of Gross's Pimco Total Return fund was quoted in the *Los Angeles Times* as being critical of Bill for his compensation and his management style. This got picked up by the U.S. financial press and spread to London, in the *Telegraph* and the *Independent* among other publications.

The turmoil prompted the Morningstar fund-tracking service to raise concerns, saying Pimco's "public reputation" had been shaken by the El-Erian exit, resulting in a downgrade of the firm's "stewardship" grade from a B to a C. Morningstar cited reports that Gross had "a severe and reputed retaliatory temperament" that makes it difficult for dissenters to speak up. These concerns were then echoed in the *New York Times* and elsewhere, further damaging Gross's investing reputation.

Then came still more piling on. Suddenly the man who had been revered for his intelligence and wisdom was being characterized—baselessly—as erratic, imperious, and a liability. "When Superstar Executives Become a Company Liability," a USNews.com headline blared on April 1, 2014. *New York Times*, April 3: "Pimco's Gross, Facing Skeptical Investors, Discusses His Dead Cat." *Bloomberg*, April 10: "Gross asks: Am I really such a jerk?"

A month later, Pimco parent Allianz declared publicly that it "stands by its chief investment officer despite fund struggles" (*Bloomberg News*). "We want Bill Gross to work as CIO for as long as he is willing and able," an Allianz exec told *Bloomberg*.

Then Again, Maybe Not

And then Bill Gross stunned the investing world by quitting Pimco outright, hand-scrawling his resignation letter with felt-tip pen and marking the time as 6:29 a.m., PST, on September 26, 2014. Gross was leaving his gargantuan Pimco fund to run a fledgling $70 million fund at the much smaller Janus Capital. Shares of Allianz fell 5 percent on the news of the surprise resignation, while the stock of Janus jumped 20 percent in pre-market trading (and 40 percent in the ensuing weeks). The news itself was enough to rock the bond markets, but the story behind it, which his lawsuit would reveal, was even more shocking.

An avalanche of media coverage depicted Bill Gross as having resigned under threat of imminent firing, scorned for his blunt style and eccentricities and leaving in disgrace and defeat. The reports, flatly untrue, were fed by leaks from Gross's enemies inside his own firm, according to his lawsuit, and enabled by a lack of a detailed, emphatic defense delivered upfront before the story got out of his grasp.

"The Long and Sometimes Wacky Reign of the Bond King," as the *New York Times* put it. A day later, the *Times* did a "folo" ("Fixed-Income Manager Made Investing Engaging with Farcical Antics") that read in part:

> But for as long as he ruled the bond markets, the king [Gross] was also the court jester. His personality quirks were famous on Wall Street. Only in recent years, as Pimco's performance slipped and investors began to bolt, did the wackiness start to seem offensive.
>
> "When you're a Master of the Universe for a while, your eccentricities are tolerated," said Russel Kinnel, the director of manager research at Morningstar, the mutual fund research company that sponsored the June conference. "Until you cease to look like a Master of the Universe anymore."

A similar point followed from the veteran financial columnist Allan Sloan in a *Washington Post* blog under the headline "When Bill Gross's Pimco funds lost market share, his oddities ceased to be charming":

> What is the difference between being a charming and colorful eccentric and being a tiresome crank? When it comes to Bill Gross, the former bond king, I think that

one of the key answers is "market share." Or, more specifically, losing market share....

[Gross] had a messy public split early this year with his second-in-command and heir apparent, Mohamed El-Erian, who left in January. That hurt Gross badly, especially because El-Erian and his allies did a far better job of peddling their version of events than Gross did his.

On November 5 came another blow: "Glory to the New Bond King," on Forbes.com, a glowing profile of LA-based bond manager Jeffrey Gundlach of DoubleLine, rhapsodizing about his new billionaire status, his $16 million Tuscan-style mansion, his collection of paintings by Warhol, de Kooning, et al., and his likely gains in the turmoil of Bill Gross's leaving Pimco. It includes this anecdote:

Just about a month earlier Bill Gross of Pacific Investment Management Co., the reigning master of the bond universe for two decades, requested an audience with Gundlach. In a scene that can only be described as Shakespearean, the incumbent bond king drove an hour up the 405 Freeway in the middle of the afternoon to Gundlach's new castle...and he was asking his nemesis for a job....

Bill Gross provided a terse no-comment for the piece. With help from his lawyers and us, Gross would blow up this extended one-sided narrative by getting the facts out in his lawsuit against the firm he had co-founded.

The lawsuit that Patty Glaser would file against Pimco and its parent, the U.S. unit of German insurance giant Allianz, portrayed an elaborate plot that the media hadn't mentioned before. Her complaint would lay out a compelling case that the controversy had masked the truth of what really was going on at Pimco: a fight over higher fees that some in the firm wanted to impose but which Bill Gross opposed as detrimental to Pimco investors and a mutiny by a "cabal" of young Turks who were bent on ousting Bill Gross and divvying up his compensation of $200 million a year among themselves.

Seth Lubove and I had to move swiftly. We reached out to Andrew Ross Sorkin of the *New York Times* and CNBC, as well as to a veteran beat reporter at *Bloomberg*, Mary Childs, giving them a heads-up, which would allow them to post their stories minutes after the lawsuit was time-stamped and filed at the court.

To ensure the right points got hammered, Seth and I wrote up a separate backgrounder laying out the same narrative that was mapped out in Bill Gross's lawsuit, though with a little less legalese. Seth, meanwhile, anticipating the inquiries that would pour in moments later, lined up a dozen waiting emails in his draft queue, ready for sending to still other beat reporters, with a copy of the lawsuit attached to each note. When the right moment came, he would fire off each one individually, one button-push at a time.

When possible, this is the kind of strategy we prefer: the surprise attack. It allows us to float our full story while the other side reviews what is in the complaint and responds to the media within proscribed deadlines. (When the shoe is on the other foot, whenever possible, we push for more than just "We can't comment" or "The litigation has no merit." It depends on the facts, the lawyers, and the case.)

"A Lust for Power"

In all the sniping and misreporting that had followed Bill Gross's surprise departure from Pimco, he hadn't yet put out his complete story to the public. The legal complaint put together by Patty Glaser and her team proved to be an ideal platform for telling it. It was brilliantly written. Filed in Orange County Superior Court in southern California on October 8, 2015, precisely at 8:01 a.m. local time, it opened with this compelling and widely quoted paragraph:

> 1. Driven by a lust for power, greed, and a desire to improve their own financial position and reputation at the expense of investors and decency, a cabal of Pacific Investment Management Company LLC ("PIMCO") managing directors plotted to drive founder Bill Gross out of PIMCO in order to take, without compensation, Gross's percentage ownership in the profitability of PIMCO. Their improper, dishonest, and unethical behavior must now be exposed.

The complaint went on to say that "Mr. Gross's ongoing success at PIMCO proved to be his undoing," citing his 20 percent share of the annual bonus pool and adding, "By forcing him out of PIMCO, the younger executives would split Mr. Gross's share of the bonus pool amongst themselves." It added, he "championed reasonable fees" for Pimco investors, while the younger executives wanted "to transform PIMCO into a high-risk, high-fee asset-management company that invested in riskier equities and leveraged real estate investments, as opposed to the stable bonds that built the firm's reputation."

The complaint also told of how Gross championed bringing in Mohamed El-Erian as his eventual successor, but "[c]racks soon began to appear in this alliance." Gross preferred his low-risk, long-term style of investing, while El-Erian wanted to steer Pimco into riskier assets such as stocks, commodities, and leveraged investments in mortgages and real estate. Gross likened his own approach to a "bonds and burgers" restaurant that serves only one thing, while El-Erian's plan was "similar to the extensive and varied menu at a Cheesecake Factory restaurant," the complaint explains.

One of the key differences between the two restaurants: how much investors must pay in fees. Fees for Gross's bond business typically ran just one-half of 1 percent of the money in an investor's account, per year (0.50 percent, or fifty "basis points"). Fees for the more exotic investments favored by El-Erian and the younger ranks at Pimco ran 2 percent (four times as high as what Gross charged), plus a 20 percent cut of investment gains. "Two and 20," in hedge fund slang.

The complaint also revealed that El-Erian chose to quit after Bill Gross offered to step aside as Pimco's co-chief investment officer and let El-Erian run the whole show solo, Gross confining himself to his Total Return bond fund. Pimco hoped to withhold news of El-Erian's resignation but told its managing directors about the move in a meeting on January 20, 2014, admonishing them that "no leak of this information to the media could be allowed," Gross's complaint relates.

That ban notwithstanding, Andrew Balls, a Pimco managing director and a former reporter for the *Financial Times*, tipped a reporter at his old paper in London, which broke the resignation story two days later, laying the fault "at Mr. Gross's feet" for his management quirks, the complaint asserts. El-Erian, upset by Gross's offer to step back, had quit in "anger and apprehension over the idea that he would have to bear sole responsibility (and blame) for the high-fee investments he had promoted at PIMCO."

Stories subsequent to the *Financial Times* piece "heaped praise on El-Erian and cast criticism on Mr. Gross." They "were fueled by additional leaks and unattributed commentary from both Balls and El-Erian himself," Gross's complaint said. It described how

Pimco tracked calls from the managing director's backup phone to a reporter at the *Financial Times* and another at the *Wall Street Journal*, in the latter case before the *Journal* published its devastating reconstruction of the El-Erian departure, painting Bill Gross as the heavy. Balls himself first denied any wrongdoing, then admitted to having briefed the reporters and reporting back to El-Erian without telling anyone at Pimco or seeking permission to do so, according to the complaint.

Bill Gross pushed Pimco to fire the leaker for his misdeeds, but the Pimco leadership refused, the complaint recounts, and "secretly" began to "align against Mr. Gross." This emboldened another person at the firm, an aggressive trader in higher-risk assets that generate higher fees, who then "hatched a plan to oust Mr. Gross from PIMCO." The trader lined up several "co-conspirators" inside the firm, and they threatened to quit unless Pimco forced Gross out of the company.

Bill Gross, alarmed for the future of the firm he co-founded, began negotiating a graceful fade-out, agreeing to resign his post as chief investment officer of Pimco while continuing to run the fixed-income business. Gross also agreed to give up his title as chairman of the investment committee and his seat on the executive committee and the compensation committee. And he agreed to cut his annual bonus in half or more "to placate the PIMCO managing directors who were seeking to ensure that they received a larger share of the company's profits for themselves," his complaint disclosed. Gross even agreed to give up his oversight of his beloved Total Return Bond Fund to run, instead, a portfolio less than 10 percent as large. Then the lawsuit revealed:

63. And then he agreed to what he considered further humiliation: Mr. Gross would be barred from the PIMCO

offices, and left to handle the remaining portfolio from another office separate and away from PIMCO's.

But Pimco and its parent, Allianz, would renege on even this humbling deal, in essence telling Bill Gross he could stay on at the firm he had run for forty years until December 2014—or be terminated immediately. A Hobson's choice if ever there was one. So he quit. Then the firm refused to pay him the $80 million bonus he had been promised for the third quarter, because he had resigned on September 25, five days before the quarter ended; never mind the even bigger sum due in the fourth quarter. Also according to the complaint, the firm violated the de facto guarantee of five years of further employment that was a consequence of his having been reelected as CIO in 2014, and the firm had denied him the opportunity to let all of his stock options and equity grants fully vest.

Seeking Damages of $200 Million

"As a direct and proximate result of Defendants' breach, Plaintiff [Gross] has been damaged in an amount to be determined at trial, but in no event less than $200 million," the complaint stated.

You might be thinking that this is a petty and vindictive spat between multimillionaires and a billionaire, but Bill Gross took the unusual step of publicly pledging that any proceeds his lawsuit exacted from Pimco would be donated to charity. Among his planned recipients: the Pimco Foundation, which he founded and subsidized in its early years. This promise shows you how much value Bill Gross places on setting the record straight and defending his reputation, not padding his bank account. The point was hammered hard by the CNBC anchor Andrew Ross Sorkin when he went on the air moments after the Bill Gross lawsuit was filed:

We have an extraordinary lawsuit that's just been filed by Bill Gross, of course, the founder of Pimco who was ousted from his own company. He is now suing Pimco in a remarkable lawsuit that was just filed moments ago in California. Gross is seeking what he says is "no less than $200 million in damages," which he says he's going to donate to charity.

Sorkin, a print journalist who has an obvious appreciation for the written word, went on to say, "It is an unbelievable story, it almost reads like a murder mystery," and then CNBC ran a "full-screen" featuring Bill Gross's mugshot, a "Breaking News" logo and headline ("GROSS SUES PIMCO"), and the full text of the lawsuit's opening salvo, as Sorkin recited the entire bite: "Driven by a lust for power and greed...."

Sorkin mentioned the El-Erian feud, a plot to deceive investors, "calls and leaks to the media," the search of Andrew Balls' backup cell phone to find his calls to the *Journal*, and the revelation that Pimco had a $1.3 billion bonus pool in 2013 and Gross was set to get a 20 percent cut. Sorkin covered a lot of ground in just three minutes and fifty-six seconds.

The story went up on CNBC.com, as well, saying the Gross complaint provided "his own colorful version of an ugly feud that led to his departure last year." It added:

Mr. Gross is seeking "in no event less than $200 million" from Pimco for breach of covenant of good faith and fair dealing, among other causes of action. But to underscore the degree to which the suit is motivated by Mr. Gross's desire to correct the public record, he has promised to donate any money he recovers to charity, his lawyer, Patricia L. Glaser, said.

Pimco's presence in the story was limited to this: "Pimco did not immediately respond to calls for comment." The story was posted on CNBC.com at 11:04 a.m. Eastern Time (just a few minutes after the lawsuit was filed in Orange County, California, where it was eight in the morning). It ran on the *New York Times* website, as well, adding to the impact. It was posted at about the same time on *Bloomberg*, which quoted a Pimco spokesman's boilerplate response: "This lawsuit has no merit and our legal team will be responding in court in due course." But that was it, nothing more. The charity angle came near the bottom of the piece. Both *Bloomberg* and CNBC tagged their stories with links encouraging readers to forward the coverage online through Twitter, Facebook, Reddit, LinkedIn, and email, multiplying the audience for Bill Gross's counter-story.

As my partner Seth Lubove and I had anticipated, all hell broke loose after that, and he proceeded to send each of the dozen emails he had prepared to get the lawsuit's message out to the next wave of beat reporters. There was an immediate shift in the tone of the media coverage as reporters focused on the plot by younger managing directors to oust their patriarch and the feud over fees.

A few days after the story of the lawsuit broke, a *Wall Street Journal* columnist called the first paragraph of Gross's complaint "the most quoted opening since 'call me Ishmael.'" He also stated that Gross's lawsuit was a bid to see "how much further he can fill his amply filled pockets at his former employer's expense."

This struck Seth and me as an outright inaccuracy, given that Bill Gross was pledging any lawsuit proceeds to charity. So Lubove requested a correction but was turned down. We got something better, however: the paper agreed to publish a letter to the editor from Gross's attorney. A correction would have been buried in a small paragraph at the bottom of the page. The letter to the editor, three days later, ran as the lead letter across two columns at the top of the op-ed pages. It was signed by Gross's lead lawyer, Patty Glaser. Headline: "Gross's Suit Has Nothing to Do with Greed."

She noted that the columnist had ignored Gross's pledge to donate any winnings to charities, including Pimco's, "as your own newspaper and scores of other publications have reported." She concluded, "Had [the columnist] included the fact that Mr. Gross has committed to donating any recovery from the lawsuit to charity, I believe it would have undermined the premise of his column and his attempt to portray my client as greedy."

After the flurry of the first few days, the media spotlight eventually shifted back to where it had been for Bill Gross before the publicity surrounding his departure: his investing views, his market outlook, his global economic vision. From then on, we focused on keeping the circle of scribes following this story up to date, making sure they had Bill Gross's responses to Pimco's responses, if any, and informing them when a key hearing was coming up in court or a new wrinkle had developed.

The *New York Times*: ". . . Besting Pimco Is the Best Revenge"

A month after the lawsuit's filing, the *New York Times* ran a story under the headline "Lawsuit against Pimco sheds light on murky investor fees." It noted, "Mr. Gross's accusation zeros in on perhaps the murkiest area of the $15 trillion mutual fund industry: How fund companies account for and disclose the billions of dollars in fees that they charge investors each year for managing their money."

Pimco did not file its full-fledged response to the lawsuit for another six months, by which time much of the frenzy had faded. In the meantime, the Gross lawsuit had prompted follow-up stories such as one published in the *New York Times* on April 27, 2016.

Headline: "For onetime bond king, besting Pimco is the best revenge." The story notes:

> Although he was fired nearly two years ago and has moved on to a rival, Janus Capital Group, Pimco remains very, very close—both physically and, it would appear, psychologically.
>
> "We were a family: Everything I did was for them," Mr. Gross said in his whispery, high-pitched voice. "That is the most disappointing thing—it just didn't make business sense."

The story went on to report that in the six months Gross had been running the Janus Global Unconstrained Fund—which started at $70 million and now was up to $1.3 billion, half of it Gross's personal money—it was "handily beating its counterpart at Pimco," up 1.8 percent versus a 1.64 percent *decline* at Pimco. Apply that gap in performance to the $300 billion that Gross used to run at Pimco, and it would be the difference between reaping an extra $5.4 billion in investment profits in a year and being *down* $4.9 billion.

The *Times* quoted Gross declaring, "I am fixated on proving that they were wrong.... It's like—no, you shouldn't have done that and the numbers will prove it." Pimco, the story noted, had seen investors pull out a staggering $376 billion in the eighteen months since Bill Gross had been forced out—another number vindicating Gross's complaint.

A month later, Bill Gross raised $4.5 million selling stamps from his personal collection, one of the richest in the world, and donated the money to charity—including the Pimco Foundation. Seth Lubove did the research on this, sensing Gross's former charges at Pimco might try to find a way to turn down the donation. He studied the foundation's bylaws and learned that Pimco would have no choice but to accept the contribution from the co-founder it had fired, who now was suing the firm in California court. And so it unfolded in the media as planned.

By late 2016, Bill Gross, even as he buttressed his investing legacy, was continuing his legal jousting with his old firm, as Patty Glaser and her partners won skirmishes in court to compel Pimco to produce long-delayed documents and knock down Pimco's efforts to force Gross into providing materials that weren't pertinent to the case.

On March 27, 2017, CNBC reported,

> Bill Gross, who was fired from Pimco four decades after he co-founded the investment firm, has settled his lawsuit against the company for just over $81 million, sources told CNBC on Monday. He also gets a "Founders Room" named after him at the company's Newport Beach headquarters, along with the launch of a "Bill Gross Award," according to a Pimco press release. A lawyer representing the Pimco co-founder filed a request in California state court to dismiss the fund manager's suit over his 2014 departure from the company. All proceeds from the settlement will go to charity—to the Sue and Bill Gross foundation.

Equally important to Bill, today, and going forward, Bill Gross's reputation is back on top, right where it deserves to be.

Chapter 11

Surviving Bankruptcy

L ong after I have left this life, it will be up to others who knew me and worked with me to decide what, if any, were the great achievements of my career, but one of them surely has to be this: I helped save the Twinkie. Twice.

This spongy, super-sweet snack teetered on the brink of extinction in 2009 as the global economy reeled in the Great Recession. The Twinkie had been a culinary and cultural standard since its invention during the Great Depression as a cheap little lift for hard times, at two for a nickel. Eighty years later it was getting squished by consumers' embrace of low-carb diets and, even more so, by high pension and healthcare costs, burdensome union rules, and revolving-door management.

Far more was at stake than popular treats: the livelihoods of almost thirty thousand workers were on the line at the Twinkie's maker, the Interstate Bakeries Corporation (IBC), whose roots traced back more than a century and whose other products included Ho Hos, Ding Dongs, Drake's Cakes, Yankee Doodles, and Wonder Bread. In my business, it is especially gratifying when I can help save jobs at a company that otherwise might shut down, and this has occurred a number of times in my career—but the Twinkies case was especially sweet. Sorry, couldn't resist.

When the U.S. economy melted down in 2008–2009 and took the rest of the world with it, waves of fear roiled the global banking system. Banks stopped lending, credit dried up for even the safest clients, and thousands of companies suddenly were at risk. All of this was happening just as Interstate Bakeries, one of the largest commercial bakers in the United States, was set to emerge from four years of reorganization proceedings in bankruptcy court.

The company had first hired my firm in 2004, when it filed under Chapter 11 of the U.S. Bankruptcy Code for protection from creditor lawsuits while it worked on a reorganization and a workout plan to pay its debts. We had been involved intensively since that time, including through much of 2008, as Interstate neared the end of its Chapter 11 journey, ready to reappear like a butterfly from a cocoon. It was taking on a "new" name it had used as a brand since 1930: Hostess. It had closed nine outdated plants, combined some overlapping distribution routes, exacted concessions from the unions that represented most of its employees, and landed new financing of $600 million in debt and equity from new investors.

A key part of this metamorphosis was $125 million in new credit from GE Capital, the giant finance business owned at the time by the conglomerate General Electric Company. Hostess needed the money to install faster and more efficient production lines to better compete on cost, volume, and freshness. Much of the gear in its forty-five plants was old and worn out, and without an upgrade the baker might not make it at all.

Then came the urgent call to my BlackBerry from two lawyers advising Hostess. "Can you get on a conference call to discuss a critical development relating to Hostess?" one of them asked me. "When?" I responded. "Now," he said.

I was in Cancun, Mexico, on holiday with my family. It was Christmas Eve 2008. GE Capital had just balked at completing its end of the deal, the lawyers told me, pushing the baked-goods giant to the verge of collapse. Without GE's promised line of credit, the reorganization plan would topple, taking the company and all those jobs with it.

Time was running out. The company's short-term "debtor-in-possession" financing was expiring in early February, just five weeks out. Now Hostess wanted my help handling communications for the next move: a lender-liability lawsuit it was preparing to file against GE Capital Corp. It was a case of Twinkies vs. GE. The lawyers said we had a great case, but even if we won it months or years later, the company would be gone by then, and all the workers would lose their jobs.

A few minutes later we reconnected on a conference call, my partner Lew Phelps joining me and the two lawyers who first had called me—Greg Milmoe and J. Eric Ivester, both of them with the New York firm of Skadden Arps Meagher & Flom, and both considered among the top restructuring lawyers in the United States. Also on the phone was the formidable New York litigator Marc Kasowitz and the Hostess CEO at the time, Craig Jung. The lawsuit idea came up, and Craig Jung said, "That's great, but by the time that gets through the courts, all twenty-nine thousand of my employees will have lost their jobs and company will be forced to close."

"I Don't Think We Have to Shut Down the Company"

"Wait a minute," I said, "didn't GE take TARP money?" The federal government's Troubled Asset Relief Program had doled out several hundred billion dollars in emergency capital to nineteen giant banks, infusing them with cash by purchasing ownership stakes in them and buying their financially suspect, hard-to-sell bonds. TARP was one of myriad remedies the feds used in the collapse, known by an alphabet soup of initialisms—TARP, TALF, FSP, TLGP, PPIP, CPFF, and more. The presumption was that the recipients would circulate this cash by loaning it out to businesses to help the economy and save jobs.

Everyone on the line was listening keenly, and Lew Phelps, tapping away at Google, cut in to tell us that, no, actually, GE hadn't received TARP money after all. "GE got HARP money," or some other acronym, Lew explains. Me: "Same thing!" And then I added, "Of course Lew would know that."

"Well, then, I don't think we will have to shut down the company. Let's get IBC's local congressmen and senators to write letters to the CEO of GE," I said to those on the call. "Let's get the unions involved. Let's see if Senators Clinton and Schumer will write him and ask, 'When the government gave you that HARP or TARP money or whatever it was, wasn't that to enable you to lend money so you can save or create jobs? Why is it you are refusing to honor your commitment to provide $125 million to this company, and in the process eliminating twenty-nine thousand good American jobs?' The media will love it. Government officials can't ignore it." Everyone on the call climbed on board.

The company's passage through Chapter 11 had been difficult. Its new $600 million financing plan (including the GE chunk) was contingent on exacting cost cuts on the labor side, and the Teamsters were defiant. Yet the union had offered to make concessions to other investors it had coaxed into bidding for the company—Grupo Bimbo of Mexico City, and Yucaipa, the private-equity fund of billionaire Ron Burkle (at the time also a client of mine).

The mainstream media are naturally sympathetic to the unions in these disputes, and Interstate Bakeries wanted to balance out the debate by increasing engagement with reporters. Two Sitrick employees had been embedded at headquarters in Kansas City, Missouri, for much of the previous year, but now the company wanted extra help from someone with expertise in dealing with the media during labor disputes. So I dispatched Lew Phelps to start spending a lot of time in Kansas City.

Soon after he showed up, he asked a local reporter covering the story to sit down for lunch. As they dined, Lew frankly told the reporter that he hoped to provide more fodder for the company's side of the story, because the unions' views seemed to predominate in the local coverage thus far.

A few days later, as Lew sat in a courtroom late one afternoon for a pivotal hearing and the reporter was sitting in the front row, as usual, the perfect opportunity arose: an attorney for the Teamsters told the court the union would rather see the company go through "liquidation" and go out of business—wiping out the jobs of 9,500 union members who drove the company's trucks—than give in to the salary and benefit cuts that Interstate Bakeries was seeking. Lew looked over to the reporter to make sure this revealing comment struck home—but the reporter wasn't paying attention. Missed it entirely.

Later that afternoon, Lew called the reporter and brought up the union rep's startling statement, repeating it to make sure it got across accurately. The next day the local paper reported:

> IBC said that if Yucaipa and Bimbo do not submit an
> offer or if their offer is not accepted, the rational thing

for the Teamsters would be to return to the bargaining table.

Frederick Perillo, an attorney for the Teamsters in the reorganization, said that would not happen, telling the court, "My client prefers liquidation to the company's business plan."

Mission accomplished. We made sure that IBC made the most of this, advising its labor-relations team to photocopy the story and post it on company bulletin boards in Hostess factories and warehouses across the country. To some workers, it was a sign their union might sacrifice their jobs to avoid setting a precedent by giving in to management's demands for cuts in pensions and other costs.

Ultimately, the Teamsters and other unions came back to the bargaining table and granted roughly $100 million a year in concessions in exchange for a 20 percent ownership stake in Hostess Brands once the company started growing again. The unions gave in by September 2008, letting the Chapter 11 reorganization proceed, and a wrap-up was now ready—until GE Capital balked and jeopardized the whole package.

Clearly, we needed to put pressure on GE Capital and get the attention of their bosses and the bosses at the parent company. GE had sought government help twice in the financial collapse. The CPFF (Commercial Paper Funding Facility) gave GE Capital access to almost $100 billion in government-provided borrowing to help it ensure that all of its overnight loans could be renewed in the short-term "commercial paper" market, which had frozen. The second program, the TLGP (Temporary Liquidity Guarantee Program), had the Federal Deposit Insurance Corporation guarantee repayment of GE Capital debt totaling $139 billion, ensuring the company's access to borrowing, and at lower rates.

To be sure, GE Capital may have had good reason to rethink the Twinkies loan. The business had been in decline for years, and the product line was a throwback. The "too big to fail" banks were under contradictory pressures from their federal overseers to shore up their balance sheets with fatter reserves for bad loans and stricter new lending, while also funding a U.S. recovery...by making more loans.

Nudging a Giant

But the GE Capital bankers had made a commitment, and nothing had changed since they had done so. My job was to find a way to nudge GE Capital into delivering the $125 million in financing as promised. Our ad hoc posse descended on Washington just as the media were looking for their first examples of how TARP was working out.

We targeted congressmen from areas where Hostess factories and distribution centers operated, and both of New York's populist U.S. senators, Democrats Hillary Clinton and Chuck Schumer. We were able to get a letter from Senator Clinton's office addressed not to GE Capital but to the CEO of its owner, General Electric: Jeffrey Immelt.

Senator Schumer went even further, calling for hearings into the matter and personally demanding that GE provide him with "daily updates" on the issue. He sent his letter to GE Capital's CEO. Even the august senator from Massachusetts, Edward Kennedy, got involved, calling on GE to make the loan and save several hundred jobs in his home state. Meanwhile, we sought out officials with Hostess's two biggest unions, the Teamsters and the bakers' union, to enlist them to contact their congressmen.

One idea we considered was putting pamphleteers in Twinkie costumes on the steps of the Capitol to hand out leaflets hailing

Hostess and humorously jabbing GE. I forget who proposed this—it might have been me, it could have been Lew, or perhaps Dale Leibach, the Washington operative we were working with at the time. But I do recall that I liked the idea a lot...until the client nixed it.

Meanwhile, back in bankruptcy court in early January 2009, Interstate Bakeries got approval to hire Marc Kasowitz's law firm as "special litigation and conflicts counsel," as the hometown *Kansas City Star* reported, "to take whatever action is required to enforce 'the legally binding commitments of the parties' that agreed to finance Interstate after it emerged from bankruptcy." This was a warning shot fired across the bow of GE Capital. Interstate's short-term DIP financing was slated to run out in a month, on February 9.

Hostess made a particularly good "actor" for this story. Food brands, more so than other product categories, have a special, more personal relationship with their customers, maybe because they appeal to our senses of sight, scent, and taste, which can evoke memories and transport us back to an earlier, comforting time in our lives. (Think of Marcel Proust's bite of a madeleine cookie in *Remembrance of Things Past*.) This provided us with an extra asset: fans of the Twinkie and its sweet siblings.

Twinkies also had a hold on the cultural psyche, renowned for their long shelf life and seeming ability to outlast any calamity. (In truth, as a *Forbes* story later told it, "Twinkies—...able to survive flood, famine and nuclear war—had a shelf life of only about 25 days." New chemistry later extended this to sixty-five days.)

In 1978 after a member of the San Francisco board of supervisors assassinated his fellow supervisor Harvey Milk and Mayor George Moscone, the killer mounted what later became known as the "Twinkie defense," arguing that the sweet snack had driven him crazy. In the 2009 film *Zombieland*, Woody Harrelson plays "an AK-toting, zombie-slaying badass whose single determination is to get the last Twinkie on earth," as Columbia Pictures put it. In one scene, he finds an abandoned Hostess truck filled with fresh pastries, but curses when they all turn out to be pink, marshmallow-frosted Sno Balls covered with coconut flakes.

Sometimes only Twinkies will do.

In finding ways to put pressure on the people running GE Capital, we offered up Hostess as a poster child for businesses challenged by the banks' reluctance to loan out some of the bailout billions they had received from the feds. Sometimes the goal when you place a story is not to rile a million readers but to get the attention of one key individual. In this case, it was the CEO.

And so one day in late January 2009, Craig Jung, the CEO of Hostess, received a call from the GE chief. Jung had been trying for weeks to reach the top levels of GE to appeal for a re-hearing, only to come up empty. Jung told us that Jeff Immelt expressed interest in working things out—but first Hostess must turn off the PR assault. This same sort of thing has happened in a number of cases in which we have been involved: we will deal, but first you must call off the hounds. But why grant that relief from the Wheel of Pain, before you have exacted what you were seeking?

We had anticipated this possibility. Jung responded that he couldn't end the campaign—the workers, union reps, and politicians weren't going to let up until Hostess got the financing that GE Capital had promised—to say nothing of the media interest. This was beyond his control.

Some weeks later, the deal was done, Hostess Brands was reborn, and the Twinkies maker emerged from Chapter 11 in February 2009. GE Capital had provided $105 million rather than the $125 million it had originally pledged, but the other investors already in on the refinancing made up the shortfall. It was a rewarding outcome to more than a year of intensive advice and arduous execution. It also was a surprise ending to a story that could have taken a worse turn, toward the loss of almost thirty thousand jobs.

The press celebrated the rescue, especially the local papers where Hostess had a presence. Senator Kennedy put out an eloquent statement: "In these very dark and uncertain economic times, this announcement is an urgently needed ray of light." Senator Schumer issued a triumphant statement, saying he had "successfully helped broker a deal between International Bakeries Corporation and General Electric that ensures the company can now emerge from bankruptcy, preserving the jobs of the 230 Upstate New Yorkers who work for Drakes Coffee Cakes."

On February 23, 2009, the *Wall Street Journal* carried a story headlined, "There Is Life after Bankruptcy for Some Companies," with Interstate Bakeries as the lead: "It was a near-death experience for the Twinkie."

Reaching out to U.S. senators and congressmen, waging a campaign on old-fashioned bulletin boards, sitting through bankruptcy court hearings, educating local and national reporters, employees, creditors, and other constituents—as you can see, handling a Chapter 11 case requires far more than the typical PR routine. Over the years my firm has built a thriving practice specializing in the arcana, vagaries, and peculiar needs of businesses undergoing Chapter 11 reorganization or some other restructuring, debt workout, or similar life-or-death maneuver.

Focus on the Fix

It is the corporate equivalent of bypass surgery. Oddly enough, I like the field, for while it can entail confrontation, discord, and brinkmanship, it is also steeped in renewal, reanimation, and the drive to set things right. If I had to pick only one of my Ten Rules for Engagement to use in Chapter 11 cases, it would be No. 5: focus on the fix. Stories on your client should explore where a company is headed next, not rehash the mistakes it made in the past.

Bankruptcy-code filings, in fact, have been a foundation of Sitrick And Company from our first days, thanks to the baptism by fire I experienced in the 1980s as the senior vice president of communications at Wickes Companies, the acquisitive owner of furniture and home-improvement retailers and consumer goods makers run by one of my greatest mentors, Sanford C. Sigoloff. Sandy had been brought into Wickes nine months after I got there, and only weeks later, bent on saving the company, the new CEO had put Wickes into Chapter 11, exposing me to a master's lessons in the black art of bankruptcy.

In my years at Wickes, I learned the ins and outs of the federal bankruptcy code. In the three decades since then, my firm has handled over four hundred companies in Chapter 11 reorganizations and roughly half that many out-of-court restructurings and workouts that otherwise would have landed in bankruptcy court. Greg Milmoe, the Skadden lawyer and former head of that law firm's restructuring practice, who called me on Christmas Eve in Cancun to tell me that GE Capital was about to crush IBC, once explained my role to a reporter for the *Financial Times* in London:

> Mike is the guy who pioneered the business of public relations in bankruptcies and distressed situations.... He developed the systems and the approach to communicate with employees, vendors, unions, suppliers— which is common sense if you think about it. But before he came along nobody did it.

I owe the late Sandy Sigoloff for that. He was one of the most gifted businessmen I have ever known. A bona fide turnaround artist with a sense of humor, he nicknamed himself "Ming the Merciless" (from *Flash Gordon*) for the sometimes draconian measures that he had to take to save companies and thousands upon thousands of jobs during his career. Sandy, who died at age eighty in 2011, was viewed in the industry as "Mr. Chapter 11" for his success in rescuing companies through bankruptcy reorganization. He had brought Wickes out of bankruptcy and expanded it with a couple of billion-dollar acquisitions, financed on the high-yield bond market with the help of the brilliant Mike Milken at Drexel Burnham Lambert.

In southern California in the 1980s, Sandy was known for starring as himself in TV ads for Wickes's home-improvement chain, Builders Emporium, an idea hatched in my group. He was depicted as a tough, demanding boss, saluted in the tagline: "We got the message, Mr. Sigoloff!" Truth in advertising.

Sandy could be a formidable presence, and soon after he arrived at Wickes, he and I sat down for an exchange that would shape my approach to client cases for years to come. We had settled into our seats on a commercial flight and were waiting for takeoff when he asked my advice on a sensitive company issue. "I think you're wrong," I told him, and explained why. Then came a pause that was a little unnerving, as Sandy stared at me with his steely blue eyes. I wasn't sure of my job status under the new management. In fact, nearly every other officer who was with the company when he first arrived had been "made available to the competition," as he used to say. I suspected that my advice was the opposite of what he wanted to hear.

"Sandy," I said, "if you're looking for someone to tell you what they think you want to hear, then you've got the wrong guy.

Just give me enough time to find another job, because I have a family."

"Thank God someone has the guts to tell me what they really think," he said. "That is what I want. That is what I need." That helped reinforce a lesson I had learned earlier in my career: the best and brightest leaders in the business world prize the unadorned truth, which is in short supply.

By now we know the bankruptcy drill, and in the ensuing years other firms have launched Chapter 11 practices, but in my view, many of them have erred by trying to make this a mindless routine: open up the book and pull out employee, vendor, customer communications, and lockstep press releases (even if not literally, close). Often they put inexperienced people on the case "to keep costs down." They don't respond to media inquiries beyond the news release, or if they do, they offer some boilerplate response.

The problem is that a reorganization—whether in or out of court—is too complicated to follow a template. Emergencies come up with employees, vendors, and customers. If you don't engage— and sometimes even when you do engage—the media will make errors in reporting on the events, sometimes critical ones. I ask potential clients, when asked whether they should hire us, if a significant error appears in a story on *Bloomberg* or in the *Financial Times* or *Wall Street Journal* at nine o'clock on a Sunday night, can the other agency you are considering get a top editor on the phone to get it fixed? We can and do.

In a Chapter 11 case, in which your constituents are already concerned that you are on life support, significant errors can have a critical if not fatal effect. You can't automate your communications, nor should they be left to people with little or no experience. As I am wont to say, it is not the place for "on-the-job training."

Getting Technical

Now for an explanation. First, let's get technical. When a company goes out of business, it files for "liquidation" under Chapter *Seven* of the U.S. Bankruptcy Code. There is no effort to keep the company alive. The focus is on liquidating the company for the preference of the creditors. But when companies file under Chapter *Eleven*, they "file for protection from creditors." They file in bankruptcy court to reorganize their affairs and mend their finances while being insulated from creditors' lawsuits. The debt is often near default or already in it and must be renegotiated, perhaps under looser terms or reduced in exchange for an ownership stake in the company-on-the-mend.

Admittedly, the stated goal of Chapter 11 isn't to protect jobs, it is to enhance the company's chances of surviving so it can pay off its debt holders, who rule the top of the heap in a Chapter 11 case. For centuries, the law has favored lenders over owners when a company fails. This is why in Chapter 11 the stock of a company can get wiped out—that is, the "equity" owned by investors who had bought shares of ownership in the company—while all efforts are focused on paying back the banks and bondholders that had loaned it money. In exchange for this payback priority and their lower risk of loss, debt holders accept a lower return on their money than that promised by a riskier investment in the stock.

Now, let's get emotional. Chapter 11 can be a rollercoaster for the people at any company that goes through it. One of our jobs is to do what we can to make sure that people at the company worry about *doing* their jobs rather than about *losing* their jobs. People fear not knowing what's coming next. Vendors must have enough confidence to supply goods on credit, and sooner rather than later. Customers need to have confidence that you will be around long enough to fulfill their orders, let alone honor your warranties on your products.

My intention here isn't to sound like some shrink or life coach. I am not known for being touchy-feely, but this needs to be understood. These are natural responses to the one feeling pervading the entire Chapter 11 process: a sense of failure. The stock of the company often falls to nearly zero or stops trading altogether. Wall Street analysts stop following it.

"Filing for Chapter 11" is so stigmatized, even today, that in the 2016 presidential campaign, critics of Republican nominee Donald Trump bashed his business savvy by citing a handful of Chapter 11 filings amid the hundreds of ventures and buildings that he has owned. So notorious is a descent into Chapter 11 that some companies will stay in denial and stall entering the process, making their plight even worse—sometimes to the point that they are forced into liquidation.

I tell my clients that a Chapter 11 reorganization, if properly handled, can and should be a new beginning, not the beginning of the end. It is important that you let your employees, customers, and other key constituents know that you believe, so you can make them believe (to take a page from a Baptist preacher). From day one, you need to talk about what steps you are taking to address the issues that made the filing necessary; how you are going to fix the business, strengthen the balance sheet, increase revenues, and enhance profitability.

This can be a difficult sell. Sometimes the leaders of a troubled company can lose the will to fight. A case in point is the aptly named Purgatory ski resort in Durango, Colorado. As I recounted in *Spin*, it was set to close down in the early 1990s because its longtime bank had refused to renew a line of credit. A lawyer who had worked with me on a case involving another ski resort called to ask for my advice in handling communications for the shutdown of this one. "We need to do damage control," he said. And that would have been that for some people in my profession. They would have put together and implemented a communications plan. But I don't always take the direct approach.

Hearing about Purgatory's hell-bent path to closing, I asked the lawyers for my new clients why the bank was balking at extending credit. Was Purgatory unprofitable? They told me the resort was in the black, but a giant, out-of-state bank had acquired the local lender and had no interest in lending to the ski industry. How long ago was the local bank sold? Within the last few weeks, they said. In that case, I told them, Purgatory won't have to close at all.

I asked my puzzled clients to imagine what the state banking commissioner would say when the *Denver Post* asked him whether, before approving the deal, he had bothered to ask the new owner of Purgatory's bank if it had any plans that would hurt the state's most important industry? What do you think the governor would say? There was momentary silence on the other end of the line, and the lawyer asked, "How soon can you have someone here?" A Sitrick partner flew in the next day.

So we set the plan in motion, getting the lawyers' okay for my personally briefing a *Denver Post* editor over the weekend and letting it be known the story might happen, but doing so entirely off-the-record, so that a story would run only if we told the editor it could run and no mention of what we discussed would appear in any form if the bank settled with my client. He agreed.

Purgatory's lawyers met with the bank's lawyers that Monday. When the bank's lawyers in effect told them to take a hike, I was given the okay to call the editor and have him send in a reporter. The story ran a day later, unleashing waves of reaction and a call for a state investigation. By the end of that week, Purgatory had a new line of credit.

In my view, the greater mission, the right mission, had been accomplished—saving several hundred jobs. In fact, the ski resort even snagged a lower interest rate.

Almost instinctively, we had shifted the Purgatory ski resort's objective from managing a shutdown to finding a way to stay open, by targeting the right pressure point and preempting the story with a better one of our own. I had recognized that this was a great story and that media pressure might persuade the bank to rethink its position. To get the media to invest the time and give the story the "play" we desired, we had offered an exclusive. The resort still is in business today (under new owners), yet it might have shut its doors had it not been for our asking that first question—why is the bank refusing to extend your line of credit?

Lawyers as Field Marshals

Senior executives can become exhausted by the workout process when a business is on the ropes. But it is critical they focus on the fix. In a Chapter 11, as much or more than any other situation, having top, experienced advisors is essential. Advisors with a track record of success. Lawyers, in my experience are the field marshals. They can make or break a case. You need good financial advisors, investment bankers where appropriate, and experienced, creative communications professionals.

Communicating to your key constituents is more than just keeping these groups informed. It is making sure they understand your objectives, accomplishments in turning things around, and for most of these constituents, how they are part of the process. Who are these constituents? Lenders, vendors, landlords, government officials, customers, your senior management team, rank-and-file employees, and yes, reporters.

Keeping reporters updated on the latest twists in the circuitous administrative processes of Chapter 11 is a more critical objective of "bankruptcy PR" than many who practice in this area think. Sometimes PR professionals advising companies in Chapter 11 will advise ignoring the media and just communicating directly to the other constituents from the outset. I think that's dangerous. I ask clients, "Whom will your customers believe—the *Wall Street Journal* when it reports that your company has only enough cash to survive three days, or an email from you the next day saying everything is great?"

Some years ago, the communications VP for a major retailer got a call from a reporter at the *Journal* who had heard that vendors were not shipping because the retailer could not pay for goods. The retailer's PR chief talked to his outside PR advisor at the time, and they concluded he should not comment. In fact, their response was, "That is so ridiculous it doesn't deserve a comment."

The story was published anyway, of course, citing a few vendors by name. This provoked what I have come to call a vendor stampede. All of a sudden, the company's other vendors began refusing delivery unless they got cash up front or upon delivery. After all, it was in the *Wall Street Journal*. Few, if any, retailers could withstand that demand. The PR team contacted vendors by phone and in writing, but the onslaught did not abate. The retailer ultimately filed for Chapter 11 and then Chapter 7: liquidation. It no longer exists today.

What should the PR chief have done? He should have asked the *Journal* reporter, before the story ran, who these vendors were and whether they would be named in the story. There is a good chance the reporter would tell him who they were. If the reporter refused to provide the names, the PR chief should have told him that he was going to appeal to his editor. (I never go behind a reporter's back.) If the editor likewise refused to identify the vendors, the PR chief should have said, "I will give you fifty other vendors. Call any of them." The company later told me they could have gotten five hundred vendors to say they were still shipping. At the very least, the story would have reported that six vendors interviewed by the *Wall*

Street Journal said they were continuing to do business as normal with the retailer, although the payments were stretched out a bit, and three others said they were refusing to ship. But that's not what the story said. And the sad thing is that, once the facts were uncovered, it turned out that the *real* reason the vendors named in the story weren't getting paid by the retailer was that the goods they had shipped were late or defective or both.

The better approach is to use the facts with the media to help you strategically position a company's Chapter 11 filing as a new beginning. We have represented several airlines prior to and during their Chapter 11 reorganizations. The CEO of one was particularly concerned that the company's filing of Chapter 11, if it occurred, could result in a dramatic drop in passengers and the ultimate failure of the company and that if it leaked Chapter 11 was one of the options being considered, it could become a self-fulfilling prophecy. He shared these concerns with me one afternoon as we mapped out our strategy.

"Why don't we preempt the news?" I asked him, and he asked what I meant by that.

"Let's set up a series of meetings with reporters and editors from key media and take them through our various options, explaining the plusses and minuses of each," I said. "The meetings will be on the record, but we will reserve the right to go off the record at times. We will do this only with reporters and editors I know."

"As part of this process," I added, "we will explain that one of the options we are considering is a Chapter 11 filing and how taking this action, if we determine it is the best course, will actually strengthen the company and its future." After further discussion that included our agreeing on the particulars of what we would say under each scenario, the airline chief signed on to the idea.

A week or so later, we flew to New York and met with key editors and reporters from various media companies. Rather than reporting on rumors or leaks, they wrote about the meeting and the paths the CEO laid out. When the company did file under Chapter 11, the move was positioned as what it truly was: a positive step to rid the company of its debt, strengthen its balance sheet, cut costs, and allow the airline to invest in and grow its business. The airline is still operating successfully today.

In another instance, a mid-sized retail client of mine had been the subject of numerous articles asserting that it was running out of cash and might not survive. When we announced the move into Chapter 11, we included an announcement that the company had budgeted $50 million for a new advertising campaign. "A company wouldn't spend $50 million on advertising if it was going out of business," one columnist wrote.

A Picnic. . .with Reporters

A week later, we invited reporters from a major newspaper in the company's headquarters city to an employee picnic. You could see the direction of the coverage change. After the picnic, another columnist in our client's hometown paper expressed similar sentiment. No company in a death spiral would hold an employee picnic.

At times I have been asked to give speeches to executive teams about to enter the Chapter 11 process, and I almost always emphasize that they have to exhibit a positive view. If they don't, their pessimism will affect the whole organization, and fear of dissolution could end up becoming a reality.

We also put in place communications programs for other key audiences, often including a script for the receptionists to make sure the right points are emphasized. The last thing you need is a key vendor or customer calling your office and asking the receptionist how things are, only for her to say, "It's really scary here. None of us knows if he'll have a job tomorrow." Also critical is an all-hands meeting of senior managers, in which they learn what's going on so they can forward the right message to their teams.

The impressions and images a company's people convey at a fragile time like this are critical to its chances for survival. The message you put out anchors the turnaround effort. Say the wrong thing, or say the right thing in the wrong way, and you can breed anxiety, alarm, and panic. Say the right thing in the right way, and you can instill calm, patience, and hope, which produce support and cooperation.

That's one reason I emphasize to clients that we use the filing as an opportunity to get out the message of a new beginning in all our communications, starting with a strong news release and more often than not granting interviews with key media, simultaneously addressing employees, customers, and vendors.

Some years after the bankruptcy proceedings I have described, Hostess filed under Chapter 11 for a second time. Strapped for cash, the company told the Teamsters and bakers it needed a new round of concessions. But the unions were unmoved. Something had to give. Eventually, the Teamsters granted the concessions that Hostess had sought and urged other unions to go along. Ten of the eleven other unions did, but more than 90 percent of the bakers' union members voted against the deal, and its 5,600 members at Hostess went on strike. Efforts to resuscitate the talks failed, and one week later, Hostess filed a motion with the bankruptcy court to begin winding down operations.

The biggest piece, Hostess's Twinkies and Dolly Madison brands, went to buyout firms Apollo and Metropoulos, which revived the Twinkie after a nine-month absence. In 2016, the business sold a controlling stake to a new owner, the Beverly Hills billionaire Alec Gores of the private-equity firm Gores Group, through his publicly traded Gores Holdings. Thus Hostess would set plans to go public yet again, coming full circle, in a way: Alec Gores and Gores Group are longtime clients of Sitrick And Company.

———

Chapter 11 was designed to help companies live on, mending themselves under court protection so they can get back to business. The obstacles to recovery are legal and financial but also emotional and psychological. Crafting the right message and delivering it to the right audiences becomes a key component of any tumble into Chapter 11 and the centerpiece of working your way out of it. Get it right, and you can secure the livelihoods of the thousands of people your company employs and help ensure a recovery that will result in creditors' getting all or part of their money back.

For companies in almost any kind of crisis, in fact, getting out the right message to the right audience is essential to survival. It is a key asset for business in general. Business is a relationship, and a relationship requires open, clear communications. Sometimes, what you say can be as important as what you do. Do the right thing but say it in the wrong way, and you are sunk. Do the wrong thing, but then say the right things afterward, and you have a chance.

And if everyone did both things right, all the time, I'd go out of business, along with a lot of my lawyer and restructuring advisor friends. Until then, we at Sitrick And Company will continue to counsel companies and CEOs, startups and their founders, celebrities and billionaires, and businesses in Chapter 11 when a company's future hangs in the balance and the jobs of thousands of workers can be saved. When crisis descends or opportunity calls, we will advise them on what to do and what to say. These people have a story to tell, although they might not always know it, and it is my job, my nearly lifelong pursuit, to help them tell it.

Chapter 12

Courting Controversy

Part One

L ooking back over a long and rather eventful career, it seems the tougher the situation, the more ferocious the criticism, the more likely it is that our firm will get involved.

A case from mid-2016 unleashed one of the biggest controversies of my career, as our firm helped expose the biggest Olympic doping scandal of all time, weeks before the start of the Summer Games in Rio de Janeiro. My partner Sallie Hofmeister (a former reporter and editor for the *New York Times* and the *Los Angeles Times*) and I gave the worldwide scoop as an exclusive to the *New York Times*, which published a stunning page-one exposé on Friday, May 13, 2016, and ran a front-page follow-up the next day.

The story told in definitive detail how some government officials in Russia had orchestrated a doping program that served dozens of Russian athletes, including fourteen members of the cross-country ski team and two bobsledders who had won two

Olympic gold medals. The *Times* called it "one of the most elaborate—and successful—doping ploys in sports history," and the story
was picked up and repeated around the world in the ensuing weeks.
There was ample time for Olympic officials to investigate the allegations and eventually ban more than a hundred members of the
Russian team from the 2016 Summer Games.

Our timing was intentional. Our clients were the director and
producer-financier of a documentary film on the doping scheme,
and they were concerned that the film's credibility and the integrity
of its central character would be attacked. By giving the *Times*
months to corroborate the film's allegations, we pre-empted such
attacks while promoting the film before it had even been sold.

This case begins, as many of my cases do, with a phone call
from someone's lawyer. Earlier in the year, I had been approached
by a lawyer who had worked with me on a number of cases in the
past, Ed Stier, who represents another Sitrick client, the private-
equity investor Ray Chambers (co-founder of Wesray Capital, one
of the first private-equity firms). Stier was looking for PR for a
small documentary, but the film was months away, the budget
was limited, and Sitrick And Company doesn't do red-carpet
movie PR.

A couple of months later, though, he returned to me with the
full story, and we could instantly see the momentous impact it might
have. Stier wanted me to help his client, the documentary company
and its filmmaker, Bryan Fogel. Cycling, perhaps even more than
filmmaking, is Fogel's fierce passion, and he was devastated by the
fall of Lance Armstrong, the greatest cyclist in history, who, after
years of denying persistent allegations, admitted to doping only
after his own teammates turned him in. This story fascinated Fogel.
Why had the authorities been unable to detect the repeated, appar-
ently widespread doping?

The same question could be asked about the Yankee slugger Alex Rodriguez, whom my firm represented in the aftermath of his steroid scandal. A-Rod was penalized only after a former ally accused him of using performance-enhancing drugs, not because Major League Baseball officials had detected any violations.

The Armstrong scandal gave Fogel an idea. What if he entered a sanctioned bicycle race, doped himself in a way so as not to get caught, and then showed in a documentary film how he did it? He started with a race in France, forgoing any performance-enhancing drugs as a base metric and finishing fourteenth among several hundred entrants (which in itself is pretty damned impressive).

The filmmaker then talked to anti-doping experts about his idea, but no one dared to get involved. Eventually, however, a scientist told him to contact a man in Moscow, one of the leading anti-doping experts in the world, Dr. Grigory Rodchenkov, who agreed to help Fogel dope himself for the next race. Meeting with Fogel over Skype, Rodchenkov told him to get a prescription for steroids and showed him, on-screen, how to inject them—not into his leg, where the bruising would be detected, but in the buttocks. Fogel filmed these lessons.

Fogel then entered a second race, and though he didn't finish as well (accident, equipment failure), he felt much stronger under the effects of the steroids. His recovery time was much faster than it was after the first race, when he could barely move and slept for the better part of a week.

During all of this, German television aired a documentary on Olympic doping, featuring a confession from a member of the Russian women's track team, a middle-distance runner named Yuliya Stepanova. Cited for doping violations, she spoke out, asserting that numerous other Olympic athletes had been doping as well, including four of Russia's gold medal winners. The documentary fingered one main character as responsible for the entire operation: Grigory Rodchenkov, former director of Russia's anti-doping lab—and now Bryan Fogel's steroid advisor.

The broadcast alleged that Russian athletes paid bribes to Rodchenkov for his illicit help, a charge he vehemently (and convincingly) denied. Ms. Stepanova claimed she gave money to her coach, who said he needed it to give to Rodchenkov. The coach may have received money from Stepanova, Rodchenkov later told us and the *New York Times*, but he never passed it along to the doctor.

With its reputation in question, the World Anti-Doping Agency (WADA), which had accredited the Moscow lab, ordered an independent investigation of the allegations, releasing its findings in November 2015. Among its recommendations: that Rodchenkov be removed from his position for aiding the widespread cheating among athletes and for destroying 1,417 lab samples to obstruct follow-up tests.

As a result of the WADA investigation, his bosses in Moscow had asked Rodchenkov to resign, and he complied. Whispering into his computer, over Skype, he told Fogel that officers with Russia's FSB (the former KGB) were in his home watching his every move. He told Bryan he needed to escape to the United States.

Bryan arranged for Rodchenkov's passage, picked him up at LAX, and drove him to a nondescript apartment that would be his temporary home for the next several months. Rodchenkov told Fogel that while he never took any bribes for providing performance-enhancing drugs to Olympic athletes, he did follow orders to provide the drugs to those on "the list" given to him by Russian government officials. Fogel now realized he had a much bigger story to tell.

"Everybody's Doping"

Rodchenkov said it was his job to run the doping program at the 2014 Winter Games in Sochi, Russia. He was under immense pressure to produce medal winners and let Russia recover from a mediocre sixth-place finish at the previous Winter Games. "Everybody's doping," he said, adding that he was convinced that few Olympic athletes could win a gold or silver medal without doping, no matter what country they were from.

It was a terrific story, but my clients, the filmmaker Fogel, and his producer-financier Dan Cogan, worried that those fingered in Rodchenkov's story, including some government officials, might try to discredit him as a rogue lab operator, though he convincingly insisted he had been doing their bidding, and that U.S. investigators might take an interest in his case, possibly turning against Rodchenkov. Moreover, Fogel fretted that the anti-doping agency and the International Olympic Committee, with billions at stake in TV contracts and sponsorships, might be reluctant to investigate at all, fearing a revelation that the entire testing system was broken. Maybe they would prefer to bury it just two months before the 2016 Summer Games in Rio.

In addition, the IOC would be deciding in weeks whether to lift a ban on the Russian track team imposed after the WADA investigation had confirmed the allegations of the German documentary and let the team compete in Rio. Fogel hoped to influence that decision with his newly discovered information, yet his documentary wouldn't be ready until well *after* the Rio Games. Rodchenkov's revelations were huge news, and Fogel wanted to make them public before the IOC made its decision.

What to do? Media from all over the world had been trying to get Rodchenkov to speak with them, but at the filmmaker's request he had refused interviews. The filmmaker and his producer suggested going wide all at once: host a press conference for all comers and release the details of the new documentary's revelations months before the film itself could be seen. Sallie and I were able to convince them otherwise, after I pointed out the drawbacks. What if no one shows up? It's unlikely you could draw much of a crowd without giving away the scoop. And even if you did get people to show up, you would probably get only a smattering of small stories because you couldn't go into enough detail for an in-depth story. Their reluctance to put Rodchenkov out there for mass questioning, moreover, further reduced the likelihood that there would be meaningful coverage.

We decided, instead, to strike preemptively, having Fogel and Rodchenkov go public in a very big way, and fast—yet by going narrow and deep, rather than going wide and shallow, as a press conference would have done. We needed the perfect Lead Steer for this mission, one with international influence but also with the heft of ink. We suggested the *New York Times*: global reach, impeccable reputation, great reporters. Fogel and Cogan agreed. It turned out a *Times* reporter, Rebecca R. Ruiz, had written about the IOC and the doping investigation prompted by the German documentary. Though Sallie and I didn't know Ruiz, we both knew the *Times*' top editor and decided to take this scoop straight to him.

We held off, however, while Fogel spent the next few weeks working on a distribution deal with a premier cable network, including an exclusive with its sibling, a cable news network. Sallie and I, concerned that if we launched this story with the cable news network alone the rest of the media might not notice and follow, suggested that the network share the exclusive with the *Times*.

Bryan Fogel and Dan Cogan got pretty far down this promising path, meeting with a dozen producers and editors at the cable news network's headquarters, before talks broke off. The news came on

Sunday, May 1, just two weeks before the World Anti-Doping Agency was to release its recommendation on whether to lift the recent ban on the Russian track and field team. Sitrick And Company had to move fast.

So the next day, Sallie and I made the pitch to the *New York Times* editor over the phone, with the paper's top investigative editor also on the call. Sallie and I cited Rebecca Ruiz's stories about the WADA investigation and pointed out that this story would show how athletes could dope through an entire Olympics, avoid detection, and take home the most gold medals.

The story was assigned to Ruiz along with Michael Schwirtz, who had spent six years reporting in Russia for the *Times* and spoke the language fluently. This was an especially astute move, as Schwirtz's language skills would prove essential to discerning the nuances in Rodchenkov's responses to the reporters' questions.

The next day, we did a run-through with Fogel and his star witness, Grigory Rodchenkov. Because of the sheer volume of the documents, we were concerned about how to present the information. We also worried that Rodchenkov's limited English might hamper the questioning.

We advised Fogel and Rodchenkov to unspool their story to the *Times* reporters pretty much as they had told it to us but with more details—what the room looked like where the swapping of samples took place and whether it was dark or well-lit, what Rodchenkov was wearing on his late-night rendezvous with FSB agents, exactly how tainted samples were swapped for clean ones through a small hole in the wall separating the official lab from a secret and illicit lab next door, and how they covered up the hole during daytime hours.

That night, Ruiz and Schwirtz flew to Los Angeles for three days of interviewing. The next morning, Wednesday, May 4, Bryan

Fogel arrived at 8:30 at a conference room at our offices with his dog, Max, a big, beautiful Vizsla with high anxiety. Fogel explained that Max could not stand to be alone and would tear up everything in his apartment if left behind—an effective strategy, from the pooch's point of view. Fogel and Rodchenkov had bonded over their dogs, displaying them for each other during Skype calls.

The *Times* reporters showed up at nine o'clock and began the interviews, spending hours interviewing Rodchenkov and Fogel and examining documents, spreadsheets, emails, and photographs showing how the elaborate doping-lab operation worked. Max the anxious Vizsla spent much of the time snoozing. We ordered lunch and worked straight through until seven o'clock that night.

At Noon, a Sudden Glitch

The next day, Thursday, the fifth, went much the same way, with Fogel's high-strung pup again napping on scene. By noon, however, there was a glitch: Fogel's attorney, Ed Stier, called me to say that producers at *60 Minutes* had just contacted him about a story airing that Sunday on Olympic doping and the Russian female athlete in the German documentary. They wanted to interview Rodchenkov.

For a variety of reasons, including fear that the film's thunder would be stolen, Fogel and Cogan unequivocally vetoed the idea of Rodchenkov's talking to *60 Minutes*. Sallie and I informed the *Times* reporters, who still were in the midst of their interviews, that *60 Minutes* was airing a doping story imminently, though without any contribution from our clients. Not to do so might make them think we had been double-dealing with a second outlet.

After three final hours with Fogel and Rodchenkov on Friday, the reporters returned to New York to spend the next week doing more reporting, checking their facts, corroborating Rodchenkov's claims, and writing a long, vivid account of what Rodchenkov had told them.

The *Times* posted the big exposé online in the pre-dawn hours of Thursday, May 12, and let the scoop run online all day long before publishing the story on page one of the print edition the next morning, Friday, the thirteenth. The thoroughness and sophistication of the reporting was worthy of the "paper of record." A two-column headline at the top of the page declared, "An Insider in Sochi Tells How Russia Beat Doping Tests." Deck: "Shadow Lab Used to Replace Tainted Samples in 2014 Olympic Quest." Lead:

> LOS ANGELES—Dozens of Russian athletes at the 2014 Winter Olympics in Sochi, including at least 15 medal winners, were part of a state-run doping program, meticulously planned for years to ensure dominance at the Games, according to the director of the country's antidoping laboratory at the time.

Most amazing of all, these allegations were leveled not by some unnamed source or just one athlete with limited knowledge. The primary source for this story was on the record and fully identified: Grigory Rodchenkov, director of the Russian-run anti-doping lab for the entire Sochi Games. He described to the *Times* misdeeds and deceptions that went well beyond what he had told anti-doping investigators months earlier. This was one of the first times a top insider in a major athlete-doping ring has stepped forward to tell all.

The story delivered riveting details: the Russian sports ministry had guided the scheme, Rodchenkov meeting weekly with the number-two official at the ministry; Rodchenkov himself had developed a cocktail of three anabolic steroids that top Russian athletes used at the 2012 Summer Olympic Games in London and at the 2014 Winter Games in Sochi (later, it would come out that the cocktail had a name: Duchess); in Sochi, Rodchenkov's over-seers had given him a spreadsheet listing athletes on the doping program and their competition schedules so he could be ready to swap out the urine specimen of anyone on the list who medaled.

Because the Sochi Games were hosted by Russia, it had control of the on-site drug-testing lab for all nations' athletes, enabling it, according to Rodchenkov, to run a tampering scheme to favor its own teams. As the *Times* reported, the Russians set up their own secret lab next door to the official antidoping lab, passing tainted and untainted samples back and forth between the two labs through a hidden hole in the wall.

The official lab was overseen by Rodchenkov and an indepen-dent observer in daytime hours. But after midnight, the *Times* story said, Rodchenkov "changed from his lab coat into a Russian national team sweatshirt and left his fourth-floor office…and made his way to Room 124, officially a storage space that he and his team had converted into a shadow laboratory."

Agents in the official lab would hand "dirty," drug-tainted urine samples of Russian athletes to agents in the secret lab, so the bad specimens could be swapped for "clean" samples. By the end of the games, more than a hundred dirty urine samples had been replaced, according to the story in the *Times*. Rodchenkov and his associates also were able to ensure that only "clean" samples from Russia's drug-taking athletes would end up in storage at the IOC's sample vault in Lausanne, Switzerland.

Russian athletes won thirty-three medals at the Sochi Games, more than any other nation and ten more than in the 2010 Winter Games, where Russia had placed sixth in total medal count. Of those thirty-three medals, one-third went to athletes named on that spreadsheet. For his work in 2014, Grigory Rodchenkov received the prized Order of Friendship from Russian President Vladimir Putin. The entire operation was so well disguised that Rodchenkov also received commendations from the IOC and from the World Anti-Doping Agency, which issued a report calling Sochi "a milestone in the evolution of the Olympic Games antidoping program."

Yes, it was—but not in the way WADA had intended.

The *Times* exposé ran at a "crucial moment for Russia," as the story noted. The Russian track and field team, suspended six months earlier, was up for consideration to be allowed to compete at the 2016 Summer Olympic Games in Rio de Janeiro. The *Times* ran a follow-up story on page one on Saturday, the fourteenth, on another stunner that emerged from the original interview with Fogel and Rodchenkov—the supposedly tamper-proof vials for Olympic drug-testing that the Russians had figured out how to breach without detection. These vessels, thought to be inviolable, had been compromised, letting Russian lab officials replace steroid-tainted urine samples with "clean" ones that had been collected months earlier from the athletes and were hidden in everyday consumer containers such as water bottles.

A Thousand Articles Worldwide

That same morning, I explained my strategy to Dennis Kneale. As the *Times* published prominent follow-ups in the coming weeks, we would line up follow-on interviews at a few other outlets, "and then we're done. Bet you we get a thousand articles worldwide." Sure enough, more than a thousand articles would follow the *Times* story in the ensuing eight weeks.

The response and fallout were swift and sweeping. A flood of media calls came in to Sitrick And Company, thanks in part to Bryan Fogel's setting up a temporary website, at my suggestion, listing his contact details and those of the firm. But we held off providing Rodchenkov or Fogel to other media for interviews, figuring the rest of the press already was reporting what the *Times* had reported first.

The Russian government dismissed the *Times* story as a political attack. "These allegations look absolutely groundless," a spokesman for President Putin told Russian reporters the day after the story was published. "All this simply looks like slander by a turncoat." On Sunday, April 15, the Russian sports minister bylined a piece in the *Times* of London apologizing for previous doping by his track and field athletes but pleading for their ban to be lifted for Rio. "Serious mistakes have been made by the federation management, along with athletes and coaches who have broken anti-doping rules and neglected the principle of fair play.... Let us be clear. We are ashamed of them," he wrote.

A few days later the *New York Times* reported that the Department of Justice had "opened an investigation into state-sponsored doping by dozens of Russia's top athletes...." The IOC called the *Times*' revelations "very detailed and very worrying," deferring to the World Anti-Doping Agency.

Meanwhile, we were working on encouraging a second wave of coverage after the crescendo of "folos" that the *Times* scoop would unleash. The goal was to ensure that WADA immediately and thoroughly investigated and vetted what Rodchenkov had said. We suggested that Fogel write a letter to the World Anti-Doping Agency, calling for an immediate investigation of the violations cited in the *Times* exposé, and slating it for delivery on the day the story ran. Sallie worked on the letter in between other matters for the next couple of days, massaging it into shape even as she connected the *Times* team with a corroborating witness who had worked for Rodchenkov.

After WADA had received the Bryan Fogel letter, the agency announced it would, indeed, undertake the probe that Fogel had requested. This, we figured, would produce another round of coverage once WADA did the testing, providing reporters with something new beyond the original story. Someone at the anti-doping agency leaked the Fogel letter to his rival—the producer of the German documentary featuring the doping confession of the Russian runner Yuliya Stepanova. The producer posted Fogel's letter on Twitter, along with video of Skype calls with Rodchenkov, which had been recorded unknowingly and surreptitiously, according to Rodchenkov.

In June, the global governing body for track and field barred the entire Russian track team from competing in the Summer Games in Rio de Janeiro. On July 18, the World Anti-Doping Agency released a hundred-page report on its investigation of the allegations in the *Times* story, confirming all of Rodchenkov's detailed claims.

The investigators got access to ninety-five urine samples from Russian athletes in Sochi stored in the IOC vault in Lausanne and chose eleven at random for inspection. All eleven showed signs of tampering, with scratches on the inner ring of the bottle caps and abnormal levels of table salt in the urine—that last detail a clue that Rodchenkov had advised investigators to search for in the samples as a way to prove he was telling the truth. He had added salt to the clean samples to give them the proper weight compared with the originals.

The very next day, the anti-doping agency took the unprecedented step of recommending that the IOC ban the entire Russian

Olympic delegation from the 2016 games—every athlete in every sport. The anti-doping agencies of the United States, Canada, Japan, Spain, Switzerland, and New Zealand were organizing to make a similar plea to the IOC. Meanwhile, an appeals court upheld the ban on Russia's track team.

Russia's President Putin responded by suspending the sports officials criticized in the report and asking for "fuller, more objective information that is based on facts," and warning, "Today we see a dangerous relapse of politics intruding into sports."

The reverberations continued in the weeks leading up to the 2016 Summer Olympic Games in Rio. Just twelve days before the start of the Summer Games, the IOC rejected the WADA recommendation to ban the entire Russian team from Rio, instead leaving it to each of the twenty-eight sports federations to decide which Russians would be allowed to compete.

This ruling presented a logistical nightmare. As the *New York Times*' Rebecca Ruiz reported on Sunday, July 24, 2016, "The worst fears of some antidoping officials were realized when, only a few hours after the Olympic committee's announcement on Sunday, the tennis federation cleared for competition all eight Russian athletes who had qualified for the Games with seemingly little scrutiny. Officials cited 205 doping samples among the eight players since 2014."

Ultimately, one-third of the Russian athletes were banned from the Rio Games for their involvement in the Kremlin's doping conspiracy, 118 competitors in total. Two-thirds of the Russian team, some 271 athletes, were allowed to compete. Russia's entire boxing team was admitted, but track and field, weightlifting, and rowing fielded no teams at all—their entire rosters were banned.

In the 2016 Summer Games in Rio, the Russians garnered 27 percent fewer medals than they had won in the 2012 Summer

Games in London, when the doping was underway; in Rio they grabbed nineteen golds (down three), eighteen silvers (down five), and nineteen bronzes (down thirteen).

Icarus Soars at Sundance

And our client's doping documentary? Bryan Fogel's film, titled *Icarus*, debuted at the Sundance Film Festival and was purchased by Netflix for one of the highest prices ever paid for a nonfiction film at Sundance. *Variety* reported, "The $5 million pact is one of the biggest ever for a non-fiction film."

As this book went to press, Grigory Rodchenkov was in the U.S. Witness Protection Program. Without him and Bryan Fogel and Dan Cogan, their lawyers—including Ed Stier—and the help of the Sitrick team, this stunning Olympic scandal might still be buried in the darkness of the IOC vault in Lausanne rather than sparking global outrage.

Still other crises sparking worldwide outrage have tested the wits and resources of Sitrick And Company, and next we will see how I handled one of the fiercest debates of my career, navigating through swirling strains of grief, anger, suspicion, prejudice, and outright racism a decade after the 9/11 attacks. I did so in defense of a project opposed by fully 70 percent of the American people: the Ground Zero Mosque.

Chapter 13

Courting Controversy

Part Two

Controversy doesn't ebb and flow these days. It surges in a tsunami of coverage, counter-coverage, and commentary transmitted digitally to a potentially infinite audience, echoed and reechoed millions of times. When this wave comes at you, you can let it crush you or you can try to ride it. That might mean redirecting a controversy with a revelatory interview or with new, solid facts, quelling it by correcting the record, or creating a different controversy of your own choosing.

The three cases in this chapter illustrate these techniques: the fight over the Ground Zero Mosque, a spat with TV networks over racy ads for Lane Bryant, and a reputational rescue for the founder of the Papa John's pizza chain. In defending the imam at the center of the proposed mosque, my firm quelled a controversy over something that hadn't yet happened. For Lane Bryant, we *created* a controversy over commercials the nets wouldn't run. And for the

Papa John's CEO, we calmed a controversy over things our client *never even said.*

———

The uproar over the Ground Zero Mosque, one of the most emotional debates in this country in the post-9/11 era, began with a whimper. In December 2009, the *New York Times* carried an aw-isn't-that-nice story on page one under the headline, "Muslim Prayers and Renewal Near Ground Zero." It told of a proposal by a local imam and a Muslim developer to build a new mosque and Islamic social center in downtown Manhattan, just two blocks from the site of the World Trade Center. They hoped to build a tower thirteen stories high with an Olympic-sized swimming pool, conference rooms, and a five-hundred-seat auditorium for Muslim cultural exchange programs, Islamic lectures, and more.

The story quoted a city planning official, an executive with the Jewish Community Center, and a local rabbi in praise of the project or the imam who was involved. It sparked no controversy at all, even as the *Times* story stated that the building's link to the 9/11 attacks was "precisely a key selling point." Building "where a piece of the wreckage fell," said the imam, "sends the opposite statement to what happened on 9/11.... We want to push back against the extremists." The story ended with a statement by the developer: "What happened that day was not Islam."

A few months later, a handful of low-traffic, anti-Muslim blogs got hold of the story and spun it in a much darker fashion. They argued this was an intentional offense aimed at the surviving relatives of those killed on 9/11, that Muslims would see it as a sign of radical Islamic conquest, and that it shouldn't be allowed to go forward. And there the spat might have stayed.

Here's the thing—even in the online era, for a story to reach full velocity and spread to the widest possible audience, most of the time it must be picked up by the mainstream media. If I had broken the Russian doping story on, say, Vice.com or theverge.com, it wouldn't have sparked the global wave of headlines unleashed by the *New York Times* unless a media outlet like the *Times* itself picked up on their story. Likewise, the fight over the Ground Zero Mosque might never have been ignited but for an item in the *New York Post*.

On May 13, 2010, the *Post* ran Andrea Peyser's column under the headline: "Mosque Madness at Ground Zero." She wrote:

> A MOSQUE rises over Ground Zero. And fed-up New Yorkers are crying, "No!"
>
> A chorus of critics—from neighbors to those who lost loved ones on 9/11 to me—feel as if they've received a swift kick in the teeth.
>
> Plans are under way for a Muslim house of worship, topped by a 13-story cultural center with a swimming pool, in a building damaged by the fuselage of a jet flown by extremists into the World Trade Center.
>
> The opening date shall live in infamy: Sept. 11, 2011. The 10th anniversary of the day a hole was punched in the city's heart.
>
> How the devil did this happen?

How indeed? The column reverberated across the media, first in conservative quarters, including Fox News and its *Hannity* show, and then across the ideological spectrum. The *Post*, a tabloid that knows how to get the most out of a good scrap, ran 230 stories on the "GZ Mosque," as Andrea Peyser returned to the topic in two dozen columns, and the *Post* itself ran twenty-three editorials opposing the project.

The nonexistent mosque provoked fierce debates around the world as well, garnering coverage everywhere as the story moved from the *Post* and *Times* in New York to the *Observer* in the United Kingdom to the *Jerusalem Post* to the *Straits Times* in Singapore to the *New Zealand Herald* and beyond. By the time I got pulled into the fight over the Ground Zero Mosque, it was as if I were parachuting into a free-fire zone.

I had joined this effort at the behest of Raymond Chambers, the "ray" in Wesray Capital. Chambers is a philanthropist and humanitarian who serves as the United Nations Secretary-General's Special Envoy for Health in the Agenda 2030 program. He asked me to take on the case and represent the imam involved in this effort, Feisal Abdul Rauf, a moderate Sufi Muslim known for his efforts to bring together people of different faiths.

Chambers was concerned, as was I, about the unrest that the stories on the mosque already were causing in New York, worrying that it might spread across the United States and to other parts of the world. We both recognized that this fight wasn't being watched just in New York but by the Muslim world. If the people of New York rejected the mosque proposed by this moderate Muslim, they would reinforce the radicals' misleading message that America is anti-Muslim. Chambers wanted Sitrick to let the world know who this imam was and why he wanted to build the mosque at that location.

A Crisscrossing of Battle Lines

Battle lines were crisscrossing all over the place. President Obama and New York City Mayor Michael Bloomberg were in favor of building the center, but former Mayor Rudy Giuliani and former House Speaker Newt Gingrich were among prominent opponents. Both Republican candidates in the governor's race in New York railed against the mosque, but then-Attorney General Andrew Cuomo spoke in support of it.

Some relatives of some of the 2,752 people who died in the towers' collapse railed against the idea, demanding that the Muslim center be built elsewhere out of respect for the hallowed ground. Other relatives saw it as an effort to heal. Some moderate Muslims said the center should move farther away from Ground Zero out of sensitivity to the 9/11 relatives, but other Muslims decried any opposition to the center as being anti-Islam.

My partner on the case was Seth Faison, formerly head of our New York office and now the communications chief at the Global Fund to Fight AIDS. We needed to get out in front of the frenzy with an illuminating story that would quell this crisis, calm nerves about the real intent of Imam Feisal, and set a path for compromise. I have always placed a lot of faith in *60 Minutes* as a premier outlet for informing and influencing a nation of TV viewers. It is the epitome of a Lead Steer. So I began working my contacts at the program and holding out an exclusive.

We realized right away that our client had a compelling story to tell. Born to Egyptian parents in Kuwait and the son and grandson of imams, Feisal Abdul Rauf had moved to the United States at age seventeen. Now in his early sixties, he had been the imam at the Farah mosque in the Manhattan neighborhood of Tribeca since 1983. In the aftermath of 9/11, he had formed the Cordoba Initiative, aimed at building bridges between Muslims and people of other faiths.

His writings spoke encouragingly of the Abrahamic commonalities among Muslims, Christians, and Jews. The FBI used him as an ally to reach out to American Muslims after the terror attacks and praised his role. The Bush administration, three times in the previous three years, had sponsored his travel to the Middle East to give speeches on how accommodating the United States had been to Muslims, aiming to help improve U.S. relations with the Muslim world.

The imam had teamed up with one of his flock, a Brooklyn-born-and-bred developer named Sharif El-Gamal of Soho Properties. El-Gamal, with undisclosed partners, had bought an abandoned building at 45 Park Place for just shy of $5 million in July 2009. The five-story structure, built in 1923, had housed a discount retail store starting in the late 1960s, then a Burlington Coat Factory retail outlet since 1990.

On the morning of September 11, 2001, the landing gear from one of the two airliners that extremist Muslim terrorists were piloting into the World Trade Center towers broke off and crashed through the building's rooftop and through two floors into the empty store. (No one was injured, as employees were gathered for breakfast in the basement before opening hour.)

The building had been vacant ever since, but in the past year, Imam Feisal had hosted weekly religious services for a few hundred Muslims inside the building every Friday night. It was an overflow crowd from his own mosque ten blocks north. Now he wanted to raze the old building and erect this new mosque.

Imam Feisal's opening salvo in trying to explain why it would be in everyone's best interest to build the Ground Zero Mosque was an op-ed published in the *New York Times* on September 7, 2010, and reprinted two days later overseas in the *International Herald Tribune*. Doubling down amid the hue and cry, the imam vowed, "we are proceeding with the community center, Cordoba House. More importantly, we are doing so with the support of the downtown community, government at all levels and leaders from across the religious spectrum."

The developer, El-Gamal, had never contacted representatives of the surviving families of 9/11 victims at the start of the process, which Imam Feisal later admitted was a huge mistake. He vowed in the op-ed to "seek the support of those families.... Our objective has always been to make this a center for unification and healing."

On the ninth anniversary of the 9/11 terror attacks, crowds of protesters converged on Ground Zero and clashed bitterly with supporters of the project. One night later, without my knowledge, Imam Feisal appeared on CNN's *Larry King Live*, in a surprisingly long interview for cable news, with anchor Soledad O'Brien. He began by plying a message of unity and tolerance, of giving back to the city and country that have given Muslims so much. He would proceed, however, despite the controversy and the latest polls showing that some 70 percent of Americans opposed building the mosque near Ground Zero.

Imam Feisal admitted, "had I known this would happen, we certainly would never have [selected the Ground Zero location]," but to back down now and build elsewhere, he said, might create a violent backlash in the extremist Muslim world. "If this is not handled correctly, this crisis could become much bigger than the Danish cartoon crisis, which resulted in attacks on Danish embassies in various parts of the Muslim world.... [I]t could become something which could really become very, very, very dangerous indeed." Feisal went on to tell O'Brien about his work for the State Department in the Middle East and his wish to bring together people of various faiths, but the damage had been done.

Days later, strains began to show up between the imam and his developer partner, as a *Times* story noted ("One Project, One Faith, And Two Men Who Differ," September 17, 2010). "Each has his own public relations firm and behind-the-scenes advisors. They have individual—not always identical—visions for the project, which they occasionally call by different names.... And amid the swirling controversy about their shared mission, they sometimes give different answers to thorny questions."

Telling It on *60 Minutes*

Our big shot at setting the story right came on September 26: a multi-segment piece on *60 Minutes*, featuring an interview of Imam Feisal by Scott Pelley. The story opened with a profile of Sharif El-Gamal, who comes across as reasonable, rational, and non-threatening. ("I'm an American, I'm a New Yorker, born in Methodist Hospital in Brooklyn, to a Polish Catholic mother, to an Egyptian father.") Then came an interview with the anti-Muslim blogger who was one of the first to use the tag "Ground Zero Mosque," followed by an interview with the imam, who exuded dignity:

> *Feisal*: I'm a man of peace, Scott. I'm extremely sensitive to the feelings of the families of 9/11.
>
> *Pelley*: Then why did you do it?
>
> *Feisal*: Because we wanted to prevent another 9/11. We wanted a platform that will enable us to strengthen the voice of the moderates.... Because it's the right thing to do. It's the right thing to do. Our community wants it. And now America needs it, and the Muslim world needs it because—
>
> *Pelley*: What do you mean America needs it?
>
> *Feisal*: I'll tell you why, Scott. We have to wage peace. The military campaign against the radical extremists

from my faith community is a military campaign. The campaign for winning hearts and minds is an important part of that campaign. We know how to do it. And we're committed to doing it. We are ready, willing, and able to serve our country and to serve our faith tradition.

Near the close of the segment, the anchor intoned over corresponding video footage, "It occurred to us that there is, of course, another Ground Zero: one hundred and eighty-four people were killed at the Pentagon on 9/11. This face of the Pentagon was rebuilt and a memorial and Pentagon chapel opened on the spot where the airplane hit. For eight years now, every weekday at two o'clock, you can hear the Islamic call to prayer in this chapel." The story then has the Pentagon chaplain saying this is "representative of America," and it closes with the final sound bite from the imam himself: "I intend to see this project succeed."

In the coming weeks, the controversy dissipated as quickly as it had erupted: no more protests, no riots, no unrest. Ray Chambers and I had achieved our goal. *60 Minutes*' featuring the mosque in the Pentagon was the capping moment.

Within a few months the imam and his developer would go their separate ways. The developer, Sharif El-Gamal, eventually scrapped plans for a Muslim community center and proposed to raze the old Burlington Coat Factory building and erect a 667-foot gleaming glass skyscraper with retail shops, restaurants, and apartments listing for $9 million to $11 million apiece. Soon after revealing his plan, El-Gamal had raised $350 million in pre-construction financing. Imam Feisal went off in pursuit of another site in Lower Manhattan where Muslims could worship.

The existence of the plan itself had set off huge controversy and coverage around the world. An entire drama can play out before the core event ever happens—if it ever does. For me, protecting my client's interests in the ensuing free-for-all becomes a kind of triage, a frantic yet strategic effort to get the right facts to the forefront to try to calm a crisis by neutralizing misinformation with real information. Getting out the facts can quell the controversy and ease or avoid a crisis. In my world, the facts rarely speak for themselves, you have to round them up, put them in the right order and context, and then purvey them to the world. From there, all else follows.

———

In the Olympic doping scandal and the fight over the Ground Zero Mosque, the high news value was obvious, but other times the real story isn't obvious at all; the bias or unfairness or some other aspect of the situation isn't readily apparent. Sometimes, someone has to connect the dots for the media and their audience. That is precisely what I did for the Lane Bryant women's apparel brand.

I came up with this strategy on the fly and in a flash, in the first call I had on the case. It was from Tom Harrison, then chairman of the diversified agency group at Omnicom, one of the largest ad holding companies in the world. One of Omnicom's ad agencies, Zimmerman, was launching Lane Bryant's new Cacique line of lingerie, a kind of Victoria's Secret for plus-size women, the brand's key constituency. The ad agency wanted to unleash a multimillion-dollar advertising campaign to launch this line.

Just one snag: ABC and Fox refused to run the spots in prime time shows, and for the commercials to be allowed to run in the few slots the nets offered, they demanded edits—cut the cleavage! (A "cleavage controversy," as some journalists later would call it.) Yet, Harrison told me, the networks were fine airing spots for

Victoria's Secret. Lane Bryant's PR agency had tried but couldn't figure out a way to persuade the networks to relent. Harrison declared, "I told them they need to bring you in to fix it."

The main objective was for the commercials to run, but I made an intuitive leap: "You don't want the networks to run the ads, at least not initially," I advised the Omnicom executive. Harrison: "What do you mean?"

And in that moment, I set our strategy: "This is discrimination against large size women! It's like *Sesame Street*, which one of these things is not like the others? They're running the Victoria's Secret ads but they won't run the Lane Bryant ads. What's the difference? The Victoria's Secret models are size zero, the Lane Bryant women are size fourteen to sixteen."

Harrison: "How soon can you get here?" So, the next day, I flew to New York, where I met with the new account in a conference room at the offices of one of Omnicom's PR firms. Before an audience of nearly a dozen or more PR people and executives from the Zimmerman ad shop, I mapped out a strategy to pick a fight with two of the most powerful TV networks in the world. I advised writing a letter to Fox and ABC, saying this is blatant discrimination, then leaking the letter to the media—give it to the *New York Post*, for starters, I advised, figuring those guys would love it, and it would go viral.

"What Are They Gonna Do, Assassinate Us?"

Another PR executive sitting there, puffing on an unlit pipe and wearing a college professor's sweater, took the pipe out of his mouth and said, "We can't do that, we'd make ABC and Fox angry." I responded: "Well, what are they gonna do? Assassinate us?" Jordan Zimmerman, founder and CEO of the Zimmerman agency that created the new ads, loved the idea, and Zimmerman and I talked it through with the client.

This was a feisty new strategy for a venerable, ladylike brand. Lane Bryant was founded over a century ago by a Lithuanian seamstress named Lena Himmelstein, who immigrated to New York in 1895 and upon learning that her family had arranged for her marriage to the man in America who had paid for her passage, refused his hand and took a job sewing lingerie in a factory to support herself. She was sixteen years old. Later she married a man named David Bryant, who died a few months after the birth of their son.

Lena paid the bills by tailoring lingerie for pregnant women and selling from her apartment. Upon opening her first store at Fifth Avenue and 120th Street in 1904, selling clothes in the front and living in the back, she took a bank loan and signed papers that had a typo, calling her "Lane" Bryant rather than Lena Bryant. And a brand was born.

On April 21 I called someone I knew at the *New York Post* about "the story." The reaction was as I expected. The *Post* loved it, playing the story prominently on page three (the de facto *second* front page of the tabloid) and punning it up:

> 'Narrow'-minded ABC refuses to air ad with buxom babe, clothing line claims
>
> ABC is issuing a "fat"-wa against full-figured models, plus-size label Lane Bryant says.
>
> The Disney-owned network refused to air the brand's lingerie ad during its hit show "Dancing with the Stars," saying it bared too much cleavage, a Lane Bryant insider said.

And Lane Bryant thinks the net's executives are a bunch of prejudiced boobs.

"The cleavage of the plus-size models, they said, was excessive, and we don't think that's the case," said the source.

"It certainly appears to be discrimination against full-sized women."

Later the story stated:

Lane Bryant said Fox, too, had originally balked at showing the ad on "American Idol."

But a Lane Bryant insider noticed that a sexy Victoria Secret lingerie spot starring a skinny model had been slotted for "Idol" for Tuesday night and complained about a double standard. "That caused Fox to change its tune," the source said.

"They wouldn't run the ad, but have you seen the Victoria's Secret spots..." the source added.

Further down, the story added: "A rep for ABC declined to comment." The story went viral from there. The ads were run all day long on CNN and other television networks (not ABC) as part of news reports, not as paid ads. Print and online media ran story after story.

Internal memos from ABC and Fox laying out the restrictions they were trying to impose "somehow" were leaked to the media. An ABC memo ruling that the ad had to run after 9:00 p.m. and would be blocked from *Extreme Makeover: Home Edition*, *Wipeout*, *Wonderful World of Disney*, *America's Funniest Videos*, and any game shows, not to mention *Sabrina the Teenage Witch*. Fox admonished: "The creative concept is problematic (i.e. the woman dressing in nothing but her underwear and a trench coat to 'Meet Dan for lunch') and would garner scheduling and perhaps time restrictions. Also…frames 9 and 11 may be unacceptable depending on how sheer the underwear appears to be."

I would continue to point out to reporters, "But they run the Victoria's Secret ads. Are you kidding?" Lane Bryant posted the *verboten* spots online and got over a million views in a few days, and other websites followed suit. Jay Leno hosted the ad's model on *The Tonight Show*, running the spot, as well.

The "bra-haha," as one writer puckishly dubbed it, simmered on for a month after we created it, spilling out in more than four hundred stories and dozens of mentions on TV and creating far more impressions, worth millions of dollars, than the ad campaign itself would have drawn. Ultimately the ads did run on network TV, but the Zimmerman agency estimated total exposure from our PR effort at some $25 million in value, a substantial supplement to the campaign's ad budget.

In our social media era, a crisis can erupt even over something that is inaccurate on its face, and that was the situation facing Papa John's. In the 2012 presidential election, the 4,600-store pizza chain with the well-known everyman CEO was suddenly singled out as Public Enemy No. 1 for his allegedly saying he was going to cut employment to avoid the costs of the Affordable Care Act. The whole kerfuffle illustrates the hazards in the social-media era of letting a story go uncorrected for even a few hours, let alone the few weeks that passed before Sitrick And Company began handling this case.

A misimpression or outright error can be sucked into the whorl of print, broadcast, cable, and online reporting, commenting, posting, and tweeting, and be repeated thousands of times before the offended or his representative have had a chance to respond to the first offender. The cascading waves of inaccuracies, if left unanswered, can hurt a brand and damage the reputation of a company, its CEO, or both.

Crisis PR and the Butterfly Effect

This can leave lasting ill effects on a business. It is the crisis-PR equivalent of the Butterfly Effect, a notion of mathematical chaos theory that says the flap of a butterfly's wings in one place on the planet can grow and expand into a typhoon by the time it reaches the other side of the world. (It cannot, but we're talking metaphors here.)

For Papa John's and its founder and CEO, John Schnatter, the flap of the butterfly's wings began with a simple, straightforward answer to a question posed during an earnings conference call with Wall Street analysts in August 2012. An analyst wanted to know about the cost of new Obamacare regulations. Schnatter offered an estimate of fifteen to twenty cents per pizza pie and assured investors the chain was well positioned to *absorb* the higher costs.

Politico.com, the HuffingtonPost.com, and *Slate*, among others, picked up the story but reported—inaccurately—that Papa John's said it was hiking prices because of Obamacare. ABC News repeated the erroneous story, and Papa John's Facebook page loaded up with snarky comments. Schnatter was the butt of jokes on late-night TV, including a zinger from comedian Stephen Colbert, who opined that Papa John's pizza was so bad that a dead raccoon found drowned in your birdbath would be tastier.

Papa John's PR problem got much worse, however, a few months later when after a speech to college students in Naples, Florida, Schnatter carefully answered a few questions about Obamacare. As *Fortune* later reported, "a passing, misconstrued comment almost instantly metastasized via the media and online chatter into accepted 'truth.' Suddenly Schnatter found himself the poster plutocrat for corporate selfishness and greed. Papa John's stock briefly plunged 9%, and the company faced its worst public-relations crisis."

The liberal blogosphere went wild. More than twenty thousand tweets, most of them mean and scornful, rippled across Twitter within a few days. It seemed everyone was reporting on Schnatter's campaign against Obamacare. Online and traditional media railed against the pizza chain, depicting its CEO as rich, cold, and heartless. (Salon.com: "Papa John's Obamacare idiocy.") On MSNBC, a host assailed Schnatter for his Kentucky mansion with a "22-car garage"—never mind that the latter was a myth.

Even as this pillorying played out, opponents of Obamacare responded by holding up John Schnatter as a national hero for his supposedly courageous crusade against the program, expressing support of a Papa John's Appreciation Day on Facebook. Yet Schnatter was neither an Obamacare basher nor a crusader: he merely had answered a few questions.

Thus far, however, Papa John's PR team—both internal and external—had advised Schnatter to ignore it, assuring him it would go away and responding rather tepidly to the media, telling ABC News among others, "We certainly understand the importance of healthcare to our customers, our employees, small business owners, and their employees." This statement failed to state explicitly the most important point of all: that the reporters were wrong—the CEO *had never said* he would raise prices to cover Obamacare, and he *had never said* he would cut worker hours to evade its requirements.

John Schnatter had been spared negative press most of his career, personifying the American success story, building a phenomenally successful company and at the same time crafting an image as a likeable, easy-going pizza man bantering with quarterback Peyton Manning in TV ads for Papa John's. "The commercials work because Schnatter comes across as likable, but more important, as an ultra-ordinary guy," *Fortune* noted.

Suddenly he was Snidely Whiplash. So one day he called his advertising advisor in south Florida to ask him: did he know anyone in PR "with a little more teeth?"

The adman was Jordan Zimmerman, founder and CEO of Zimmerman, who had called on me for the Lane Bryant case two years earlier. This happens to us a lot: a satisfied client refers a new client, or a past source of previous referrals keeps sending new ones our way. What unfolded next is well told in the reconstruction of the entire saga in *Fortune*:

> Michael Sitrick's Gulfstream-200 taxied down the runway at Clark Regional airport, across the river from Louisville.... The Winston Wolf of public relations had arrived. Wolf, if you recall, was the fixer in *Pulp Fiction*. Played by Harvey Keitel, he washed away assassins' splatter and gore. Sitrick cleans up the messes of companies, celebrities, and others, and he's a strategist who isn't averse to treating PR as combat....
>
> To Sitrick, Papa John's troubles seemed relatively straightforward. "You need to correct the record," Sitrick told Schnatter. "Every day that goes by is not good for you."

And so it was that we arrived to ease John Schnatter's pain by setting the record straight on the facts, always with the facts. What bothered me was that the media had gotten it wrong on several levels. First and foremost, Schnatter had not said what they reported he had said. Second, they were portraying a false picture of who he was. He wasn't some smug heir who wanted to cheat his workers out of healthcare benefits. He cared deeply about his employees.

"How's That Working So Far?"

Schnatter was a self-made entrepreneur who had set his sights on a career in pizza at age fifteen. By twenty-two, he had helped his father revive a failing tavern in Jeffersonville, Indiana. There, in a former broom closet that he converted into space for a new oven, he started making pizzas for tavern customers, and that, in much-retold company lore, is where Papa John's began.

We had to right this wrong. In my initial conversation with John Schnatter, he said that his internal and external media advisors had told him to ignore all the bad press, that it would go away. He asked me what I thought about that advice. "How's that working so far?" I asked the CEO. "Awful," Schnatter told me. "I agree. We need to address it and address it fast," I responded.

My first step was to get the facts: among my first questions was whether Schnatter actually had said what he was reported as saying. Did he say he was going to cut jobs because of Obamacare?

Schnatter replied he had not.

"Can we prove it?" I asked. "It's not that I don't believe you, it's that we have to prove it to the media. They have been reporting that you made this statement as fact."

"We do have proof," Schnatter said. "The college taped the speech and the Q&A, and I have a transcript."

"Great," I replied. "Please email it to me. What about the statement that you were going to raise prices on your pizzas because of Obamacare?"

"I never said that, either, and we have a transcript of that call, too. I'll send you that, as well."

I tapped a longtime colleague to join him on the case, Terry Fahn, who had interned with us while he was still an undergraduate and trained and practiced as a litigator in Patty Glaser's firm in Los Angeles for several years. I value Fahn's good judgment and strategic-communications skills and consider him one of the best researchers I've ever worked with. Terry is also more conservative in his approach, and I use him as a sounding board and a check and balance for me—a trait I try to encourage among my senior people. Although I do reserve (and exercise) the right to make the final decision.

Fahn began researching what actually had been said in the media and by whom while we plotted strategy. I had already identified the "silver bullet" in the case: what the Papa John's founder *really* said, in two particular moments that sparked much of the firestorm, had been recorded verbatim, and that evidence now could be used to prove all the reporting was wrong.

In the first instance, a transcript had been made of Schnatter's comments during the earnings call with Wall Street analysts in August. Asked to estimate the cost impact of the new healthcare requirements, Schnatter had said, "Our best estimate is that the Obamacare will cost eleven to fourteen cents per pizza, or fifteen to twenty cents per order from a corporate basis." He assured investors the chain would be well positioned to *absorb* the higher costs.

It is important to note that the CEO had said that the new healthcare act would *cost* the company an extra fifteen cents or so per pizza. He didn't say that Papa John's would raise its prices by that amount, or by any amount. He said the chain was well positioned to "absorb" the higher costs. Yet when *Politico* and other websites reported the analyst call, they asserted that the CEO had said he would raise prices, and everyone else in the media followed. Without checking.

The backlash went into full swing with the re-election of President Obama in November, when media reports stated that the Papa John's CEO had announced plans to cut jobs and reduce worker hours to deprive employees of coverage otherwise mandated by the Affordable Care Act. This faulty reporting emanated from a speech Schnatter gave to a college in Florida.

Doing a favor for a friend, the Papa John's CEO had agreed to speak to a class at Edison State College, near his vacation home in Naples, covering his career and how he built the Papa John's chain. Near the end of his speech, a student asked him about Obamacare, and a local newspaper reporter in the audience followed up. The *Naples Daily News* reporter got her story right—the rest of the media pretty much got it wrong.

Fortunately, as Schnatter had told me in our initial phone session, the college had *taped the entire exchange*. As the tape revealed, when the student asked Schnatter about Obamacare, the CEO answered, "The good news is 100 percent of the population is going to get health insurance. I'm cool with that. We're all going to pay for it. There's nothing for free. And this way I get to provide health insurance, I'm not at a competitive disadvantage because I offered it to our employees and the other guy didn't."

None of that would get reported.

Then the *Naples Daily News* reporter asked the pizza entrepreneur whether he believed Papa John's franchisees (who are independent owners of their stores) might cut back on employees' hours so they wouldn't qualify as full-time workers entitled to Obamacare. Here is the exchange:

> *Schnatter*: Well, in Hawaii there is a form of the same kind of health insurance....
>
> *Reporter*: My understanding is that if you're a full-time employee, which is thirty-five hours or over, you'd be covered. Or if you're part-time, then you wouldn't be. So wouldn't some business owners just cut people down to like thirty-four hours a week so they wouldn't have to pay for health insurance?
>
> *Schnatter*: It's common sense. It's what I call lose-lose.

Thus, John Schnatter *never* said that he or the company's seven hundred wholly-owned stores would cut jobs to avoid covering workers. He hadn't endorsed it as a good idea. And in point of fact, the pizza chain did provide healthcare coverage to all corporate employees and all full-time workers in its company-owned stores.

Setting the Record Straight

Our effort to set the record straight began with an op-ed from Schnatter himself, which we got to the *Huffington Post*, the online news and politics site that had been one of the first to run stories saying Schnatter was cutting jobs. This was tantamount to putting Daniel in the lion's den, offering the CEO's own story to the same online critics who had been savaging him. Papa John's op-ed opus opened with a clever lead, then made a blunt, spare declaration of innocence that, in my view, should have been said from the very start:

Reading what has been written about statements I made on the effect of the Affordable Care Act on our franchisees reminds me of a quote from Lewis H. Lapham, former editor of Harper's magazine: "People may expect too much of journalism. Not only do they expect it to be entertaining, they expect it to be true."

Many in the media reported that I said Papa John's is going to close stores and cut jobs because of Obamacare. I never said that. The fact is we are going to open over hundreds of stores this year and next and increase employment by over 5,000 jobs worldwide. And, we have no plans to cut team hours as a result of the Affordable Care Act.

Clearly there was some misunderstanding somewhere.

Schnatter's column not only said that what was printed was inaccurate, it proved it. He laid out the exact exchange with the reporter in Naples, adding, "The reporter asked what I believed Papa John's franchisees would do in response to Obamacare, not what Papa John's would do. ... Since our franchisees own the restaurants they operate, whom they hire, how many hours they give each employee, and what they pay each employee is up to them, not me or Papa John's. Like any small business in these economic times, our franchisees are under a tremendous amount of pressure on costs."

Immediately after the op-ed ran, Fahn began contacting every major reporter and blogger who had written inaccurately about the college speech or the earnings call with Wall Street analysts, sending them a copy of the op-ed, telling them we had transcripts of both conversations, and asking for a correction. Subject line: "We

Are Public Relations Counsel for Papa John's." Key opening salvo: "Your assertion about what Papa John's founder Schnatter said is not accurate and paints him in a false light." Last line, dignified and courteous: "We would appreciate a correction." The vast majority complied.

Much of the heat dissipated after that, and in mid-January, *USA Today* carried a favorable profile of Schnatter, noting he "makes no apology" for his self-made wealth and that "his only regrets" are that the media "misconstrued" his remarks and "that he didn't respond to 'false stories' quickly enough."

Then came the capper. A *Fortune* reporter named James Bandler put in a call to John Schnatter's office. Schnatter referred it to me, and I called the reporter:

> *Sitrick*: Hi, James, how are you. John Schnatter asked me to return your call.
> *Bandler*: You just answered my question.
> *Sitrick*: What question?
> *Bandler*: How this [story] turned around so fast.

I tried to disabuse Bandler of that notion, but the *Fortune* reporter just laughed. "We are going to do a story on this," he said. "It's a good lesson for our readers."

When I told Schnatter about it, he was all for it.

On March 18, 2013, the *Fortune* story reconstructing the entire Papa John's furor ran under the headline: "The Education of Papa John: How America's most famous pizza guy got schooled on the hazards of politics and media." It featured a full-page photo of John Schnatter flipping a pizza and included a picture of me, at the photographer's request, looking more than a little stern. The story read:

Like more than one figure caught in a media cyclone, Schnatter turned to one of the most accomplished practitioners of the dark arts of public relations. He and the Svengali began plotting a counterattack, engaging lawyers to pursue Papa John's tormentors. Will their counteroffensive work?

The answer, as the story would detail, was *yes*, our counteroffensive did work, and it worked extremely well. In riveting detail, it exonerated John Schnatter of all accusations and indicted a wild-pack media for getting it wrong. A prominent pull-quote summarized the story perfectly: "The web exploded with articles saying Papa John's would *cut workers' hours* because of Obamacare. But Schnatter hadn't said that."

The story closed on a humorous note: John Schnatter took the writer on a quick tour of his Kentucky manse, making sure to include the underground garage—the one that MSNBC had said held twenty-two cars. The *Fortune* writer impishly noted that Schnatter "may have a 17-room mansion and four putting greens, but by God, he has only a four-car garage."

It wasn't John Schnatter's fault that controversy descended on him, that the media blithely reported him saying things he never said. The problem, as I told him and adman Zimmerman, was that the CEO hadn't immediately called the media on their errors. Ultimately, Schnatter did tell the true story and, with some help from Terry Fahn and me, was able to correct the record.

When the media decide to make you the poster child for whatever controversy will fuel their content and coverage, it is dangerous, if you have a response, to simply step aside and go silent. If they have it wrong, it is imperative to fight back—vociferously and unrelentingly—as early as you can, marshaling the facts in great detail.

Many of my clients ask me to find a way to launch or reposition their businesses, fight the shorts, support or defend them in take-overs or litigation, or to ease their pain and embarrassment. If I believe I can help them, I will analyze the facts and attempt to find a way to achieve their goals, sometimes coming up with a new plan, sometimes picking from an established arsenal of methods and maneuvers, and sometimes a little of both. If the facts as reported are fundamentally wrong, I will put all of my firm's resources into correcting the record. If the charges are true, I will come up with a plan, focus on the fix, and devise and publicize real, concrete ways to make amends.

No One Is Impervious to Attack

Even the richest and most famous people and the largest cor-porate behemoths, however impervious to attack they may seem, can be crushed. The fixer in me feels some inner need to set things right, to quell a crisis and when appropriate establish a new narra-tive, one that will set the record straight and cast my client in a more accurate or at least a better light. This often involves correct-ing bad facts, unearthing new ones, and shaping how the story is perceived, giving voice to those who might not be heard—and exonerating those the media have wrongly convicted and sentenced to infamy.

My simple and clear priority is serving clients and achieving their objectives, by whatever strategy is workable and necessary. The tactics, which may include placing a story or killing a story, are merely tools toward that end. My aim is to keep fixing crises for clients and perhaps never retire, because I enjoy it too much. My father is my role model in many areas. In this instance, he is ninety-two and still going to work each day running his firm: J. Herman Sitrick Advertising.

So I and my colleagues at Sitrick And Company will take on more clients in companies that need to be launched, companies and individuals in crisis and panic, more stories and narratives that need to be redirected and told in a truer and more positive way—more cases that will test my mettle.

While our clients benefit from these efforts, if you will indulge me for a moment, so, more often than not, do readers, viewers, investors, policymakers, politicians, and other consumers of the truth in the news. As I like to say, if you don't tell your story, someone else will tell it for you. The controversy and conversation will rage on with or without you. Today the bigger risk usually lies in responding inadequately or failing to respond at all. *Most times, you must engage.* I hope you have enjoyed this book and found it helpful.

Best of luck to you.

Epilogue

DENNIS KNEALE
September 2016

For fifteen years as a journalist on the other side of the table, I watched Mike Sitrick work his magic. In the most perilous business crises and in the most painful personal scandals, this Merlin appears on the scene to quell the outcry and ease the fallout. The more difficult the situation, the more ferocious the criticism, the more likely it is that he will get involved. His cases span the globe: Russia, Japan, China, Brazil, Europe, and the United States.

I played a part in several of the cases he profiles in this book. As one of my old colleagues in journalism would say, "When Mike calls, you know there's almost always going to be a story you want." When I was the managing editor at *Forbes*, and thereafter as an anchor at CNBC and then at Fox, I felt the same way. Mike doesn't call with "fluff." He understands what makes news and what a journalist will want and need. Quite simply, I was a Lead Steer for

Mike Sitrick, and my readers and viewers were better off for it. What Sitrick And Company does is not what most people think of as PR. It is more akin to high-level management consulting.

Since leaving journalism, from my standpoint as his co-writer, researcher, and editor, I have spent months studying how he does it. I have learned how he views his relations with reporters, the paramount importance he gives to the facts, and why he insists that social media is often but a means to an end. He has explained how he worked with some of the best lawyers and other professionals in the nation to resurrect the image of Michael Jackson, exonerate the chairman of Hewlett-Packard, and help bring about change at the top of the Walt Disney Company.

He also has shared insights on how to make short sellers go away and how to restore the reputation of a legendary investment professional (and save the Twinkie). Mike Sitrick should be spent by now, but if you know him, you know he is anything but. He cites as his role model his father, who is still working full-time at age ninety-two.

Over the years I have had countless email exchanges and phone interviews with Mike. (At a time when the live, real-time phone call is a rarity for many of us, it remains the canvas on which Sitrick does his best work.) But face-to-face meetings have been rare, so I was pleased to arrive at Sitrick's New York office one mild but muggy mid-September morning in Manhattan as we prepared to wrap up our work together on this book.

My aim was to get his undivided time to discuss a few big thoughts, tie down some final loose ends, and bring the reporting of this book to a close. That's a lot more difficult than one might assume, for Sitrick is forever keeping track of ongoing email threads, fielding calls from flustered or panicked clients, reaching out to reporters, and meeting new prospects. In a single day, recently, he worked on a dozen separate cases.

He had arrived by jet a day earlier, in time for a charity dinner. Later he had meetings with the general counsel for one billionaire client to discuss a lawsuit, with private-equity legend Thomas H. Lee (*not* the Mötley Crüe rocker Tommy Lee), and with a *New York Times* reporter to pitch her a story on a new client (and to try to get her to include, in a second story, points that are important to another client of his). The next day he would meet with another reporter from CNBC and the *Times*, and the day after that he had a meeting with a new client in New York.

Sitrick strolled into his Times Square offices on the twenty-sixth floor on time at 10:00 a.m. (after an 8:00 breakfast meeting) and said he'd see me in five minutes, but he couldn't get free for half an hour. When I finally entered his office, I saw that he was every bit as trim as when I met with him seven months earlier, on a sunny Saturday in Pacific Palisades, near LA, thanks to his daunting ritual of doing pushups and crunches every morning. The vacation goatee he had just started growing back then is a fixture now, giving him a devilish glint that his wife tells him she likes.

Our chat starts with the broad view: why do this at all? Is it for the money? And though I long have regarded wealth creation as a major driver of all business, for Mike Sitrick this wasn't a motivation at all. He tells me he could have stopped working after he left Wickes Cos., where he built his bankruptcy expertise before going out on his own in 1989, though he adds he couldn't have supported his current lifestyle. Certainly, he could have stopped years ago. "It's not money-driven," he tells me. What, then, keeps him going?

"I feel a commitment to my clients, and I love the game," Sitrick answers. That's it. He prefers laconic over loquacious. He admits to getting tired, sometimes, of never having any weekends or evenings or vacations to himself and his family. There never is time off, though he insists there is no other choice. "There's no such thing as hitting the off switch," he explains.

When he was on vacation with family in Italy a few years back, at a nice dinner out, his phone rang, and he lost the better part of an hour on an urgent matter. "Had I not taken the call, there would have been a quote in a story that embarrassed the client and created problems," he says. "It's not like it can wait until tomorrow, because, most of the time in what we do, it can't."

Mike Sitrick doesn't charge his clients a premium for late-night calls, weekend calls, or anything of the sort. "You're either a professional or you're not," he says. He tells the story of a rival PR exec who balked when a client asked him to attend a weekend meeting. The PR man declared, "Saturdays are for my family, Sundays are for my God." The client retorted, "And your agency is for someone else." Fired on the spot.

Some of the better insights on the Mike Sitrick Method come from the people who work with him—his firm partners and staff; the two executive assistants, who have been with him forever (Anne George in New York, having started with him thirty-plus years ago at Wickes, and Stephanie Bruscoli, with him twenty-one years in Los Angeles); and some of the reporters, editors, and producers who have gotten Sitrick exclusives. And above all, past clients, who share a certain satisfaction and gratitude coupled with a kind of bewilderment at what Sitrick is able to pull off.

There emerges a fuller picture of Mike Sitrick than I had seen in the years I had known him, a little, before taking on this assignment. His enigmatic, deadpan demeanor and his high-profile clientele could lead a journalist to regard him warily, and the formidable impression he makes has grown with his fame in the PR profession.

So it is surprising to learn that Mike Sitrick turns out to be a *supermensch*. I base this observation on what I was told, again and again, by other people who know him far better than I.

The star New York litigator Marc Kasowitz, described by CNBC as the "toughest lawyer on Wall Street" and by *Bloomberg Financial News* as an "uberlitigator" and has been a close friend of Sitrick's for more than twelve years, tells me Mike is one of the really good guys, loyal to his clients, family, and friends, yet hard-charging and very focused, so that when you meet him you could get a tougher impression. Sitrick, he adds, understands how to meld what the writer wants with his clients' needs, and he is inalterably devoted to the facts—a good thing.

Stanley Gold of Shamrock Holdings of the Roy Disney fight tells prospective clients that Sitrick will be 100 percent devoted to his clients, 24/7, no questions asked, and San Francisco lawyer James Brosnahan, who was named among the top thirty trial lawyers in the United States in the *Legal 500 US* and worked with Mike on the Pattie Dunn case, speaks of Mike's empathy for his clients and his willingness to do whatever it takes to come to their rescue (though Mike will insist that I add "within the law and the appropriate ethics"). Another nationally-recognized lawyer, Patty Glaser of Los Angeles, who *Chambers and Partners* describes as a "trial icon," calls Mike the "epitome" of imagination, street smarts, and relentlessness.

Dan K. Webb, a former U.S. attorney in Chicago and the former Iran-Contra prosecutor, who today is one of the leading trial lawyers in bet-the-company cases, has worked with Sitrick on half a dozen cases in the past seven years. From their first case together, Webb spotted two "enormous strengths" in Sitrick—having the ear of all the right journalists and his ingenuity and perseverance in getting the job done for his clients.

Lew Phelps, now of counsel to Sitrick And Company and the longest-serving professional there after Sitrick himself, says Mike has an innate ability to snag the cases that are the crisis PR equivalent of Center Court at Wimbledon—or lifting cases to Center Court importance. Sitrick often ends up defending the players who have the most to lose and who look most likely to lose it. Sitrick has a soft spot for the underdog, taking on impossible cases to prove himself...to himself.

Inside Sitrick And Company, the founder is known as a demanding boss who expects his people to give their all, but who is willing to work harder than anyone else. He is a relentless representative of his clients' interests and a stickler for the minute details of a strategic plan. His extensive network of reporters, editors, and producers—journalists he knows well, on more than a one-time basis—may be the most important asset of the firm, in Lew Phelps' view.

Sitrick's colleagues describe him as a magnanimous boss who can surprise them with his generosity. A few weeks after Phelps joined the firm, a client called Mike Sitrick directly to complain furiously about something he had done. Sitrick felt it was a misunderstanding at best and overblown at worst, but it needed to be addressed. Phelps feared he would be fired, and he braced for the worst when his new boss strode down the hallway and leaned into his office, telling him, "We have to call the client and fix this. Come on."

Sitrick escorted the apprehensive new hire back to his office to call the client together. At that moment, when it felt like Phelps might break down, Sitrick turned to him and asked: "Are you scared?" Yes, Phelps said. "Don't be," the boss told him, "I'll handle it." And he did.

It was the message that Phelps needed to hear, delivered at the right moment, as he would recount later, and he never forgot it. It won his loyalty from that day on. It also embodied the approach that Mike Sitrick takes with clients in crisis—don't be scared, we will handle it. And invariably he does.

I won't elaborate further on Mike the *mensch*, lest we make him feel like he is attending his own funeral. Besides, Mike's colleagues would rather talk about his nose for news—his ability to handle the most difficult cases, not just enduring or neutralizing a situation but redirecting it or, occasionally, even creating news to serve the client's larger objectives.

While most of his cases involve businesses, giant corporations, or corporate executives, Sitrick also specializes in cases involving celebrities and the trials (literally and figuratively) of the rich and powerful, as you have seen in this book. Although a significant percentage of Sitrick's cases involve what he calls the more routine, day-to-day tasks of strategic communications—launching and repositioning brands, handling investor relations—the firm is best known for its work on cases where the stakes are bet-your-company, bet-your-career, or even bet-your-life.

In taking on these high-profile cases—celebrity matters, as well as headline-grabbing business stories—his firm is able to build relationships with media at the very highest levels, far more so than if it handled only routine M&A and investor-relations work or just celebrity cases. These are stories almost any journalist would want, and reporters are open to Sitrick's pitches—an advantage for his non-crisis clients, too.

Forty-five minutes into our wrap-up interview, Sitrick was offering a few final thoughts on his brand of crisis management— crisis fixing, really, as he practices it—speaking between intercom buzzes, client calls, texts and emails, and interruptions from partners who need him, now, when suddenly, and subtly, interview time seemed to be over. Mike dismissed me without really dismissing me (he is too smooth and too polite to do otherwise), and he was on to the next matter, our conversation never having quite ended. Conversations with him can be like that, they don't so much end as pulsate on and off, only to recommence later, smack in the middle of where you were the last time you spoke to him.

My best guess is that Mike Sitrick will continue handling cases and quelling crises for clients for years to come. This is what he is best at, and it isn't just his clients who benefit. Journalists and media outlets are beneficiaries of Sitrick's work as well, feeding on the exclusives, leaks, profiles, and controversies that he brings to their attention. Readers and viewers benefit, too, as he feeds their appetite for scandal, celebrity, controversy, resurrection, in-depth analysis, opinion, and debate.

It's a virtuous circle, starting with consumer demand for sizzling content, which fuels media focus on providing it, which sets up an eager market for the goods that Mike Sitrick can deliver. His biggest stories bring more news consumers to the media, which hunger for still more stories to feed the crowd, which Sitrick And Company is happy to provide (when it suits the interests of the client).

Enough cases, perhaps, to fill a third book by Mike Sitrick.

Acknowledgments

The results discussed in this book, achieved by the firm that carries my name, are the product of the enormous skill, hard work, and dedication of the people who make up that firm. Some of those people are mentioned in this book. Others are not, because of space considerations or the vagaries of the cases with which they have been involved, but that should not be interpreted as an indication that their contributions have not been substantial. They have been and continue to be so.

And it's not just the client-facing people here. As anyone who has dealt with me knows, I could not do my job without my recently-retired executive assistant of more than two decades, Stephanie Bruscoli and my new executive assistant Nicole Morneault. And when I am in New York, the same goes for Anne George, who started working for me while we were at Wickes together before I started the firm. We have worked together for approximately thirty years. Then there is Ron Novak, my CFO and right arm; Patt Carney, my recently-retired long-term controller and Nop Meevasin and their staff; and Eric Carr and David Salinas, who head our IT group and keep things running.

When I was writing my last book, my wife Nancy asked who would get the dedication. I jokingly answered, "My father. He is my mentor," which is true. I met Nancy when she was a freshman and I was a sophomore at the University of Maryland at College Park. We have been together ever since. After all our years together, she took me seriously and was a bit hurt. Of course, I was going to dedicate it to her, my wife and lifelong best friend, just as I have dedicated this book to her.

Nancy has put up with my seemingly never-ending evening and weekend work, travel that has left her alone for days and nights on end, and parent-teacher nights where she was the only parent who showed up. She and my three daughters—Julie, Sheri, and Alison—have made a lot of sacrifices to allow me to pursue my passion and my career. And I am eternally grateful for their sacrifices and for their being in my life—now with their husbands, Terry, Kevin, and Jesse, and most important of all, my grandchildren. I have two sets of twin granddaughters—one set from each of my older daughters: Sarah and Hannah, identical twins, and Stella and Layla, fraternal twins; plus two grandsons, Matthew and Oliver, one each from the same daughters, and, very recently, Anabelle Leilani, from my youngest, Alison.

People have asked me why I still work this hard. The answer is I love what I do. I love the challenge. I love helping people right wrongs (I know that sounds corny). I love the challenge and the battle. When I stop liking what I do, then I will retire. Having said that, my father will turn ninety-two a few months after I turn in this manuscript and is still going into the office of J. Herman

Sitrick Advertising every day. Throughout much of my career, I would call my father every day for advice. I almost always took it and have learned a great deal from him in business and in life. I still talk with him nearly every day no matter where in the world I happen to be.

The other person who deserves credit is my mother. Unfortunately, she passed away before the publication of this book. When I was a young boy and would tell her I felt sick and didn't want to go to school, she would tell me, "Get out of bed and go to school. Work through it." Truth be told, at five feet tall, she was the tougher of my two parents. Another life lesson: tough it out. My parents—especially my mom—were the personification of tough love, though if truth be told it was lots more love than "tough." I owe enormous gratitude to my parents, as well as my late in-laws, Florence and Seymour Eiseman.

There are lots of other people who deserve my thanks: my two brothers, David and Ron. Ron has served as outside general counsel for our firm, and besides the thanks I owe him and David for support as my brother, my firm and I owe Ron, along with his life and law partner Shelly, a great deal of thanks for all they have done professionally for our firm. I owe a great deal of gratitude to the colleagues with whom I have worked—especially Lew Phelps, Tony Knight, and Jeff Lloyd, the first two of whom have moved from partner to counsel and Jeff who has retired. I would also be remiss if I didn't thank Members of the Firm: Jim Bates, Tom Becker, Terry Fahn, Brian Glicklich, Sallie Hofmeister, Anita Marie Laurie, Seth Lubove, Tom Mulligan, Stuart Pfeifer, Angela Pruitt, Wendy Tanka, Tammy Taylor, Mark Veverka as well as Lt. General Steve Blum (USA ret.) and Holly Baird—not to mention clients, lawyers, and myriad others. I have been fortunate to work with and learn from so many smart and wonderful people.

And of course, a special thank you to Dennis Kneale, who has worked tirelessly to help me create this book: checking facts, talking to my colleagues—inside and outside of the firm—who have worked with me on the cases cited in this book, to augment and provide checks and balances for my recollection of events, helping me to put this whole thing together.

It's been a long journey from the South Side of Chicago. I have loved every minute of it—well, *almost* every minute. I hope I will be able to duplicate my father's passion and dedication and still be doing this into my nineties. Nancy said she married me for better or worse, not for lunch. In the meantime, I hope you enjoy this book.

AUTHOR NOTE

Michael Sitrick is the chairman and CEO of Sitrick And Company, a strategic communications firm famous for handling high-stakes, bet-the-company crisis cases. *Fortune* calls him "one of the most accomplished practitioners of the dark arts of public relations," comparing him to the "fixer" in *Pulp Fiction*, and the *New York Times* hails Sitrick And Company as "the city's most prominent crisis management firm." He published his first book, *Spin*, in 1999.

Dennis Kneale is a writer and media strategist in New York. He started his career at the *Wall Street Journal*, served as managing editor of *Forbes*, and was an anchor at CNBC and Fox Business Network.

Index